Federico García Lorca
and *The Public*

Federico García Lorca in the family home in Granada, dated and signed by the poet for his friend Campbell Hackforth-Jones.

Rafael Martínez Nadal

Federico García Lorca
and *The Public*

A Study of an Unfinished Play and
of Love and Death in Lorca's Work

SCHOCKEN BOOKS · NEW YORK

Published in U.S.A. in 1974 by
Schocken Book Inc.
200 Madison Avenue, New York, N.Y. 10016

Copyright © 1974 by Rafael Martínez Nadal

Library of Congress Catalog Card No. 74-5346

All quotations from Federico García Lorca's works by
kind permission of Francisco García Lorca.

Printed in Great Britain

CONTENTS

Page

FOREWORD [to the English Edition]   9

INSTEAD OF A PROLOGUE

  Lorca's Last Day in Madrid   11

INTRODUCTION

  What I know about *The Public*   19
  The Manuscript   20

PART I: THE PUBLIC

 I SYNOPSIS

  The Theme   27
  Cuadro I   33
  'Roman Ruin'   36
  Cuadro without title or number   40
  Cuadro V   47
  Final *Cuadro*   52

 II ANALYSIS

  The Structure   55
  The Characters   59
  The Poet   64
  Surrealism and Cultural Tradition   70
    Forms – metamorphosis – void   82
    Ruins – arches – grass   92
  The Public and *When Five Years Have Passed*   96

PART II: LOVE, DEATH, HORSES, THEATRE

I LOVE IN THE WORK OF GARCÍA LORCA   107
Eros: Surrender or Frustration   112
Frustrated Love in Women   114
The Case of Doña Rosita   121
Frustrated Love in Men   124
'Ars Amandi'   128
Norm of Yesterday   142

II DEATH IN THE WORK OF GARCÍA LORCA   155
'A box of joy'   157
Theory and divertissement of the 'duende'   159
Religious thought in the work of F. García Lorca   161
The 'Lament'   169
Life in death   172
Social awareness   179
The rest is silence   183

III THE HORSE IN THE WORK OF GARCÍA LORCA   185

IV THEATRE IN THE WORK OF GARCÍA LORCA
More about Cultural Tradition   218
Passion for the Theatre   221
Author and Public   225
Reality and Dream   228
Theatre within the Theatre   230
Lorca's Main Works   235
Works by Lorca Mentioned in the Book   237
Index   243

ILLUSTRATIONS

1 Federico García Lorca in the family home in Granada, dated and signed by the poet for his friend Campbell Hackforth-Jones. By kind permission. *frontispiece*

2 Coloured pencil drawing by Lorca, 1927. *opposite page*
By kind permission of Campbell Hackforth-Jones. 32

3 First page of the manuscript. 33

4 First appearance of Juliet in the sepulchre scene in Verona. 64

5 Horse's song to Juliet.

6 Song of the Mad Shepherd.

7 Dialogue between Director and Juggler in the last *Cuadro*. 65

8 Last page of the play. 96

9 A drawing by Lorca published in *Una rosa para Stefan George*, a poem by the Argentinian poet Ricardo E. Molinari. (De luxe ed. Limited to 42 copies.) By kind permission of R. E. Molinari. The drawing is a graphic representation of several recurrent themes in Lorca. The roots and trunk of the tree are made up of the word *muerte* (death). In the base triangle: *Tierra para tu alma* (earth for your soul). Tree-top: above, *aire para tu boca* (air for your mouth). Bordering the left side, *Siempre y siempre tierra, tierra, tierra* (always and always, earth, earth, earth). Inside the left semi-circle, five times the word *cuerpo* (body). In the top circle, *y nunca* (and never); *nunca* repeated six times in the semi-circle on the right. Top of trunk and centre of the tree-top, *muerte* (death). Inside left branch, *agua para tu amor* (water for your love). Inside right branch, *fuego para tu ceniza* (fire for your ashes.) 97

FOREWORD

to the English Edition

Federico García Lorca belongs to a cultural renaissance that took place in Spain between 1868 and 1936, labelled 'period of nefarious liberalism' by the present Spanish regime and 'second golden century' by some American critics. But it was not only to literary merit that Lorca owed his lightning rise to fame.

The Spanish Civil War was only a few weeks old when General Franco supporters arrested him in his native Granada and two or three days later – 18th or 19th August 1936 – without accusation or trial he was dragged from prison and assassinated at dawn in the ravine of Víznar, outside the city; his body was never found. He was 38. Because this crime went unpunished, as many thousands did, and because no investigation was ever conducted, Lorca's death became and remains the symbol not only of the horror of all civil strife but also of fascist mentality and methods. In a matter of weeks he became world famous.

His tragic death served his fame abroad just as his exceptionally brilliant personality had served him when alive; it aroused wide interest in his work. This interest survives. Now, thirty-eight years later, when for most people the Spanish Civil War and its brutalities are past history, Lorca is probably still the western poet best known and most translated both in Europe and elsewhere. Famous composers have written operas round several of his plays; many of his poems have been set to music; his famous lament for a bullfighter has inspired choreographers; painters have taken Lorca's symbols and characters; and films have been made about his life and work.

At first sight this interest is baffling. In spite of brilliant flights of imagination, provocative metaphors and images, the down-to-earth nature of the rural tragedies and the boisterous gaiety of the farces, Lorca's poetry is fundamentally obscure, at times almost incomprehensible. Yet it is so full of ancient resonances that as one well-read lady once confessed to me: 'There are lines of Lorca that come to mind quite unexpectedly. One doesn't understand their meaning, yet they haunt the memory.' This book is an attempt to clarify not only Lorca's most difficult play – still unpublished – but the nature and variations of the love and death themes in his work and their most recurrent symbols.

I owe a debt of gratitude to my wife Jacinta Castillejo, without whose help I would never have undertaken this task, and to Margaret Crosland for making valuable suggestions, reading the proofs and preparing the index. Special thanks are due to my friend Kathleen Raine not only for looking over my script but for spending many hours on the revision of my translations of Lorca's texts. However, I take full responsibility for anything un-English in my approach.[1]

R.M.N.

[1] For Lorca's life and death consult:

Marcelle Auclair:
Enfances et mort de García Lorca
(Seuil. Paris. 1968)

José Luis Cano:
García Lorca. Biografía Ilustrada
(Ediciones Destino–Barcelona. 1962)

Ian Gibson:
The Death of Lorca.
(W. H. Allen. London. 1973)

INSTEAD OF A PROLOGUE

Lorca's Last Day in Madrid

On that 16th July 1936, two days before the outbreak of the Spanish Civil War, Federico was having lunch at my house. 'But come and collect me around one o'clock,' he had said the evening before. It was the request he always made when he wanted to be sure of keeping a promise. It would either mean waking him if he had not gone to bed until the early hours, or dragging him away from the visitors who used to call on him after midday, the only time when one was reasonably likely to find him at home.

Shortly before two o'clock I called at the light and airy apartment where the Lorca family lived, on one of the upper floors of 102 Calle de Alcalá. Federico was still half dressed, wrapped in a white bathrobe, giving that impression of cleanliness, health and freshness he always radiated when he first stepped into the street at his usual late hour, as if he were putting on, though only briefly, his better self of five or ten years earlier. One visitor still lingered in his room – an old, out-of-work actor seeking a letter of introduction. Federico finished off the letter and, as he handed it over, I saw him slip a twenty-five peseta note into the visitor's pocket.

From the doorway of his house to the taxi rank, a mere fifty yards' walk, he had to stop three times to shake hands and exchange a few words with people: the proprietor of the bar on the corner, sitting in the doorway of his establishment; a university student and a lady who happened to be passing by.

'Federico,' I said, 'it's impossible to walk down the street with you any more. It's like being with a famous bullfighter.'

'You're right, it's too much,' he said drily.

In Federico the disquiet that all Spaniards felt about the political situation took the form of depression, of lack of direction. Not since the publication of the *Gipsy Ballads* could I recollect having seen him so depressed as during those last days in Madrid. This man of unerring instinct and usually so sure of himself, suddenly, though for quite different reasons, again gave the impression now of feeling alone, hesitant, his helm lost. Now as then, he shrank from public contact and took refuge among a small circle of old friends. During lunch he asked me the same question several times. 'But what do *you* think is going to happen?'

Then, turning to my mother, 'Doña Lola, what do you advise me to do? Shall I stay in Madrid or go to Granada?'

This dilemma had haunted him since the assassination of Calvo Sotelo.[1] My mother took refuge in proverbs. Halfway through the meal he seemed to cheer up. He mentioned the success of his play *Doña Rosita* in Barcelona and lavished praise on the leading actress, Margarita Xirgu. He talked of his forthcoming visit to Mexico, of how that country and its people attracted him, of the poets and writers he hoped to meet there, and he repeated what I had heard him say on other occasions: 'It is only among the peoples of Spanish America that one senses the real potential of our language and the responsibility of being a Spanish writer.' Over dessert the conversation returned to the topic that was worrying him. 'If only the Morlas[2] were staying on in Madrid, I would go to them. I hate sleeping alone in my apartment these days.'

My mother cut him short. If that was the only thing preventing him from remaining in Madrid, the room usually occupied by my brother Alfredo, who was working in Barcelona at the time, was vacant, and he could have it for as long as he liked. My sister and I urged him to accept.

'I'd be only too pleased, but the 18th is my father's saint's day and mine too.'

[1] José Calvo Sotelo, Finance Minister under the dictatorship of Primo de Rivera and leader of the Monarchist Party under the Republic. He was assassinated on 13th July 1936 as a reprisal for the assassination, a few hours earlier, of the left-wing Lieutenant Castillo; these were the last two victims of right and left extremists in the wave of crime that preceded the outbreak of the Civil War.

[2] Carlos Morla Lynch, Chilean diplomat, at that time Minister Counsellor in Madrid. With his beautiful wife Bebé he ran an unorthodox literary salon much frequented by Lorca and his young friends. In 1957 Carlos Morla published *En España con Federico García Lorca*, extracts from his extensive diary.

The recollection of the day and of his family stirred his imagination and he at once gave us a rapid, lively picture of St. Frederick's Day on their estate, *La Huerta de San Vicente*: servants and members of the family busy from the crack of dawn; messages of congratulation; arrival of relatives and friends; presents and drinks; his mother, an intelligent and energetic woman, discreetly superintending everything and everyone; and in the centre, dominating his children, relatives and friends, the patriarchal figure of his father, Don Federico, a formidable man if his patience was over-tried by clumsiness or stupidity, but full of human warmth, sparing of word and gesture, unpredictable in his pithy, humorous sallies. He did not fail to spot the frailties of those closest to him, yet he never lost sight of the human, emotional and cultural life that surrounded him. His irony was therefore without malice, his affection without sentimentality.

'Neither my brother Paco nor Isabelita will be there this year,' Federico ended. 'If I didn't go, my parents would be terribly disappointed.'

Lorca belonged to his family and his world as a tree belongs to its native soil. He rose from the table and, smiling, spoke to my sister. 'Look, Lolita, Rafael and I will decide whether to go or not over a good cognac outside Madrid, in Puerta de Hierro.'

We took a taxi. As we drove down the Calle de Goya, Federico urged me once more to go with him to Granada, and reminded me that in the previous December I had promised him and his parents to spend a fortnight with them at *La Huerta*.

'My parents are expecting you and you cannot let them down. Besides, I would have left for Granada earlier had I not been waiting for you, so that we could travel together.'

It was true that I had made the promise. As for his second point, although I knew well enough how he was exaggerating, there was some truth in it. Federico was interested in talking to me because we had not met since January, and because one of the lectures I had delivered in Scandinavia in April had been on the subject of his poetic and dramatic works. In Stockholm they had spoken of the pressing need for some of his plays to be translated into Swedish. Federico knew all this from a report published in the Madrid newspaper, *El Sol*, and from a private letter from his friend Alfonso Fiscowich, then the Spanish Minister Plenipotentiary in Stockholm. With the generous praise that he usually lavished on any of his friends' efforts, Federico over-rated my minor success as a lecturer. As our taxi was going down through the Parque del Oeste, Federico persisted, 'You are so involved in my work; you must come with me to Granada. I want you to be there on my saint's day and see the village where I was born and get to know the people and places of my early childhood.'

I repeated what I had been telling him since my arrival: I did not like in any way the political atmosphere I had encountered in Spain and I had no intention of moving from Madrid that summer. Again he asked the same question, which seemed to be directed more to himself than to me: 'But what do *you* think is going to happen?'

It was warm at Puerta de Hierro, but not excessively so. The tables outside the tiny kiosk-bar that Federico patronized were deserted. We sat down and ordered two large glasses of Fundador. The taxi driver drank at another table with the waiter. Federico was humming, absent-minded rather than sad. I broached various topics in order to draw him out of his reverie, but they were dropped as soon as they were introduced. At last I too fell silent. After a long while, as though continuing aloud some inner conversation, he said: 'So you won't come to Granada.'

'No, Federico.'

'And you really think it will be all right for me to stay in your house?'

'Of course.'

After a long pause, he went on, 'What would you do if you were me?'

I could not reply, and we ordered two more glasses of Fundador.

Deep in concentration, with his elbows on the table and his eyes gazing into the distance, Federico smoked incessantly. The cigarette in his fingers seemed awkward, so did the short puffs he took. How strange! Although he smoked heavily at times, he never gave the impression of being a habitual smoker. The cigarette between his fingers always seemed the first.

It was then that he said, without changing position or altering his tone of voice: 'Rafael, these fields are going to be strewn with corpses.'

Had I not commented upon this remark of his to my family that same night, and, in particular, had I not noted down some hours

14

later the conversation of that day, I could not now be so certain that I had not invented that sentence. Suddenly, stubbing out a cigarette which he had just lit, he rose to his feet: 'My mind is made up. I'm going to Granada, come what may.'

The decision seemed to cheer him up. In the taxi on the way back to Madrid, he talked about his plans: the Biblical trilogy he had been brooding over for some years.

'I'm enormously attracted by the story of Thamar and Amnon. No playwright since Tirso de Molina in the 17th century has done anything serious on that superb incest. Though perhaps I'll write *The Destruction of Sodom* first. I've thought it all out. Just think what a marvellous ending I'll have for the second act.'

Lot leads the two angels to his house, trailed and spied upon by some of the young men of Sodom.

'At the back of the town square, on the left,' he went on, 'will be Lot's house with a large open gallery where the banquet will be held. The whole scene will have a Pompeian ambience, Pompeii after Giotto.'

As the taxi carried us back towards the centre of Madrid, his words created squares and houses, filled them with speech and movement, with poetry and sexuality. The conversation between Lot, his wife and the two angels was set in the gallery, punctuated by the asides of Lot's two daughters who were starved of men and wondering if the coldness of the visitors was not due to the same cause as that of the men of Sodom. The dialogue would then shift from the gallery to the square below, where the townsmen were gathering to discuss the arrival of the mysterious strangers, and to extol their beauty. The scene would develop on two planes, with the rising rhythm of counterpoint interrupted by a chorus of voices demanding that the strangers be yielded up to them. His description of this scene brought to mind the 'awake the bride' chorus in his later play, *Blood Wedding*, to be cut short here by the appearance of Lot and his daughters on the gallery. Then came Lot's desperate struggle to save the two guests by offering the virginal beauty of his daughters to the men of Sodom on condition that they left his guests alone. In a desperate effort to correct unnatural desires Lorca's Lot even tore open his daughters' tunics to uncover their breasts, 'hard as those of young slaves in a Tunisian market' was Federico's expression. But the chorus would continue to chant incessantly the words from Genesis: 'Where are the men who came in to thee this night? Bring them out to us, that we may know them.' The two angels would then appear at the door of Lot's house, smite the men of Sodom with blindness and lead Lot, his wife and daughters out of the city, while the multitude in the square 'wearied themselves to find the door'. Federico ended: 'Then there'll be the distant song of a shepherd boy, cut short by a sharp, sustained note on a violin. The actors, scattered over the stage, will at once remain frozen in their positions, as though the reel of a ballet film was suddenly stopped. The curtain will then descend slowly.'

The play would end with Lot's second inebriation, when he lies with his younger daughter. Federico had worked out every detail of this drama.

'What a marvellous theme!' he said finally. 'Jehovah destroys Sodom for its sin and the result is the sin of incest. What a superb indictment of the decrees of justice, and those two sins, what great demonstrations of the power of sex.'[1]

In the Gran Vía we stopped for a few minutes at the German bookshop to buy copies of some of his works that he wanted me to send to my Scandinavian friends, and then at Thos. Cook's to reserve his sleeping-berth on the Andalusian express. We reached his house. The sudden burst of enthusiasm with which he had described his *Destruction of Sodom* in such detail had now passed. As he began to pack his bags – a task that always made him nervous – he looked sad and tired. Listless and clumsy, he jumbled together his books, clothes and papers. The cases would not close. Perspiring and dismayed he collapsed into a chair.

'No good, I can't go.'

I laughed, took out his things and repacked them. The cases closed perfectly.

'You see, Rafael? Plenty of travel, successes and projects, but I'm more of a simpleton every day.'

We were on our way out when he went back to his room, opened the drawer of his desk and took out a package: 'Take this and keep it for me. If anything happens to me, destroy it all. If not, you can return it to me when we next meet.'

---

[1] The third drama of the Biblical trilogy would have been *Cain and Abel*. On several occasions Lorca referred to his project as a bitter anti-war drama. Apparently it was an attempt to fuse 'today's madness' with the Biblical legend. 'To begin with nobody will understand what the drama is about,' he once said to me.

Before going to the station he wanted to call at my house to take leave of my mother and my sister.

'Doña Lola, I'm going away for the sake of my parents and because I want to spend the summer writing at *La Huerta*.'

Installed in the sleeping-car, Federico untied the parcel of books he had bought and there and then inscribed them. These were the last inscriptions he wrote in Madrid and probably the last he wrote in his life.

They were addressed to Magnus Grønwold, the Norwegian Hispanist; Jacob Nielsen, the theatre director; Ernesto Dethorey, a Spanish journalist in Stockholm, and Alfonso Fiscowich. I undertook his commission to put them in the post, but the one addressed to Fiscowich was returned to me some days later.

Someone went by down the corridor of the sleeping-car. Federico turned away quickly, stuck the forefinger and little finger of each hand in the air, to ward off the evil eye, and chanted: '*Lagarto, lagarto, lagarto*.' ('Lizard, lizard, lizard.')

I asked him who the man was.

'A Member of Parliament for Granada. The evil eye. Real poison.'

Federico stood up, obviously unnerved and upset.

'Look, Rafael, you go now. Don't wait on the platform. I'm going to pull the blinds down and get into bed. I don't want that creature to see me or talk to me.'

We gave each other a quick hug and for the first time in my life I left Federico on a train without waiting for its departure, and without laughing and joking until the last moment.

When I got home, I opened the package Federico had entrusted to me. Apart from personal papers, there was what appeared to be the first draft of five *cuadros*[1] from his still unpublished play *El Público*. I took it that his request to destroy the whole package could not possibly apply to that manuscript.

---

[1] *Cuadro*. One of the parts into which an Act may be divided by the lowering of a curtain. When this occurs the Act consists usually of two or three *cuadros*.

I say five although I am convinced that the text was complete when Lorca gave it to me in Madrid and when I received it in London. I feel sure I saw the missing part because my attention was drawn to the fact that the sheets were held together by a folded piece of paper on which was written 'Act IV', not 'cuadro'. Have I imagined this 'Act' or has it disappeared in a mysterious way?

INTRODUCTION

What I know about *The Public*

One night – in the late autumn of 1930 or beginning of 1931 –
Lorca read *The Public* to a group of friends in the house of the
Morla family. 'You'll see what a play it is! Most daring, using a
completely new technique. It's the best thing I've written for the
theatre.' That was how he spoke on the way to the gathering.
There he read with enthusiasm but at the end there was a long
silence, due not to admiration or emotion, but to confusion or
surprise. 'Stupendous,' said someone without conviction, 'but
impossible to stage.' And another, more sincere: 'I must confess I
understood nothing.'

The gathering ended and we left the house together. Lorca
spoke, not with resentment, but with confidence: 'Either they've
taken in nothing or they were afraid, and I sympathize with them.
The play is most difficult and for the time being impossible to put
on. But in ten or twenty years it will be a great success. You'll see.'

I know that he read the play to other friends and that, according
to him, the reception was somewhat warmer. Yet his attitude towards the play had not changed. For the time being it was not
ready for presentation. When, three years later, he published two
cuadros in the Madrid literary magazine *Los Cuatro Vientos*, I asked
him why he did not publish the whole play. 'Because I am correct-
ing and polishing it; then it will be really good, with no concessions made to facilitate its performance. One of these days I'll
read it to you.'

That day arrived quite unexpectedly another three years later.
It must have been about the tenth of that same July 1936. At about
10 p.m. he telephoned me: 'Hurry up and come to dine with me
and another friend. I will read you both the final version of *The*

Public.' I could not join them for dinner and when I finally reached the garden restaurant Lorca was already reading the last *cuadro*. But I did get a chance to glance at the text. It was typed on foolscap paper, with a good many corrections in ink. I begged him to let me have it for two days: 'No. Tomorrow a friend of mine is going to begin typing it. But I promise to let you have a copy as soon as it is finished. This is the type of drama I must launch when I finish the biblical trilogy I am working on.'

There should exist, then, at least two complete versions of this play. The one he read at the Morla home in 1930 and the one I saw in 1936. Do they still exist? Are they being kept secret by one of the poet's friends? Or were they lost or destroyed – like so many other documents – during the Spanish Civil War? Or could they be buried in a garret among the old papers of some dead friend?

In 1958, as soon as I received the manuscript which I had confided to a friend in Spain, I informed Lorca's heirs of its existence and requested permission to arrange for a very limited facsimile edition. For several reasons the poet's family begged me not to publish the document until they could get hold of one of the complete versions. Time passed and this was not accomplished. I therefore thought it my duty to put an end to the mystery that had surrounded this play, and to satisfy the legitimate curiosity of all those interested in Lorca's work and in the theatre in general, in 1970 I finally published in Spanish (Dolphin Book Co. Ltd., Oxford) this study of a text which will only appear in its entirety when the poet's heirs authorize a facsimile edition.[1]

The Manuscript

The manuscript consists of sixty-two pages of different sizes and types of paper; some are written in ink, others in pencil, some on one side only, others on both; some are full of corrections in a nervous handwriting, in others the writing is more relaxed with fewer corrections as though the text had already undergone a first revision. As in many of the author's manuscripts the punctuation here is very irregular and to indicate which character is speaking

[1] This English version includes the new chapter on the death theme written for the second Spanish edition for publication in Mexico.

different abbreviations are loosely employed: *Di-; Direct.; Direc.; Director.; Dire-; Director.*

Other indications of the speed with which this draft was written are a number of mis-spellings, syllables omitted or transposed, and some Andalusian idioms, errors of concordance, hesitations, etc.

The manuscript pages are divided into five groups – corresponding to different *cuadros* – plus two loose sheets.

1 – *Cuadro I.* Eight sheets. The first seven are on writing paper from the Havana Hotel *La Unión,* in quarto, Lorca's favourite size. On the first, well up and in the centre, we read: *Director's Room.* To the right, still higher, almost on the top edge of the sheet, one can read in minute handwriting the title of the play: *The Public – Drama in twenty cuadros and one assassination.*

2 – *Roman Ruin.* Probably *Cuadro II,* one of the two that Lorca published in *Los Cuatro Vientos.* There, and in subsequent re-editions, it has appeared as *Roman Queen,* due, no doubt, to a misreading of Lorca's difficult handwriting (Reina=Queen; Ruina=Ruin). The first three pages are in octavo, the rest are sheets of lined paper from a large exercise block.

3 – *Cuadro* without number. For a view of 'the poet at work' there is nothing better than the eighteen sheets of this block. The first five and a half are written in pencil, then follow the same number in ink, then three and a half pages in pencil and the rest in ink. There are many corrections, deletions, stains and blots. Probably this is the first *cuadro* of Act II.

4 – *Cuadro V.* Seventeen numbered sheets of poor quality paper in octavo, all written in pencil with few corrections. The text differs little from the one published in *Los Cuatro Vientos.* It could well be a corrected version, though it is written in pencil, at great speed, without the mistakes Lorca usually made when copying his own texts.

5 – Final *Cuadro.* Ten sheets of the same type as the previous one but in ink. Again, very few corrections. Of all the *cuadros* this is the one with the clearest handwriting. One perceives a certain satisfaction in the way the last three stage directions are annotated, in spite of the mis-spelling of the Spanish word for Juggler (*prestitidijaladr* instead of *prestidigitador*). Also a certain confidence in the clear date at the end of the play.

There remain two loose sheets of the same size and type of paper as the last ones. First, a stage direction:

CUADRO 6
The same décor as in the first 'cuadro'.
To the left a large horse's head resting on the floor. To the right, a huge eye
and a group of trees with clouds resting against the wall.
[The stage Director walks about in agitated fashion. The Judge dressed in
black is sitting on a chair.]

Underneath it three vertical lines indicate that the text continues on another page. I feel sure this stage direction corresponds to the last *cuadro*, as there are several allusions to this decor.

The second sheet contains the *Song of the Mad Shepherd*, headed by a stage direction:

BLUE CURTAIN

[(*To the left*)] *In the centre a great wardrobe full of white masks with various*
expressions. In front of each mask there is a little light. The Mad Shepherd
comes from the right. He is dressed in rough furs. On his head he wears a
funnel of feathers and little wheels. He plays on a hurdy-gurdy and dances in
slow rhythm.

Although there is no indication as to where this monologue would take place, it could well precede 'Roman Ruin' (in this case the tune of the hurdy-gurdy would fade into the melody played by the Figure dressed in Vine Leaves). Yet I feel inclined to believe that the Mad Shepherd sings on this side of the blue curtain behind which is the decor for the last *cuadro*.

The manuscript allows us to deduce that Lorca started to draft this play in Havana, in the hotel *La Unión* where he was staying. The first pages reveal, too, how Lorca started to write this drama. It is obvious that when he began writing he had no idea of the title . . . or that he had thought of one completely different. In fact, on the back of page two we see the title, subtitle and list of characters of the play he no doubt thought he was going to write. It reads:

> *Samson*
> [*Drama*]   *poetic mystery in forty 'cuadros' and one assassination*
> *Characters...Samson*
>   *Philistine*
>   [*The Dove*]
>   *Delilah's skeleton*
>   *The child with the Dates*
>   *The Lovers*

22

For Lorca to start a play without having decided on its title is of no consequence. That he apparently chose a title, without having a clear idea of his plot is something very exceptional. Lorca's usual way was for him to confide his dramatic projects to his friends. By describing to one a scene, to another a dialogue, to another a full act and by studying the reactions of his many 'confidants' the dramatic piece would gradually take shape in his head with such precision that he could then retire for one or two months to his parents' country estate. During these months final form was given to a play that had taken several years to mature. This was his way of working.[1]

Not so with *The Public*. Before Lorca's journey to New York I remember him talking about his plan for a play based on the story of Samson and Delilah, but what he told me on that occasion bore no relation to the idea of *The Public*. None of his friends, not even those in close contact with him in New York, ever heard him refer to this latter play. So the manuscript under discussion is almost the equivalent of those first confidences. The comparison of this draft with any of the other two complete versions would be an experience similar to that of seeing the transformations to which Picasso subjects the pictures he improvises for the ciné camera.

Samson . . . No. *The Public*. – What an intimate scene this change of mind conjures up. Suddenly the poet decides to give form to a theme which has been obsessing him for many years. He takes a sheet of paper and in the centre, just underneath the heading of the hotel, slowly and deliberately writes the title of a play he had mentioned to some friends. Then adds the subtitle and list of characters; some of them do not belong to the world of the biblical drama as he had explained it to me on one occasion. He puts the sheet aside and on the back of another begins to write, at

[1] Lorca did not limit this type of 'confidence' to his literary or educated friends. The following anecdote illustrates this characteristic of his. One day we were both invited to lunch at the house of a well-known lady in Madrid society. The hostess, anxious lest the much sought-after young writer should let her down before her friends – he had a well-deserved reputation for missing appointments – asked me to collect Lorca at his house. When I arrived he was not in. As I enquired from the concierge whether he had left a message, there came from the bottom of the stairs leading to the porter's lodge, unmistakable laughter. Lorca was already having lunch with the concierge. 'Nothing would induce me to miss this exquisite rice with chicken.' And without further thought for the waiting aristocrat and her guests continued with the meal while describing to his hostess the final scene of his drama *Blood Wedding*, still to be written.

first with agonizing hesitation. He is not sure what he is going to say and how to say it; he is not sure of the characters he is going to create or of the order in which they must appear. In any case what flows from his pen has nothing to do with the planned title; he then uses, as his second page, the reverse of the sheet bearing the title of the Samson play. Probably before the end of this *cuadro* Lorca became aware that the key title was being offered to him by the Servant in the first words of the play:

SERVANT: Sir.

DIRECTOR: What?

SERVANT: There is the public.

And he wrote *The Public* in the only blank space left on the original page.

The comparison between the two titles is of interest. The 'forty *cuadros*' of Samson are reduced to twenty (in actual fact only to six). 'Assassination' is retained but Lorca forgets to change 'Drama' into 'Mystery'. Forgetfulness, no doubt, for throughout the play one notices a far-off echo, or rather a modern variant of the technique of the old Mystery play – a not uncommon phenomenon of modern theatre as, for example, in *Waiting for Godot*. Very likely the 'Child with the Dates' has become the Child who in 'Roman Ruin' heralds the entry of the Roman Emperor; 'The skeleton of Delilah' has become the dead Juliet, the one who says to the horses who want to make love to her . . . '*but I command, I direct, I mount you. I cut your mane with my scissors*' (like Samson's hair). Finally, 'The Lovers' of the first title may have turned in *The Public* into the figures with little bells and vine leaves. This manuscript is no doubt the draft for the version I heard him read in 1930 or 1931.

PART I
THE PUBLIC

I

SYNOPSIS

The Theme

If either of the two versions of *The Public* is ever published, particularly the second, the one that Lorca considered final, it will be evident that by reason both of the theme and the technique employed this is indeed his most daring work.

The five *cuadros* at our disposal (about two acts and a half) suffice to prove that in 1930 Lorca, in his efforts to bring the most intimate problems on to the stage, was experimenting in techniques and ways of expression similar to those which twenty or thirty-five years later were to characterize the *avant-garde* drama of Europe and America. In this draft Lorca appears more defiant, though less coarse than, say, Genet and richer in symbols than Beckett. His obscurities spring from the soundings of human motivations, not from any deliberate plan to multiply interpretations. He shows, too, a greater capacity than Tennessee Williams for intermingling real or historical characters with creatures of his fantasy; Ionesco would have envied his wit, the unexpected situations and dialogues, the quick replies, his theatrical resourcefulness. Lorca's debt to Pirandello is no greater than that of any of the authors just mentioned.

The first impression on reading this early draft is one of labyrinthine confusion. At times one perceives a poetic charm amongst surly and thorny expressions, and here and there a central idea seems to emerge. But the reader is lost in the incidents and dialogue of a plot that would seem without logic, without real towropes, as in the dream of an entangled sub-conscious. Let us look,

for example, at the beginning of the first scene with all its alterations, by no means the most difficult piece:[1]

> *The Director of the open air theatre. Seated. Wears a cutaway. Blue décor.*
> *On the wall the print of a great hand. The window-panes are X-ray plates.*

SERVANT: Sir.

DIRECTOR: What?

SERVANT: The public.

DIRECTOR: Show them in.

> *Enter four white horses [and three men wrapped in one piece of cloth covered*
> *with rubber hands and whistles].*

DIRECTOR: What can I do for you?

THE HORSES: [Ha guaa maa taa (*leaping*).] *They play their bugles.*

DIRECTOR: This might do if I were a man capable of sighing. My
theatre will [not ever] always be an open air theatre. (*furious*) [All my
life, all my fortune, all my effort.

VOICE: All your blood.

DIRECTOR: All my blood to flee to Greece. So as not to leave a single
dove alive in Greece.

THE HORSES (*shuddering*): Jaaee quaaa maeraa taua taua.

THE WRAPPED MEN: Neither Persia, nor France nor India.]

DIRECTOR: But I have lost all my fortune. If not I will poison the open
air. A little syringe for removing the scab of the wound will be
enough for me. Out of here! Out of my house, horses! [Horses of
my heart] The bed for sleeping with horses has already been
invented (*crying*) My little horses. Open air theatre! (*they exit; to the*
Servant) Continue (*he sits behind his table. Exit Servant*)

SERVANT (*reappearing*): Sir.

DIRECTOR: What?

SERVANT: The Public.

DIRECTOR: Show them in.

> *The Director changes his fair wig for a dark one. Then three men dressed*
> *identically and with identical long black beards appear.*

The opening dialogue, sharp and crisp, reminds us of the beginning of Lorca's later rural dramas *Blood Wedding* and *Yerma*; the

---

[1] This is an exact, shortened translation of the beginning. Suppressed text appears
between brackets. Other deleted words will only be given in translation to illustrate
a specific point. I have unified the indications of characters.

windows that are X-ray plates give the play an unmistakable surrealist tone emphasized by the entrance of the four horses, cal-
culated to surprise and to produce a plastic effect that, no doubt,
would have pleased the Cocteau of *Orphée*; the entrance of three
bearded men all looking alike is a clear echo of the entrance of the
horses and an obvious disguise which is only partially shed in the
conversation with the Director and in the development of the
plot. Inevitably the beginning of *Six Characters in Search of an
Author* comes to mind but, as we will see, the resemblance –
Director of a theatre, interventions of unreal creatures – is of form
rather than of substance.

Yet, what can be the meaning of the hand and the X-ray window plates, of horses that invert the syllabic order of words, of
men whose disguises disappear in part when they are forced to
pass behind a mysterious folding screen? How are we to understand the scene entitled 'Roman Ruin', in which we meet an
Emperor in constant search of the One and assist at a dance-game
of two figures, one dressed in vine leaves, the other completely
covered with tiny bells? One Spanish critic has spoken of this
scene, one of the two published in Lorca's life-time, as 'the poetic
idea of superimposition of forms, the basis of surrealist aesthetics.'
But if the reader is convinced that surrealism in Lorca is never
more than an auxiliary tool he will be inclined to interpret that
dance-conversation as the dialogue of impossible love more
closely connected, as we will see later, with the ancient myths
of metamorphosis than with surrealist aestheticism.

What can be the meaning of *Cuadro* V where a '*red nude man
crowned with blue thorns*' is dying in a perpendicular bed inter-
polating in his dialogue with the male nurse words from the passion of Christ? Then half way to what may be *Cuadro* III, when we
are presented with the theatre *under the arena*, suddenly the background wall opens wide and we find ourselves in the crypt of the
Capulets in Verona. Juliet jumps out of her sepulchre and sings
a song that will be discussed later. Then three of the white horses
appear and court Juliet, who is protected by a black horse:

THE THREE WHITE HORSES: We want to sleep with you.

FIRST WHITE HORSE: We want to sleep with you because we are real
horses, cab-horses who have broken down the wooden partitions
and the windows of the stable with our pizzles.

THE THREE WHITE HORSES: Undress, Juliet, and uncover your rump for the lashing of our tails. We want to resurrect. (*Juliet takes shelter with the Black Horse.*)

BLACK HORSE: Mad, more than mad. There is your concrete form.

JULIET (*bracing herself*): I do not fear you. Do you want to sleep with me? Yes? Then it's I who now want to sleep with you but I command, I direct, I mount you and with my scissors will cut your manes.

BLACK HORSE: Who goes through whom? Oh love, love that needs to pass it light through dark heat! Oh sea resting in twilight and flower in the arse of the dead!

Lorca can be a very difficult, obscure and at times even an esoteric poet but in the most seemingly incomprehensible poems in *Poet in New York*, in the 'Casidas' and 'Gacelas' of the *Divan del Tamarit*, in the 'surrealist' dramas and prose writings, or in those metaphors that are like little secrets within the apparent clarity of the *Ballads*, Lorca always tells us something, nearly always something precise and clear. Once we grasp his main ideas or his line of thought the obscurities disappear.

However, nothing is so confused as the state of this manuscript. Characters unfold as if parading through a gallery of mirrors that in reflecting them transform their faces and costumes; conscious and subconscious planes are superimposed. Shakespeare's Juliet, a Roman Emperor, a Centurion, talk to the characters created by the poet – creatures taken from real life or from his own inner world – intermingling Biblical or Shakespearean words in a text which comprises both Lorca's best lyricism and the crudest Spanish popular expressions. The confusion partly vanishes when we realize that behind these obscurities there is a precise theme, a thesis, or in modern jargon a 'message'. What Lorca is trying to say can be summarized as follows:

(1) Love is a phenomenon motivated by factors alien to the will of man:

> *And what if I tell you that the principal character was a poisonous flower? What would you think? Answer*

says Man 1 to the Director of the open air theatre in the first scene of the play when they discuss Romeo and Juliet.

(2) Thus love can manifest itself on all levels and with equal intensity or drama. Nor is the participation of two sexes, even of two human beings, poetically speaking, essential:

Romeo can be a bird and Juliet a stone. Romeo can be a grain of salt and Juliet a map

says Man 1 to the Director in the opening scene, and in *Cuadro* V the idea is taken up by Student 2 and driven home by Student 1:

STUDENT 2: Anyhow, must Romeo and Juliet always be a man and a woman for the scene in the crypt to take on such a true and poignant form?

STUDENT 1: No, it is not necessary and this is what the Director of the open air theatre has set himself to prove.

And this is what Lorca is trying to prove: poisonous flower – the love-in-idleness of Shakespeare – love is pure chance. Titania in love with a donkey is an allegory. This is for Lorca the message of *A Midsummer Night's Dream*. He thinks that *Shakespeare's anguish used ironically the invention of the flower's* elixir to illustrate the fortuity of love. Lorca was of course well aware that the poetic magic of this famous comedy is such that the spectator accepts all the planes or levels interwoven in the play as one accepts the incongruities of a beautiful dream. We close the book or see the last curtain fall and soon realize that Puck in his last speech has woven a subtle net in which interpretations and questions remain entangled:

And this weak and idle theme
No more yielding but a dream.

Deliberately Lorca rejects all fiction and to prove the fortuity of love chooses as his model the, in 1930, thorny theme of homosexual love. Nightmare – no mere dream – in an atmosphere of oneiric surrealism as far removed from the palace of Theseus and the lyric forest near Athens as *The Garden of Earthly Delights* of Hieronymus Bosch is from the garden of Botticelli's *Spring*.

The love which did not dare to whisper its name is one of the four or five capital themes which run throughout the whole work of Lorca. He was well aware that what in essay, novel or poetry was relatively easy or permissible, on the stage would be unacceptable alike to the individual and to society's moral mask:

'What shall I do with the public? What shall I do with the public if I take away the railings from the bridge? The mask would come to devour me. I once saw a man devoured. The strongest youths of the town with blood-stained pointed sticks were sinking balls of old newspaper into his arse and once in America the mask hanged a young man from his own intestines.'

Thus speaks the Director in *Cuadro* i and then in what looks like *Cuadro* III he returns to the same idea:

'*In the middle of the street the mask fastens our buttons and stops the indiscreet blush that at times rushes to our cheeks. In our bedroom when we pick our nose or delicately explore our arse the plaster of the mask presses our flesh so hard that we can barely lie down on our bed.*'

But fear should not prevent us from bringing the mask to the stage as Man i suggested in the first *Cuadro*:

DIRECTOR: Sir, it is quite plain. You cannot imagine me capable of bringing the mask on stage.

MAN i: Why not?

DIRECTOR: And the morals? And the spectators' stomachs?

MAN i: Some people vomit when an octopus is turned inside out and others pale at the word cancer pronounced with the correct insinuation. But, as you know, against all that we have the tinplate, the plaster and the adorable mica, and in the last resort, cardboard, accessible to all fortunes.

Yet for Lorca all that is theatrical gimmickry. '*One has to destroy the theatre or to live in the theatre,*' he says through the Director's mouth in the closing scene, and when the Juggler asks the former: '*Why did you choose such a well-known comedy instead of presenting an original play?*' the Director answers: '*To express what happens every day in all the great cities of the world and in all countrysides by means of an example accepted by everyone in spite of its originality, an example which only occurs once.*'

Thus slowly the skein begins to unwind and at least one of the aims of the poet seems clear: to present for the first time on the Spanish stage, perhaps for the first time on any European stage, fully conscious of its dangers, the then difficult problem of homosexuality; and, more important still, the no less difficult task – though not new to the theatre – of determining the real personality of each individual and the true nature of all desire. Had Lorca wished to write a play acceptable to the morality of the day he would have disguised his intention under a guignolesque fable or a conventional plot, with more than one interpretation. But what he does is to analyse in depth – poetic depth – the themes of love and of superimposition of masks – or personalities – in an effort to uncover ultimate reality.

Coloured pencil drawing by Lorca, 1927

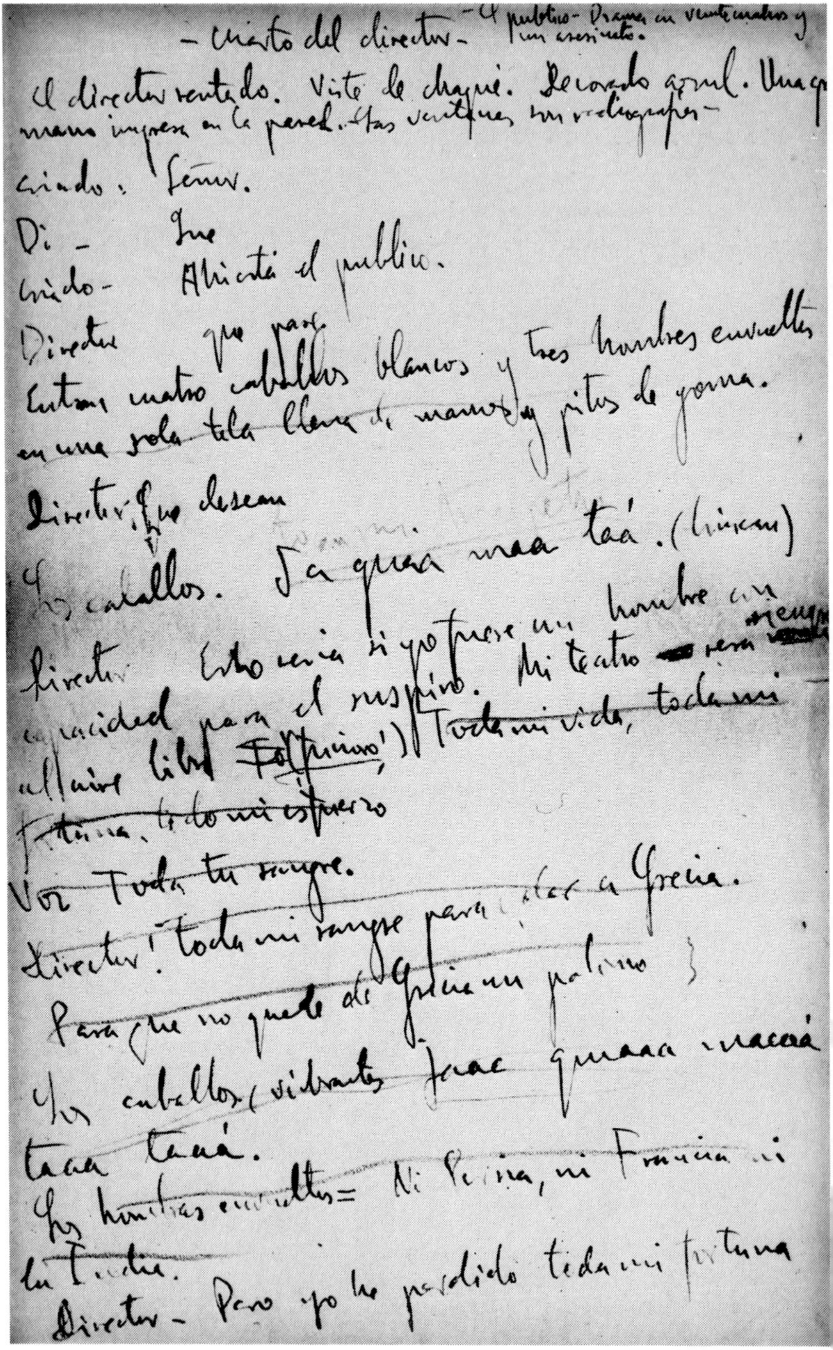

First page of the manuscript.

Those who come to this play in search of propaganda, justification or eulogies will be disappointed. Love for Lorca may be at all levels irresistible impulse, dramatic agent. But in the last resort, for him, love's real word is deceit, a broken mirror, a footprint in water. In each one of us there is a conflict of disguises which hide the ultimate reality:

'*When they have shed the last dregs of blood, truth will be a nettle, a devoured crab, or a piece of leather behind window panes.*'

The symbolism of the décor in the first scene seems to have a precise meaning. Love=chance; that is to say, destiny or law. An analysis in depth will only be complete when we meet the skeleton, death. A hand printed on the wall, windows that are X-ray plates.

Let us see if a more detailed analysis of each scene confirms and deepens these tentative conclusions.

Cuadro I

Once the theme is known and the poet's standpoint understood, it becomes possible to unravel the plot, to clarify some symbols and metaphors. Some will offer a variety of interpretations; others, at least for the time being, will keep their secret.

After the horses' exit three bearded men call on the Director of the Open Air Theatre to congratulate him on the success of his production of *Romeo and Juliet*. In reality they come in search of truth, the truth in the theatre, the truth behind Romeo and Juliet, behind love 'the poisonous flower'. The Director, as we know, resists through fear of the mask. But the three men insist that it is imperative to bring the mask on to the stage. Against the Open Air Theatre, the theatre with the appearance of truth, the first of the three men defends the theatre under the arena, the theatre underlying apparent realities, the theatre of the dead where the true roots of all drama are to be found. *I will have to shoot myself* – he says – *in order to inaugurate the real theatre, the theatre under the arena*. The director refuses because he fears the public and the mask.

A conflict of hidden intentions between the three men and the Director culminates in the triumph of the latter:

DIRECTOR (*getting up*): Gentlemen, I do not argue. But what do you want from me? Do you bring a new play?

MAN 1: Can you imagine a newer play than we with our beards . . . and you?

DIRECTOR: And I?

MAN 1: Yes, you!

MAN 2: Gonzalo!

MAN 1 (*talking to Man 2 but looking at the Director*) I still recognize him and I can still see him that morning when he shut up that hare, which was a prodigy of speed, in a little brief-case full of books. And then I remember that day when he stuck a rose behind each ear, the day he discovered the centre parting. And you, do you recognize me?

DIRECTOR: This is not the plot. Please (*aloud*) Helen, Helen! (*He runs to the door.*)

Men in black beards and coat-tails; Director in morning coat and dark wig. But Man 1 wants to unmask the Director at all costs and scores a first point in his favour with the symbolism of the hare to which we will refer later.

The Director receives the buffeting and calls for Helen but it is too late. The first man will not be robbed of his initiative. *I will drag you to the stage willy-nilly*, he says to the Director. And in order to carry out his threat immediately asks for a folding screen which has the power to reveal the true personality of all who pass behind it. Man 3 produces this infallible lie-detector and places it in the centre of the stage. At this moment the horses' trumpets are heard offstage. Man 1 invites the horses to enter and be seated; in the drama which is about to begin, a play about unmasking, there is room for horses and men. Man 2 and Man 3 push the Director and from the other end of the screen appears *a youth dressed in white satin with a white ruffle round his neck. This part must be played by an actress. She carries a little black guitar.*

MAN 1: Enrique! Enrique! (*He hides his face in his hands.*)

It seems that in an unspecified past intimacy between the Director (Enrique) and Man 1 (to whom all the others refer as Gonzalo) did exist. We also discover that Man 2 courted, or is still courting, Man 1 and that at one moment some kind of intimacy must have existed between the Director and Men 2 and 3. Compelled also to pass behind the folding screen, Man 2 reappears as *a woman dressed in black pyjama trousers with a crown of poppies on her head. In her hand a lorgnette with a fair moustache attached which she will use at certain moments in the play.* The masks, at least the most obvious, have thus fallen; the relationship that exists or once existed between Man 1 and the Director is now uncovered and there is a faint outline of character. The Horses sit down to watch the play. The Director – Enrique in order to accelerate the process of unmasking, calls again for Helen, the woman he loved when his theatre was in the open air projecting the seemingly real world.

HELEN: (*Enters from the left dressed as a Greek. Her eyebrows are blue, her hair white and her feet of plaster. The dress, completely open at the front, discloses her thighs covered with rose-coloured tights. Man 2 raises the moustache to his lips.*) The same again?

DIRECTOR: I would rather live this way than die under the knife of Gonzalo.

Man 3 begins to court Helen but the Director unmasks him. In a fury Man 3 passes quickly behind the screen and reappears without a beard, pale-faced and with a whip in his hand. He wears leather cuffs with gilded studs.

MAN 3 (*whipping the Director*): You always talk, you always lie and I am going to finish with you without mercy.

HORSES: Mercy, mercy.

HELEN: You could go on beating him for a whole century and I would not believe you. (*Man 3 goes to Helen and presses her wrists.*) You could go on torturing my fingers for a whole century and you would not succeed in extracting the faintest moan.

MAN 3: We'll see who is the stronger.

HELEN: I, and always I. (*Enter the Servant.*)

Tired of recriminations and duplicities, Helen begs the Servant to take her away at once. The Servant carries her in his arms and the two reappear on the other side of the screen without transformation.

Man 1 – Gonzalo – is the only one who does not pass behind the screen. He has conducted the dialogue and does not hide his true personality. At the end of the *cuadro* Director and Man 1 are standing face to face.

DIRECTOR: Can we start?

MAN 1: When you wish.

HORSES: Mercy, mercy.

Slow curtain.

In spite of the apparent confusion, this first scene complies with the accepted rules for presentation of characters and theme. Let us follow the development of the latter and the transformation of the former.

'Roman Ruin'

The challenging words at the end of the first scene seem to indicate that we are about to witness a drama without masks or deception, perhaps in the form of flashbacks or the re-enacting of broken intimacies. In any case it seems legitimate to expect, once the masks have fallen, a final search for the ultimate truth hidden behind words and gestures. Yet at first sight we find in this second *Cuadro* – if, as I believe, 'Roman Ruin' is the second – two masks and two speaking costumes. Intended contradiction? Mere theatrical effect? Let us look more closely at this scene and try to find out to whom the voices of the two main characters might belong.

More than half this scene is taken up with obscure amorous dialogue between a figure completely *covered with red vine leaves, playing a flute while seated on a fallen capital, and another figure completely covered with little golden bells dancing in the centre of the stage.*

Game, challenge or test. To the suggestion of a possible metamorphosis the answer must be another mutation which will always assure the proximity of the beloved. Lyricism and scatology intermingle:

FIGURE WITH BELLS: If I should turn into a cloud.

FIGURE WITH VINE LEAVES: I would turn into an eye.

F.B.: If I should turn myself into dung.

F.V.L.: I would turn into a fly.

F.B.: If I should turn into an apple.

F.V.L.: I would turn into a kiss.

This following or pursuit of the beloved, in whatever form, will always have a dramatic end:

F.B.: And if I should turn into a moon-fish?

F.V.L.: I would turn into a knife.

The dance is now interrupted and the recriminations of a love that could never be satisfied begin to fall back into the game of metamorphosis, now with slight variations:

F.B. (*with timidity*): And if I should turn into an ant?

F.V.L. (*with energy*): I would turn myself into earth.

F.B. (*stronger*): And if I turn into earth?

F.V.L. (*weaker*): I would turn into water.

F.B. (*exhilarated*): And if I turned into water?

F.V.L. (*growing weak*): I would turn into a moon-fish.

F.B. (*trembling*): And if I should turn into a moon-fish?

F.V.L. (*getting up*): I would turn into a knife, into a knife sharpened during four long springs.

New interruption of the dance, new recriminations and another effort to resume a game no longer possible. The perfect union being thus unobtainable there remains only the other form of love: hatred or sadism.

F.V.L.: And if I should turn into a grain of sand?

F.B.: I would turn into a whip.

F.V.L.: And if I turn into a bag of little spawn?

F.B.: I would turn into another whip. Into a whip made with guitar strings.

F.V.L.: Don't beat me!

F.B.: A whip made from ship's ropes.

F.V.L.: Don't beat my belly!

F.B.: A whip made from the stamens of an orchid.

F.V.L.: You will end by blinding me.

Dialogue of impossible love with a sadistic slant, a style Genet used thirty years later in *Les Bonnes*. After the first interruption of the erotic game the Figure with Bells laments: *You enjoy interrupting my dance and dancing is the only way I have of loving you.* A little later the

Figure with Vine Leaves mourns: *But you are not a man. If I had not this flute you would escape to the moon, the moon covered with little lace handkerchiefs and drops of woman's blood.* The Figure with Vine Leaves can only retain the object of his love with the sound of his flute, an instrument of which Cirlot quoting from Marius Schneider says in his *Dictionary of Symbols*: 'Erotic and funerary sorrow . . . phallic symbol by its shape; feminine by its tone.' If we remember the traditional double meaning that the moon has in the personal symbolism of Lorca, as death-woman, it seems likely that it is used here as a feminine symbol. If that be so, the Figure covered with Vine Leaves would seem to fear that without his flute the Figure covered with Bells would either go to women to make love, or become effeminate. Both figures want to love each other while remaining men. But what type of men? . . . *For I am a man* says the Figure covered with Vine Leaves – *for I am just a man; more man than Adam, and I want you to be more man than I. So manly that there must be no rustle of leaves when you go by.*

The Figure with Bells answers a few lines further on with another combination of antitheticals: *I am indeed a true man. So manly a man that I faint when the hunters awaken. A man so manly that I feel an acute pain in my teeth when somebody breaks a stem however minute. A giant. A giant so gigantic that I can embroider a rose on the fingernail of a newly born baby.*

This strange cat and mouse game goes on. Each figure wants to dominate the other and, at the same time, be dominated to a degree that becomes impossible to both.

F.B. (*approaching and speaking softly*): And if I should turn myself into a capital?

F.V.L.: Poor me.

F.B.: You would turn into the shadow of a capital and nothing more. And then Helen would come to my bed. Helen! My love! While you would be lying underneath the cushions covered with perspiration; perspiration that would not be yours, but the perspiration of coachmen, stokers, and doctors operating on cancer. And then I would turn myself into a moon-fish and you would be nothing but a little powder-box passing from hand to hand.

When the Figure covered with Vine Leaves seems defeated he blows a silver whistle and a child drops from above announcing the arrival of the Roman Emperor who enters accompanied by the four white horses of the first scene and a Centurion. The Emperor is looking for the One. The two figures pretend to be that one. The Centurion insults them and Lorca introduces the first note of irony which, with Andalusian exaggeration, comes to relieve the tension of the scene:

CENTURION: The Emperor will detect which one of you two is the one. With a knife or with a spit of his saliva. Curse you and all your sort. On your account I am roaming the roads and sleeping on sand. My wife is as beautiful as a mountain. Gives birth to children from four or five places at the same time and snores at midday under the trees. I have two hundred children and will have many more. Curse upon your sort.

In the dispute to prove who is the One, the Figure with Vine Leaves springs forward:

F.V.L. (*to the Emperor*): You know me. You know who I am. (*He sheds his vine leaves and a nude of plaster whiteness appears.*)

EMPEROR (*embracing him*): One is one.

And a few lines further:

CENTURION (*to the Emperor*): It is indeed difficult but here you have it.

F.V.L.: He has it because he will never be able to have it.

F.B.: Treason! Treason! (*The Figure covered with Bells pulls one of the columns and this unfolds into the screen of the first scene. Behind it the three bearded men and the Director appear.*)

MAN 1: Treason!

F.B.: He has betrayed us!

DIRECTOR: Treason! (*The Emperor is embracing the Figure with Vine Leaves.*)
Curtain

The new characters who have appeared will be examined later; but for the time being it is enough to call attention to the end of this scene in which the column of the ruin unfolds into the screen of the first scene. What was happening in the 'Roman Ruin' was being watched by the three men and the Director from his room. The Director and Man 1 seem to identify themselves with the figures in the Ruin. And if we remember that a few minutes before, the Figure with Bells had exclaimed *Helen, my love!* (which the Director will also repeat in another scene), a suspicion arises:

have we not witnessed another unfolding rather than an identification? On the one hand, we have the Director – Enrique – Figure covered with Bells; on the other Man 1 – Gonzalo – Figure with Vine Leaves. If this interpretation proves correct – and we will see whether the following *cuadros* confirm it – the scene enacted in the Ruin (first encounter in the accepted challenge of the first scene) will in effect be the casting off of yet another mask, an intermediate stage between the Open Air Theatre and the Theatre Underneath the Sand where the next action takes place.

Cuadro without title or number

This is the section that presents the greatest problems. Complexities and interest increase in this first draft. Oneiric atmosphere and apparent incoherence are now intensified. One would think Lorca was quickly jotting down an explosion of ideas and images that no doubt later would have been ironed out and polished. But the reader is struck by the originality of the outline, the richness of the imagination, the freedom of the experiment.

The stage direction gives us the key to this scene:

> *Wall of sand. To the left and painted on the wall [the sectional cut of a tree shooting towards the roof] a transparent jelly-like moon. In the centre a huge green leaf.*

The deleted version discloses the intention of the poet more clearly. Lorca first thought of the section of a tree trunk as seen at ground level, as might have been seen by Alice in wonderland, or by Walt Disney in one of his rare poetic moments. Lorca changes the trunk to a jelly-moon and adds an immense green leaf, in the centre of the stage. The correction obscures but does not alter the intention. That green leaf could be a blade of grass, or the leaf of a trefoil seen from below, and in 'close up'. There are other examples of similar visual angles in the work of Lorca.

We are about to witness the theatre under the sand to which the characters referred at the end of the first scene. The Horses and Man 1 confirm this later on in the *cuadro*.

MAN 1: Enough, gentlemen!

DIRECTOR: Open Air Theatre!

WHITE HORSE 1: No. Now we have inaugurated the true theatre. The theatre underneath the sand.

BLACK HORSE: So that the truth of the tombs may be known.

THE THREE WHITE HORSES: Tombs with advertisements, with gas spotlights and long rows of seats.

(A repetition of what Man 2 and Man 3 said in the first scene.)

MAN 1: Indeed. We have now taken the first step.

Theatre underneath the sand. Below the surface, behind each one of the personalities or masks of the individual; theatre of desires that consciousness would prefer to forget, 'so that the truth of the tombs may be known.' The truth of passions now dead is presented in the limelight of the stage and in front of 'long rows of seats' very likely empty, for there is nobody to sit on them – an idea Ionesco was to use later in *Les Chaises*. Perhaps, too, 'the truth of the tombs' may be a vision of the past in a strange life of the dead. The work of Lorca provides examples which would justify each reading.

The poet sets in 'Roman Ruin' the verbal game of metamorphosis and the encounter of the Emperor with the *one* for whom he was searching. In the theatre under the sand he explores the roots of the impossible love. The scene opens with a conversation without precedence in Spanish drama, probably without precedence in any drama:

MAN 1 (*enters*): This is not what is needed. After what has happened it would not be just that I return to talk to children and to observe the euphoria of the sky.

MAN 2: Bad place this.

DIRECTOR: Did you witness the struggle?

MAN 3 (*enters*): Both should have died. I have never witnessed a more bloody feast.

MAN 1: Two lions. Two demigods.

MAN 2: Two demigods if they did not have arses.

MAN 1: But the arse is man's punishment.

DIRECTOR: Just as roses have thorns. . . .

MAN 1 (*furious*): The thorn is essential to the rose, it protects and builds, the arse is man's failure, man's shame and man's death.

In this scene the differences between the types rather than the characters incarnated by each man, become clearer. Types, ideas and feelings in tune with the obsessions felt by the author with greatest intensity during his stay in New York, although they can be detected also in the rest of his work.

The first part of the scene is taken up with a discussion in which the idiosyncrasies of the three visitors begin to take shape and that of the Director becomes stronger. It is a question of ascertaining which one of them would be capable of killing the Emperor, who is still in the Ruin, in order to attain freedom from the sexual obsession tormenting them all. The discussion ends with the triumph of Man 1, ready to dare where the others dare not. When he is about to depart, the Director stops him with a *ritornello* to the dramatic game of metamorphosis which the two, disguised as the Figure with Vine Leaves and the Figure with Bells played in the 'Roman Ruin'.

DIRECTOR: Wait. And if I turn into a little dwarf of jasmine?

MAN 2 (*to Man* 1): Let's go. Don't let him deceive you. I will accompany you to the ruin.

DIRECTOR (*embracing Man* 1): I will turn myself into a pill of aniseed containing the essence of the rushes growing near all rivers and you would be a great Chinese mountain covered with living, minute harps.

MAN 1 (*half closing his eyes*): No. No. I would not then be a Chinese mountain. I would be a skin of ancient wine that will fill your throat with leeches. (*They fight.*)

As in 'Roman Ruin' the game ends in a fight – now physical. Struggling, they exit stage right. Man 3 proposes to Man 2 that they push them 'into the well' and thus be free. The latter objects – *you free, I more enslaved than ever* –. They fight too and in their turn disappear on the other side. Then:

> The wall opens and we see the sepulchre of Juliet in Verona. Realist décor. Rose-trees and ivy. Moon. Juliet is lying over the sepulchre. She is dressed in an operatic white dress. Her two celluloid-coloured breasts are uncovered.

Juliet jumps out of the sepulchre, laments her solitude and sings a song that will be discussed later. The song is interrupted by a tumult of voices and swords coming from the back of the stage. Juliet complains about the noise and its cause:

42

JULIET: More people every day. They will end by invading my sepulchre and occupying my own little bed. I do not care about their discussions on love or on the theatre. What I want is love.

HORSE 1 (*appearing*): Love! (*The horse brings a sword in his hands.*)

JULIET: Yes. A love that only lasts a moment.

Like Troilus, Lorca's Juliet laments the brevity of the act.

Horse 1 tries to convince Juliet that in order to *drive away the passive marble walls* – clear allusion to the sepulchre and to the resurrection – the only thing she has to do is to mount on his rump and let herself be carried away.

JULIET: Where?

HORSE: To darkness. In the darkness there are soft branches. The wings' cemetery is one thousand surfaces thick.

Should we understand by this the cemetery of dreams? The dreaming friend of the Young Man in *When Five Years Have Passed*, sings, in his sleep: 'I return for my wings/ let me return. I want to die being/ spring./ I want to die outside/ the sea.' Wings of dream? Pegasus' wings? There in the cemetery of wings, the Horse promises Juliet *the most hushed of the darkness . . . moss without light. The touch devouring little worlds with the tip of its fingers.*

But it is a disillusioned Juliet who listens, aware of the brevity of life and of the fleeting nature of all things. In tears she utters the key words of the drama about the inherent deceit of the word 'love'. Besides, she is a Juliet who sees life from the realm of death, who perceives death at the very moment of birth, who looks upon everything as a constant somnambulistic repetition, fatally vanquished by death:

> *The moon softly pushes the inhabited houses, causes the fall of columns and offers the worm tiny torches for penetrating inside the cherries. The moon carries the meningitis masks to the dormitories, fills with cold water the bellies of pregnant women and at the slightest inattention throws handfuls of grass over my shoulders.*

The uproar offstage increases and the Horse sings and dances a poem which on this level seems an echo of the central theme of love as heard in the first scene.

Juliet laments that on the previous night forty people came to disturb her sleep: *Now they are four, four young men who wanted to stick on me a little phallus of mud and were determined to paint on me a moustache of ink.*

Juliet refers to the constant uproar offstage, which could be the revolution to which several characters refer or the approaching entry of the Director and the Men. The insistence on four interrupting the tranquillity of her dream to leave on her, incarnation of pure feminity, signs of the opposite sex, provokes the entrance of the Black Horse.

(Enter Black Horse. With a tuft of feathers of the same colour and a wheel in his hands.)

BLACK HORSE: Four boys? Everybody. A world of asphodels and another of seeds. The dead go on discussing and the living use the surgical knife. Everybody.

Asphodel, the plant associated with the dead, the plant eaten by the dead to become visible. Asphodels from the world of the dead and seeds from the world of the living – for Lorca two halves of a whole – come to Juliet's tomb in Verona; the dead to continue their polemics about the two facets of love; the living to probe with the surgical knife of analysis.

The conversation that ensues between Juliet, the White Horse 1 and the Black Horse is full of classical, biblical and literary echoes, but on the entrance of the Three White Horses the conversation acquires a tone of vital anachronistic urgency in these domains of death. What the Three White Horses seek is to make love to Juliet and thus to achieve the resurrection of the Horse. She rejects them but a little later her maternal instinct confuses her:

JULIET: Must I then be silent? A newly born baby is beautiful.

THE THREE WHITE HORSES: It is beautiful. And it will trail its train in the sky.

The plastic, vigorous image, both old myth and Chagallian print – is interrupted by the unexpected entrance of the Director and Man 1. The former wears the harlequin costume in which we saw him after he had passed behind the folding screen of the first scene. Man 1 confirms that they have already taken the first step in the theatre under the sand but, addressing the Horses, accuses three of them of cheating, *still swimming on the surface.* He orders them to leave immediately because he knows only too well they

44

are not looking for Juliet, they are looking for the satisfaction of a desire *which hurts me and which I read in their eyes*.

Simulation, deceit and masks are also to be found amongst horses or, as Horse 1 says, *like the horses, nobody forgets his mask*.

Man 1 affirms that he, who never wore a mask, struggled to unmask the Director and see him naked. Instantly a revealing verbal duel takes place which ends in a physical fight.

MAN 1 (*struggling*): I love you.
DIRECTOR (*struggling*): I spit on you.
JULIET: They are fighting.
BLACK HORSE: They love each other.

White Horse 1 orders Man 1 to leave the Director alone. The three horses separate the fighters.

DIRECTOR: Slave of the lion, I can be [lover] friend of the Horse.
WHITE HORSE 1 (*embracing him*): Love.

Man 1 does not believe that the time for the horses to carry away a nude, *a nude I have made white with my tears*, has already come, and calls desperately for Enrique.

DIRECTOR: Enrique? There you have Enrique. (*He quickly takes off his suit and throws it behind a column, leaving him in a Ballerina Costume. From behind the column emerges the Costume of Enrique. This character is the same white Harlequin with the pale yellow mask.*)
HARLEQUIN COSTUME: I am cold. Electric light. Bread. They are burning rubber.

With the Ballerina Costume the Director takes the name of Guillermina, but when the horses address him as such the Director reacts:

DIRECTOR: Not Guillermina . . . I am not Guillermina. I am the 'dominga' of the little negroes.[1] (*Takes off the 'tutu' and now appears dressed in all-over tights covered with little bells. He throws the dress behind the column and exits followed by the horses. Then enters the Ballerina Costume.*)
    The Ballerina Costume: Gui- Guiller- Guillermi- Guillermina. Na-namir – namiller – namillergui. Let me in or let me out. (*Falls asleep on the ground.*)

[1] *Dominga de los negritos*, in Spanish. An allusion to the 'Negra Dominga', a black Cuban dancer and courtesan of great beauty. In 1892 the well-known Nicaraguan poet Rubén Darío wrote a poem in praise of her secret graces.

45

Here we have a further proof that the Director is at the same time the Harlequin called Enrique, the Ballerina Guillermina and the Figure covered with little Bells. From this moment the scene takes on a more accelerated rhythm, but the surprises continue. Juliet asks for a sleeping draught and the Black Horse offers her sand. Man 1, wanting desperately to retain Enrique, shouts: *Into a moon-fish. I only desire that you be a moon-fish. That you turn into a moon-fish!* Man 2 and Man 3 enter in great haste, the former in the woman's costume with which he reappeared after passing behind the screen. Now Man 3 courts Juliet who tells him that nobody better deserves his love than his girl-friend, the transformed Man 2. In a rage Man 3 strips him of the black pyjamas, the poppies and the wig and throws everything offstage. From the opposite side enters the Pyjama Costume.

(*The face of this character is white, smooth and oval as an ostrich's egg. Sits on the steps and slowly beats his smooth face with both hands until the end of the scene.*)

There remain on the stage Juliet, Man 3, the Black Horse and three costumes – the two shed by the Director and the one which belonged to Man 2. The end of the scene has a visual and dramatic effect which is typically Lorquian.

BLACK HORSE (*shaking his wheel*): Closing time!

JULIET: It is raining heavily.

MAN 3: Wait, wait. The nightingale is going to sing.

JULIET (*trembling*): The nightingale, oh my god. The nightingale!

BLACK HORSE: Do not let it surprise you. (*He takes her quickly and lays her on the sepulchre.*)

JULIET (*falling asleep*): The nightingale!

BLACK HORSE (*on his exit*): I will be coming tomorrow with the sand.

JULIET: Tomorrow!

MAN 3 (*by the sepulchre*): My love, come back! The wind breaks the leaves of the maple-tree. What have you done? (*He embraces her.*)

VOICE (*outside*): Enrique!

HARLEQUIN COSTUME: Enrique!

BALLERINA COSTUME: Guillermina. Finish and be done with it. (*Cries.*)

MAN 3: Wait, wait, now the nightingale begins to sing (*a ship's siren is*

46

heard). He leaves his mask on Juliet's face and covers her body with the red cape.

MAN 3: It rains too much. (*He opens an umbrella and goes out in silence on tip-toe.*)

MAN 1 (*entering*): Enrique, how is it you are back?

HARLEQUIN COSTUME: Enrique, how is it you are back?

MAN 1: Why do you mock me?

HARLEQUIN COSTUME: Why?

MAN 1 (*embracing the costume*): You had to come back for me, for my inexhaustible love, after having conquered grass and horses.

HARLEQUIN COSTUME: And horses.

MAN 1: Tell me you have come back for me.

HARLEQUIN COSTUME: I am cold. (*In a weak voice.*) Electric light. Bread. They were burning rubber.

MAN 1 (*embracing him with violence*): Enrique!

HARLEQUIN COSTUME: (*in a weak voice*): Enrique.

BALLERINA COSTUME (*very weakly*): Guillermina.

MAN 1 (*throwing the costume to the floor and running upstairs*): Enriqueee!

HARLEQUIN COSTUME (*on the floor*): Enriqueeeeee.

> *The egg-face figure continues to beat his face with both hands. Over the noise of the rain, sings the real nightingale.*
>
> **Curtain.**

Cuadro V

The stage direction establishes three points of interest:

In the centre of the stage a bed, facing the public and perpendicular as if painted by a primitive . . . At the back, arches and stairs leading to the boxes of a great theatre. To the right the façade of a university building.

Three simultaneous actions take place but only two are visible, disconnected in appearance and at different levels of reality. The characters taking part in one are invisible to those performing in the other. On the perpendicular bed we shall see the death agony of *a red nude figure crowned with blue thorns*, a double of the Figure

47

covered with Vine Leaves just as the latter was a double of Gonzalo, Man 1. The similarity between the passion and death of the 'red nude' and that of Christ is obvious: a perpendicular bed instead of a cross, a crown of blue thorns, and the constant filtering of words, figures and symbols from the Passion in a dialogue which flows with the natural incongruity of a dream:

NUDE: I want to die. How many glasses of blood have they extracted from me?

MALE NURSE: Fifty. Now I'll give you the gall and then at eight I will return with the lancet to deepen the wound on your right side.

NUDE: It's the one richer in vitamins.

NUDE: How far to Jerusalem?

MALE NURSE: Three stations if there is enough coal.

NUDE: Father! Take away this cup of sorrows.

MALE NURSE: Shut up. This is the third thermometer you have broken.

And a little later:

MALE NURSE (*to robbers*): Why do you arrive at this time?

THE THIEVES: The prompter has made a mistake.

MALE NURSE: Have you already had your injection?

THE THIEVES: Yes. (*They sit on the end of the bed holding lighted candles. The stage is darkened. Enter the prompter.*)

MALE NURSE: Is this the proper time to give the warning?

PROMPTER: I do apologize. But Joseph of Arimathea's beard has got lost.

MALE NURSE: Is the operating theatre ready?

PROMPTER: There only remain the candlesticks, the chalice and the ampoules of camphorated oil.

MALE NURSE: Hurry up. (*Exit Prompter.*)

NUDE: How much longer?

MALE NURSE: Not much. The third bell has already rung. When the Emperor puts on his Pontius Pilate disguise.

It is not difficult to trace some of the most obvious sources of this type of dialogue to which the avant-garde theatre of the fifties so often resorted. In the early thirties it began to appear in the pages of *The New Yorker*, and was used by circus clowns and harlequins and in the first films of the Marx Brothers. It matters little whether Lorca was or was not the first Western playwright to use this type of dialogue in a dramatic play, or to determine to what extent there are comic undertones here, or whether there is a sideways glance at the surrealists or a desire to *épater*; what matters is that in *The Public* Lorca uses a new type of dialogue which fits the internal logic of the play, its peculiar concept of time and the incidents of the action.

Through the Male Nurse we learn that people are searching the ruin for Gonzalo, that the tumult is due to the public demand for the death of the Director of the theatre and for the poet to be dragged away by the horses. The students and the ladies, who go in and out of the theatre, inform us too that a revolution has started and that the horses have succeeded in escaping with the Director. All this sparked off, it seems, by the fact that the public, led by Helen – here as wife of the Professor of Rhetoric – has found out that the passionate Romeo was a man of thirty and Juliet a boy of fifteen. It is the student who tells us that the Director set himself to prove that it is not necessary for Romeo and Juliet to be a man and a woman for the scene in the sepulchre to become 'alive and heart-breaking'. Perhaps the lost Act IV would have given us the key to this first performance to which ladies and students refer, and to the start of the revolution, if we are to take the words of this scene in their literal sense. The students tell us also that the Judge has already arrived at the theatre and that before the couple are assassinated they are going to be forced to repeat the scene in the sepulchre.

Cuadro V, in terms of the action, is limited to what happens in the 'great theatre' and, as a consequence, to something we cannot see. But we are kept informed by the flow of students and women in and out of the building who keep up a running commentary. But they are not the only vehicles of information because the action taking place in and around the bed is a transposition of that invisible drama on to a higher level where reality, myth and fiction meet.

The red nude dying in the perpendicular bed, besides being the Figure covered with Vine Leaves, Gonzalo and Man 1, is also the Romeo who has been stripped of his clothes and forced to repeat the performance before his death inside the theatre. We witness the assassination of the red nude, dreamer of a complete integration with the chimerical *one*. According to Lorca, Romeo is condemned to die by the lack of understanding and hypocrisy of people who do not want to listen to a truth unpalatable to their masks. The echo of the words of the Passion are intermingled with truncated quotations from Shakespeare's *Romeo and Juliet*.

MALE NURSE (*aloud*): When are you going to start the death knell? (*One bell is heard.*)

THE THIEVES (*raising their candles*): Holy, Holy, Holy.

NUDE: Father, into thy hands I commend my spirit.

MALE NURSE: You are two minutes fast.

NUDE: But the nightingale has sung already.

MALE NURSE: True. And the chemists are all open for the agony.

NUDE: For the agony of man, man alone on platforms and in trains.

MALE NURSE (*consulting his watch and aloud*): Bring the shroud. Very carefully, or the wind which is going to blow will take off your wigs. Quick.

THE THIEVES: Holy, Holy, Holy.

NUDE: All has been consummated. (*The bed turns round on its axis and the nude disappears. On the other side of the bed appears the dying Man 1, still in white tie and tails and with a black beard.*)

MAN 1 (*closing his eyes*): Agony!

At this moment the students who come out through the arches confirm the death of Romeo inside the theatre. The new generation, the students, protest against what has happened.

STUDENT 4: What is unacceptable is that they have assassinated them.

STUDENT 1: And that they have also assassinated the true Juliet who was moaning under the seats.

STUDENT 4: The repetition of the act has been most beautiful because they really love each other with an incalculable love though I do not justify it. When the nightingale sang I could not stop my tears.

STUDENT 3: Nor anybody else, but then they set their hands to knives and walking sticks. Words were stronger than they are and when doctrine lets loose its hair it can run without fear over the most innocent truth.

The two actors have been assassinated but in the dialogue that follows Lorca seems to indicate that the cause of their death, 'the innocent truth', persists and will reappear. Student 5, vital and gay, comes on stage, carrying in his hand, as an amorous souvenir, Juliet's shoe. When he is told that the Juliet he fell for was not a woman but a boy of fifteen, he cries: *But I want her. She looked most beautiful and if she was a boy in disguise I do not care.* And a little later . . . *I who climb up the mountain twice a day, and when I finish studying, guard a huge herd of bulls with which I have to fight every minute and win, do not have time to think whether she is a man or a woman or a boy but only to see that she pleases me with a joyous desire.* Between Student 5 and Student 1 a relation is established at once, which in spite of the natural, free and gay tone, seems at times to mirror the relation between Man 1 and the Director. Both students demand a freedom to love similar to that enjoyed by the 'flower people' of America and England and which their idol, the poet Allen Ginsberg, expounds without inhibition.

Embracing each other, Students 1 and 5 run through the arches shouting *Joy, joy, joy.* But the dying Man reminds us of that other truth which for Lorca was still more obsessive than love in all its manifestations. The 'alone you are and alone you will die.' *Agony. Solitude of man in dreams full of lifts and trains where you reach incredible speeds. Solitude of buildings and corners, of beaches where you will appear no more.* In the meantime, women in trailing dresses and students struggle, like the characters in *Last Year in Marienbad* to find the non-existent exit.

STUDENT 1: Some door must be the true one!

WOMAN 2: Please! Don't let go of my hand!

STUDENT 1: When dawn comes the skylights will help us.

WOMAN 3: I begin to feel cold in this dress.

MAN 1 (*in a weak voice*): Enrique, Enrique.

WOMAN 1: What was that?

STUDENT 1: Quiet!

(*The stage is dark. The torch of Student 1 illumines the dead face of Man 1.*)

CURTAIN

The *cuadro* and the discourse come to an end. What surprise awaits us in the last scene?

Final *Cuadro*

Same décor as the first scene, says the stage direction, but immediately one notices subtle, important alterations. *To the left, on the floor, a large horse's head* (which was not in the first scene). *To the right a huge eye* (instead of the large hand printed on the wall) *and a group of trees with clouds leaning on the wall* (instead of the X-ray plate windows). The stage direction ends thus:

> *Enter the stage Director accompanied by the Juggler. The Juggler wears tails, white tie, an ankle-length white satin cape down to his feet, and silk hat. The Director wears the same dress as in the first act.*

The Director returns to his room as if from a journey in which all has been lost. The scene is an epilogue where theme, plot and symbols meet in a final *ritornello,* almost like echoes of problems and desires perceived in the realm of death. All that is left of the horses which broke in on the first scene, and which as key symbols constantly appear throughout the play, is that stony horse's head on the floor. The large hand printed on the wall – a likely symbol of inescapable destiny, has been replaced by a huge eye, the impassible eye that sees everything. The X-ray windows have disappeared for it is no longer necessary to take off dresses and masks: because what we are going to see next is the skeleton of the play. As the Director himself says: *We have broken down the doors, lifted off the roof and there remain the four walls of the drama.*

Almost the whole scene is a dialogue between the Director and his visitor, briefly interrupted by the entrances of Gonzalo's mother and the Servant, that is to say a dialogue between the Director and Death, here disguised as a Juggler. The conversation – no chess match – is almost a replica of the first conversation between the Director and the three bearded men with the difference that in the first scene Gonzalo and his friends incited and challenged the Director to put on the stage, boldly, complex problems of life. Now, in this last scene, when everything has been consummated, the Director sees how the problems remain without possible solution: *A juggler cannot solve this problem, neither can a doctor, nor an astronomer, nobody,* are his first words. When the

Juggler criticizes with irony the Director's approach to the play, the latter – or Lorca – clarifies the purpose behind the action: *To express what happens every day in all the great cities and in the fields . . .* and adds: *Had I raised the curtain on the original truth the stalls would have been blood-stained from the very first scenes.*

Lorca, through the Juggler, summarizes too an interpretation of *A Midsummer Night's Dream*, to which we will refer later, and returns to the central theme of the play, *the profile of a hidden force.* The Director has broken *all the doors of the drama* in order to demonstrate that from the highest point of view, any moral or religious code *is a wall which dissolves itself in the smallest drop of blood.*

At this moment the servant enters in great haste followed by the white Harlequin costume and a Lady *dressed in black; her head covered by a thick black veil which hides her face.* She is Gonzalo's mother in search of her son.

DIRECTOR (*irritated*): When the performance ended he quickly went down to the cellar under the stage together with that young man who is accompanying you. Later the Prompter saw him lying on the Imperial bed in the prop room.

LADY: I will bring a case against you. Where is my son? This morning the fishermen brought me a huge moon-fish, pale, decomposed, and shouted at me: Here is your son! As a thin trickle of blood flowed ceaselessly from its mouth, the children laughed and painted the soles of their boots red. When I fastened my door I heard how the people of the market dragged him towards the sea.

By the end of this speech it is clear that the mysterious Juggler is one of the many disguises that Lorca has given to Death. Gonzalo's mother wants to leave the room but cannot find the exit.

JUGGLER: Madam, there is no exit that way.

LADY: You are right. The vestibule is completely dark. (*She goes to the opposite door on the right.*)

DIRECTOR: Not that way either. You will fall through the skylight.

JUGGLER: Madam. Allow me, I will show you the way. (*He takes off his cape and covers her with it. He makes two or three passes, pulls the cape quickly and the lady disappears. The Juggler brings out a great white fan and begins to fan himself while singing very softly.*)

DIRECTOR: I feel cold.

JUGGLER: What . . . ?

DIRECTOR: I say I feel cold.

The Servant who also feels cold enters and asks the Director whether he should switch on the central heating. The Director refuses because he will not be beaten by a vulgar trick. He raises the lapels of his tailcoat and puts on his gloves.

JUGGLER (*swinging his fan*): But is cold a bad thing?

DIRECTOR (*in a weak voice*): Cold is a dramatic element like any other.

SERVANT (*at the door, shaking, pressing his hands against his chest*): Sir!

DIRECTOR: What?

SERVANT (*falling on his knees*): There is the public.

DIRECTOR(*falling face down on the table*): Show them in! (*The Juggler sitting near the horse's head fans himself with great joy and whistles. All the left angle of the décor opens out and reveals a sky with long clouds brightly lit and a slow rain of white gloves, rigid and well spaced out.*)

VOICE (*offstage*): Sir!

VOICE (*offstage*): What?

VOICE (*offstage*): The public!

VOICE (*offstage*): Show them in!

The Juggler waves the fan about fiercely.

Snowflakes begin to fall on the stage.

Slow Curtain.

Saturday, 22 August, 1930.

II

ANALYSIS

The Structure

The circular conception of the play is evident. It ends where it began, in the room of the Director of the open air theatre. Director and Servant close the drama with the very words they used at the beginning of the play. Yet a closer reading will show that it is a spiral rather than a circle. Themes, symbols, situations and words reappear but each time the level is higher, the poetic analysis deeper. The drama ends in the place where it began, true, but the few alterations in the scenery to which we have referred make all the difference. The presence of death in the guise of an elegant, detached juggler, turns the room into a place of transition between life and death. The voices that repeat offstage the words: 'Sir! What? The Public! Show them in!' at the end of the play, in addition to creating an obvious and intentional theatrical effect, offer us two suggestions, both perfectly possible and with precedent in Lorca's poetic world: somnambulistic repetition, echo of ending life, or announcement of the coming of new characters or public to the world of the dead, where, perhaps as in that of the living, changing forms, dresses and masks may also be found.

This circling movement into the kernel of the theme is characteristic of the drama. Lorca's point of departure is a concrete problem – homosexual love; but he ends by discussing the problem of human love in all its manifestations. He begins with the masks of his characters to reach general conclusions on the mask or masks of every man, on the multiple personalities in secret conflict that make up the 'whole' man. One of the deleted passages reveals the poet's intention clearly. It is in the scene that takes place in Juliet's sepulchre:

WHITE HORSE 1 (*addressing the Director*): You are fighting a collection of dresses.

THE THREE WHITE HORSES: A ballerina, a priest, a warrior, a courtesan.

If in the search for our true personality we go on shedding masks and costumes we will in the end find ourselves faced with a fight between costumes, personalities in their own right, all authentic, fully alive in one moment of our memory, repeating a precise gesture, as occurs with the harlequin costume or with the egg-shaped face at the end of *Cuadro* V.

But truth, the truth that the three bearded men and the Director were looking for, the truth about love, where can this be found? One mask is superimposed on another, one dress hidden beneath another, and when all costumes and masks have been shed the last truth will be 'a nettle' at the foot of the whitewashed wall of a cemetery. According to the Juggler this search for truth is due to a misunderstanding: *You cry* – he says to the Director – *because you have not yet realized that there is no difference between a person and a dress.* These words are crossed out by Lorca no doubt because they constitute another way of referring to the veracity of each one of the multiple personalities of the individual already mentioned in the play.

Yet the Director persists in his search for ultimate truth right up to the last scene, when everything has been lost. *And if the dogs whine tenderly* – says the Director to the Juggler – *one must raise the curtain without fear.* That is to say, one must take on stage, examine and show to the public all manifestations of love – or of pain – that the poet may detect, whatever their form or level, whether his voice be heard by thousands, by one or by nobody. For Lorca the duty of the poet is to unmask the truth even if he is punished by blindness or is left to preach in the desert. Or in another Lorquian metaphor: *I knew a man who swept his roof and cleaned his skylights and railings only out of courtesy to the sky.*

Characters and their doubles reappear, themes, sentences and words recur, but we are never in the same place. The play begins in the room of the Director of the open air theatre, continues in a Roman ruin where we saw the first encounter with the impossible love, a ruin just a little below the surface (*descend to the ruin*, says one of the men); then follows the scene leading to Juliet's sepul-

56

chre and to the theatre *underneath* the sand, to continue in *Cuadro* V back in the world of the living, of social conventions where judgments are passed and punishments – crucifixion – ordered, without it being realized that all who die for love, for unmasking truth, are in a sense re-enacting the Passion of Christ. Then there is a return to the Director's room with the changes we have noticed. If in previous scenes the characters spoke of grass, sand and sepulchres, now, in this last scene, everything is seen as from above or somewhere near the sky. The predominant words are roofs, clouds, skies. Aloofness due to elevation, to an effort for human understanding. Lorca believes that only by knowing the roots can we understand the branches, only by penetrating the darkest depth do we obtain the perspective that never loses sight of human destiny and suffering: *If you climb another step, man will seem to you a blade of grass*, says the Juggler, but the Director contradicts with energy: *No. Not a blade of grass but a navigator*.

We know how the theme of love is viewed. On all levels it is outside human control; it can always be a drama. One could, of course, argue that by comparison with the fruitful love between man and woman, homosexual love bears the stigma of frustration, of the stillborn, of the lost seed. But Lorca would never have accepted this. What characterizes his attitude as a man and as a poet is that he sees everything as *sub specie mortalitatis* even in moments of maximum gaiety. When the Juggler says that he can, with the greatest ease, change a navigator into a sewing needle, the following dialogue develops:

DIRECTOR: This is precisely what is done in the theatre and this is why I dared to play a very difficult poetic game hoping that love will burst out with great impetus and give new form to the costumes.

JUGGLER: When you say 'love' it astonishes me.

DIRECTOR: Why does it astonish you?

JUGGLER: I see a landscape of sand reflected in a foggy mirror.

DIRECTOR: And what more?

JUGGLER: That dawn never quite comes.

DIRECTOR: It is possible.

JUGGLER (*peevishly and beating the horse's head with his fingertips*): Love.

DIRECTOR (*sitting on top of the table*): When you say love you astonish me.

JUGGLER: Why astonish?

DIRECTOR: I see how each grain of sand turns into a live ant.

JUGGLER: And, what else?

DIRECTOR: That night falls every five minutes.

JUGGLER (*staring at the Director*): It is possible.

For any reader well acquainted with Lorca's symbolic terms, the meaning of this dialogue may be relatively clear. He presents here two different types of love in opposition, each accusing the other. For the Juggler who is Death, defender of the reproduction of the species *per se*, the word 'love' in the mouth of the Director, defender of the legitimacy of homosexual love, awakens the idea of a 'landscape of sand' – wasted seed – reflected in a foggy mirror, without possible dawn – life. For the Director the word 'love' in the mouth of the Juggler – Death – produces a similar astonishment. In that very mirror he sees all those grains of sand turn into ants – men; and he sees how they die – it becomes dark every five minutes. Later on we shall learn how this is not the only occasion in which Lorca expresses in dramatic form the idea, not without precedent in Spanish and European literature, that the fruit of love is nothing but food for Death.

From this standpoint, moral, human or divine law means little. Before the sufferings, blood and death of men, moral precepts vanish. When the Juggler asks the Director: *Who ever thought that one can break open all the doors of drama?* the Director answers: *It's only by breaking down all the doors that drama can justify itself, seeing with its own eyes that the law is a wall that dissolves in the smallest drop of blood*, to which we have already referred. The Director, who cannot envisage a possible solution, will not here, or in a supposed life after death, accept deception.

> *It disgusts me to see a dying man outlining with his finger a door on the wall and quietly going to sleep. True drama is a circle of arches where the wind, the moon and creatures come in and out without finding a place to rest.*

Man alone with his destiny, with no possibility of rest or, as the dying Man 1 said in *Cuadro* V, man passes through life, like a shooting star, *at incredible speed.*

The Characters

In *The Public* Lorca is trying a new form of dramatic expression; a drama of ideas and abstract passions, not of characters and plot in the traditional sense. As in *The Prodigious Cobbler's Wife, Don Perlimplín, Yerma, The House of Bernarda Alba* and *Doña Rosita* Lorca presents in *The Public* a theme rather than a plot. But in those plays the characters are taken from every-day life. If Yerma, the Mother in *Blood Wedding*, Bernarda Alba or Doña Rosita are larger than life, it is not because the poet has conceived them *a priori* as symbols of their respective obsessions but because they are swept along by the power of their feelings. Even in *The Prodigious Cobbler's Wife*, where Lorca *did* wish his protagonist to represent the eternal struggle between truth and fantasy, the young, playful, sulky Zapaterita, so feminine in her bitter-sweetness, is more real than other creatures poised between dream and reality.

In *The Public* and in *When Five Years Have Passed* the characters lack proper names and, at first sight, real personality. It seems likely that Lorca meant these people – Director, Men, Emperor, Students, Centurion – to be generic with no life outside his mind. Even when given a proper name, this is generic: Helen=Woman. The only exception is Juliet who, though archetypal, is more real than all the other characters in the drama. Yet one feels so much human suffering, such inner truth in these nameless creatures that at moments, quite suddenly, they seem to us more true and concrete than if they had proper names and descriptive adjectives. Let us have a look at each one of them.

The drama, as we know, revolves round the Director and three men: three attitudes, three variations. Within the diffuseness common to the three bearded men, Man 1 is the one drawn with greater clarity. The sketch is not only of a type but also of a character, without doubt the most important after the Director. As we have already noted he is the only one who hides neither his true personality nor his most intimate desires. He appears to embody the homosexual type that in the 'Ode to Walt Whitman' Lorca defined as 'pure' or 'classic'. *They should triumph* says he, in the unnumbered scene, referring to the struggle that took place in the

'Roman Ruin'. And when Man 3 asks *how?* Man 1 answers: *By both being men and not letting themselves be dragged down by false desires. Being entirely men. Can a man ever stop being just a man?* Perhaps this is why Man 1 is the only one aware of the impossibility of realizing his desires. At times this Man 1 – and on another plane the Black Horse in Juliet's sepulchre – seem to share a platonic idea of love. The condemnation of the arse made by him in that revealing un-numbered *Cuadro – man's failure, shame and death –* seems to find an echo later on in the same scene, but applied now to the union between man and woman. It occurs in the already quoted marginal comment by the Black Horse to Juliet: *Oh love, love that needs to pass its light through dark heats.* In opposition to these implied condemnations of all forms of carnal love, Man 1 aspires *to the pure beauty of marble that glitters, protecting intimate desires beneath a flawless surface.* It is perhaps opportune to remember that this is the character that under the disguise of Figure with Vine Leaves, hides *a plaster white nude.* And when the Roman Centurion says to the Emperor that at last he has found the 'one' he was looking for – *It seems difficult but there you have it* – the very Figure covered with Vine Leaves answers sharply: *He has it because he will never be able to have it.*

Sometimes Man 1 may belie this dominant feature of his character, but there is no doubt that he is conceived as a seeker of ideal beauty, exempt from all carnal desires, though the road to that goal may be through the enjoyment of the flesh. Man 3, who does not share the concept of ideal beauty enunciated by Man 1, and even less his implied condemnation of sexual satisfaction, recalls what happens in real life when people are in a state of natural innocence, without moral or religious bias: *When the moon comes out, the children in the fields assemble to shit together.* Instantly Man 1 cuts him short: *Behind the rushes, by the edge of fresh, lingering waters we have found the footsteps of the man who coarsens the freedom of nudity.* He alludes no doubt to the exhibitionists, voyeurs and corrupters in all countries.

Man 2 seems to embody the hesitant and effeminate, those whom Lorca lashed in 'Ode to Walt Whitman' with the epithets of 'woman's slaves, bitches of their boudoirs'. Man 3 would appear to slink eternally around his own instincts, always ready to deny what he loves and feigning attraction to the opposite sex. It is Man 1 who uncovers Man 3's real nature in one of their many disputes. Man 3 accuses the others of not being real men and declares himself ashamed of being in their company. Immediately Man 1 challenges him. If what Man 3 says is true, the remedy is very simple: *There behind the revellers is the Emperor. Why don't you go and strangle him?* When it is a question of ascertaining which of the four would be courageous enough to kill the Emperor, Man 1, realizing that Man 3 is the most frightened of all, speaks to the Director: *That's the one. Do you recognize him now? He is the valiant one that in the café and in the books rolls up our veins in long fish bones. That's the man who loves the Emperor in secret and looks for him in the dockside pubs. Enrique, look him well in the eyes. Look what little bunches of grapes fall over his shoulders.*

The last words, perhaps an allusion to the effeminate Dionysus of some representations, not only disclose the true psychology of Man 3 but throw light on the mysterious figure called the Emperor. If Man 3 loves the Emperor in secret and looks for him in the dockside pubs, if the final proof of hatred towards homosexuals is to kill him, it seems legitimate to assume that at least in some sense this Emperor is the personification of homosexual love. If we remember besides that the Emperor roams the world in constant search of the 'one', it could also embody the chimerical union of two halves, the longing for a total love. Or could it not be that for Lorca homosexual love in its highest form is nothing but the expression of an ideal love, without urge for the survival of the species?

In any case why did Lorca personify these ideas in a Roman Emperor? Why should the Emperor have to disguise himself as Pilate? If he was thinking of any specific Emperor, I feel inclined to believe that the model must have been Hadrian in love with Antinous. But what is certain, and of great importance, is that this Emperor, with all his symbolic plurality, is both in perpetual conflict with Helen and perpetually defeated by her. In the first scene, when Man 3 fiercely presses Helen's wrists and challenges her: *We'll see who is the stronger*, Helen replies with calm security: *I and always I.*

In the unnumbered *cuadro* we witness a new encounter of these two opponents:

MAN 1 (*to the Director*): I'll bring you the Emperor's head!

DIRECTOR: It will be the best gift for Helen.

MAN 2: Stay, Gonzalo, and allow me to wash your feet.

MAN 1: The Emperor's head burns the bodies of all women.

DIRECTOR (*to Man 1*): But you don't know that Helen can polish her hands in phosphorus and quicklime. Go with the knife. Helen, Helen, my love.

MAN 3: My eternal love. Let no one name her here.

DIRECTOR: Nobody name her (*trembling*). Let's be calm. It's much better. It will be possible if we forget the theatre. Let no one name her.

MAN 1: Helen.

DIRECTOR (*to Man 1*): Shut up. Later I will be waiting behind the walls of the great store-house. Silence.

MAN 1: I prefer to finish once and for all. Helen!

Dressed as a Greek in the first scene, as the Centurion's wife (giving birth to children through four places simultaneously), or as a Picassian vivandière-cow in the 'Roman Ruin', or as the Professor of Rhetoric's wife in the unnumbered *cuadro*, Helen is at all levels of dream or reality the woman who conquers and annuls the type of love represented by the Emperor and practised by the Director and the three men. And yet under all those disguises, Helen is an abstraction, a motif, at times a coarse deformation of herself, never a real being. She is a type conceived for or by the homosexual. Such a representation of woman could not possibly satisfy Lorca, who has shown such a deep understanding of feminine psychology. In contrast to Helen, dehumanized by the cliché or irony of the homosexual, Lorca sketches in Juliet the only really feminine character of the drama. In spite of the strange texture of the play, the great transformations that everything undergoes in the sepulchre scene and the fact that she speaks from death, she remains without serious distortion the most 'living' character. It is a Juliet who resembles other Lorquian heroines rather than the impassioned Capulet's daughter although, as we shall see later, clear echoes of the Shakespearean lover converge in her.

The other figures appearing in the play spring from the world of reality, history or legend, but never in a clear or total way. The Centurion *of yellow tunic and grey flesh* accompanying the Emperor is not so much a true Roman Centurion as a centurion from the

Andalusian Holy Week processions; a figure of fun rather than an attempt at historical reconstruction, half-brother of those other 'yellow centurions of grey and sleepless flesh' who in Lorca's 'Martyrdom of St. Olalla' 'arrive in heaven rattling of their silver armour'.

The ladies in *Cuadro* V who come in and out of the theatre belong to a world of reality which, through them, penetrates the dream-world of the play. At first sight the Students too seem to belong to the real world. Yet we have seen how at certain moments they act as if they are echoing what is happening in the surrealist world of the Director, the men and their doubles and doubles of doubles. But Ladies and Students, rather than entering into the play, limit themselves to reacting to its external manifestation – the performance of *Romeo and Juliet* which has unleashed the revolution.

The Male Nurse remains imperturbable in a frontier region between dream and reality, but the thieves are those of the Passion of Christ who turn here into good companions helping the Red Nude in his transit. Gonzalo's mother, who enters during the last scene to claim her son, is a Pirandellian character seen in reverse, a person of the real world penetrating the world of the imagination. A strange character is the Servant, nearly mute, impassive companion to the Director right up to his death. As we will see later he is the elder brother of the Servant in *When Five Years Have Passed*, both very possibly modelled on the idealized English butlers of so many novels, plays and films of the period. There remain the horses, but it would be difficult to unmask their meaning without studying them in connection with all the other horses in Lorca's plays and poems. So we will look at them in the corresponding section.

A detailed examination will confirm the first impression. Whatever their origin, Men and Horses, Ladies and Students, Servant and subsidiary characters, all are illumined by a strange dream-like or nightmarish atmosphere. A detailed analysis will also confirm that characters, theme and plot converge round the Director in such a way that one wonders whether Lorca had not conceived the play – quite apart from the theme – as a dream, nightmare or delirium of the Director seconds before his death. In the very centre of the stage, always in the limelight, looming larger than everyone else, the Director often seems to us a double of Lorca himself. Many of his ideas about the theatre, the solitude of individual men, the freedom of love, are to a great extent Lorca's personal views as we see them expressed with greater or lesser frankness in the rest of his work. Perhaps by unravelling the play still further the profile of the Director and his creator will become clearer.

The Poet

Theme, subsidiary themes and final conclusion – the absolute solitude of man – are felt with such depth, with such equilibrium and precision, with such brutality intermingled with tenderness, that in this seemingly first draft of an experimental drama one hardly perceives the skill with which Lorca has avoided the most dangerous pitfalls in the so-called drama of ideas: discursive tone, over-simplification, condemnation or propaganda. In avoiding such dangers the dramatist – who is only concerned with human understanding – is greatly assisted by the poet, creator of new forms, bearer of an old cultural tradition.

After the surprise of finding that such a daring experiment was made in 1930, the first thing one notices is the poetic nature of the play. The quotations so far given are enough to support this assertion. Themes, characters and situations are conceived and treated in a manner of which only a poet would have been capable. Only a poet could have changed the original idea, however interesting or polemic, into a new contribution to the saga of man's destiny; only a poet could have enshrined in words and metaphors such plurality of meaning, so many reverberations; only a poet could make the coexistence of opposites or the intercommunication of kingdoms and spheres appear 'natural'.

From the very first words uttered by the Horses at the beginning of the play – *And your shoes* (the Director's) *were baked with sweat but we learnt to understand that the moon bore the same relation to the apples that rotted on the grass* – right to the *I knew a man who swept his roof and polished railings only as a courtesy towards the sky* – of the Director to the Juggler in the last *cuadro* – the poet takes us from the particular to the abstract, from the human and minute to the cosmic or universal. The method he employs is always love, a

64

First appearance of Juliet in the sepulchre scene in Verona.

sobre mis hombros. No me mires caballo con ese deseo que tan bien ~~conozco~~ ...

~~...~~ ... Verona a las hermosas casas que... los ... las veía pintadas en mis libros pero los recordaba siempre al poner p...

Caballo. Amor que solo dura un momento.

Julieta. ~~Si, Un~~ ... y Julieta viva, alegrísima, libre del ~~...~~ durante ... de ~~tropas~~ — Julieta en el ... Julieta la orilla de la ciudad.

(El tumulto de voces y espadas vuelve a rugir en el fondo de la escena).

Caballo. Amor. Amor Amor
~~Julieta~~ Amor del caracol col col col
que saca los cuernos al sol
Amor Amor Amor
del caballo que lame
la bola de sal
(baila)

Julieta Ayer eran cuarenta y ~~...~~ estaba dormida. Venían las niñas ... y la joven violada por el perro tapándose con los geranios ... ajustaba ... hebras del queso ... de leche de sirena pero ... ahora son ... ... que me han querido poner un jubito de barro y estaban decididos a pintarme un bigote de tinta

Caballo. Amor Amor Amor
amor de ~~...~~
y de la ~~niña~~ en el caracol col col col
que saca los cuernos al sol
Amor Amor Amor
de Júpiter en el establo ~~...~~ ... para sal

Horse's song to Juliet.

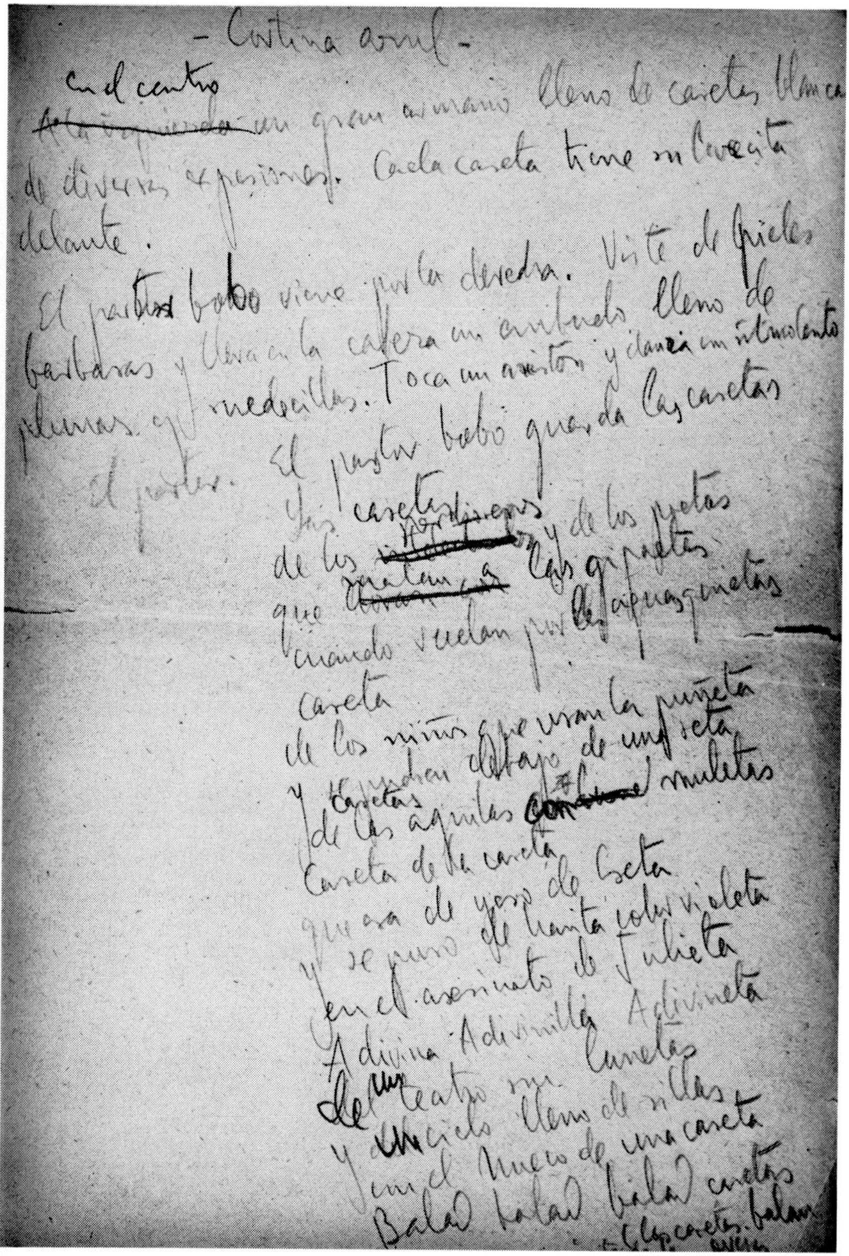

- Cortina azul -

en el centro un gran armario lleno de caretas blancas de diversas expresiones. Cada careta tiene su lucecita delante.

El pastor bobo viene por la derecha. Viste de pieles bárbaras y lleva en la cabeza un embudo lleno de plumas y ruedecillas. Toca un aristón y danza con ritmo lento.

El pastor. El pastor bobo guarda las caretas

Las caretas [illegible]
de los [illegible] y de los poetas
[illegible]
que [illegible]
cuando vuelan por [illegible]
careta
de los niños que usan la puñeta
y se pudren debajo de una seta
caretas de las águilas con muletas
Careta de la careta
que era de yeso de Creta
y se puso de tinta color violeta
en el asesinato de Julieta
Adivina adivinilla adivineta
de un teatro sin lunetas
y un cielo lleno de sillas
y en el hueco de una careta
Balad balad balad caretas
[illegible] caretas balad [illegible]

Song of the Mad Shepherd.

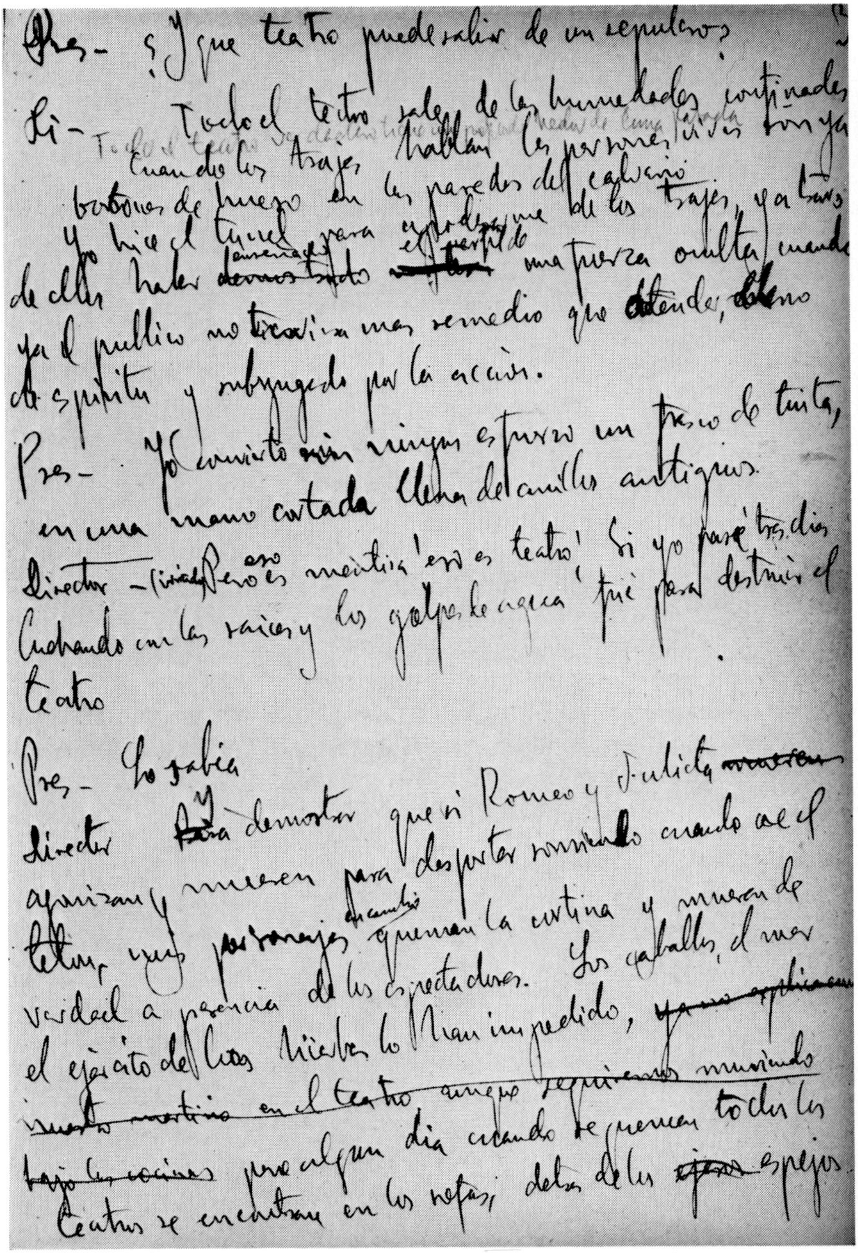

Dialogue between Director and Juggler in the last *Cuadro*.

love never limited to human beings. The form in which he expresses his Franciscan outlook is also that of a poet, now in control of prose and dialogue, both precise and clear-cut. When the Three White Horses tell Juliet that she has still the meadows and mountain-filled horizon, the Black Horse interrupts: *Juliet, don't pay any heed. In the meadows is the peasant who eats his own mucus, the huge foot which crushes the little mouse and the army of earthworms which wet the vicious grass with their dribble.* And just a little before in that same scene Juliet laments: *When I was very small I saw the beautiful cows grazing in the fields of Verona, later I saw them in my picture-books but I always remember them when passing the butcher's shop.*

In this play the poet has placed himself at the service of the dramatist. Corrections and erasures prove Lorca's sustained effort to restrain his lyrical vein. At times he may give the impression of going too far in this direction and of falling into coarse humour. In *Cuadro* V the students discuss the first effect of the revolution:

STUDENT 4: The first bomb of the revolution swept off the Professor of Rhetoric's head.

STUDENT 2: To the great joy of his wife who will now work so hard that she will have to instal two taps on each of her teats.

Expressions like this not only help to lighten the tension of the drama, they help to intensify by contrast the nightmarish atmosphere of the whole play. This and other similar Andalusian student puns fulfil in the play a function somewhat similar to that of a fly alighting on a loaf of bread, a clearly defined pin, or a bicycle painted with *quattrocento* richness of detail in a picture by Dalí, Miró or Domínguez.

In *The Public* Lorca introduces a few brief poems, but it is precisely on these occasions that we perceive most clearly how strong is his determination not to give way to lyrical temptation. They are, as we will see later, cast in an anti-poetic language but in popular poetic form because this fits the dramatic purpose, the circumstances in which they occur and the characters who voice them. Only in one instance has Lorca allowed his Pegasus a little flight, although the reins are kept short. It is in the middle of the unnumbered *cuadro*.

(The background wall opens and the sepulchre of Juliet in Verona is seen. Realistic scenery. Rose-trees and ivy. Juliet lies in the sepulchre. She is dressed in a white opera gown. Her breasts of rose celluloid uncovered.)

JULIET (*jumping out of the sepulchre*): Please, help me! I have not met a single friend in all this time in spite of having gone through more than three thousand empty arches. A little help, please. A little help and a sea of dreams. (*Sings.*)

> *A sea of dream,*
> *A sea of white earth,*
> *And the empty arches through the sky.*
> *The train of my dress through seas and sea-weeds,*
> *The train of my dress through time.*
> *A sea of time.*
> *Beach of woodcutter worms*
> *And dolphin of crystal through the cherry trees.*
> *Oh pure amianthus of the end! Oh ruin!*
> *Oh solitude without arches! Sea of dreams!*

This appearance of Juliet immediately after the dispute and fight between Director and Man 1 and between Men 2 and 3, is an example of the structural rhythm and equilibrium of the play. The Director and the Men, still in the world of the living, prisoners of their own unsatisfied instincts and desires barely understood, debate and fight amongst themselves. Juliet, perfect embodiment of normal love, though in the world of the dead, goes on longing for love and sings her 'solitude without arches' in a beautiful poem full of echoes not always easy to decipher.

The component elements of the poem – solitude, time, empty arches, dream – are mentioned by Juliet herself in the brief monologue before the song. To a certain extent this poem plays on the themes and ideas that recur in other works by Lorca but acquire a precise form at the opening of Act 3 in *When Five Years Have Passed*. There the sibylline Harlequin sings and dances a poem which is closely connected with this one of Juliet's. The two complement each other and contribute to a better understanding of their respective meanings. In both the poet establishes an opposition between dream and time but also a correlation and final fusion. What the Harlequin alludes to in a difficult metaphor, is the very heart of Juliet's song – a grave, cold, desolate meditation on the brevity of life and dream and on man's utter loneliness.

Juliet speaks from the realm of Death, Harlequin from its threshold . . . if this Harlequin is not – as I suspect – the disguised Angel of Death, or Death herself coming to receive those who arrive at her lair.

Dream drifts above Time
Floating like a sailing ship.
Nobody can force open seeds
In the heart of dream.

Thus begins Harlequin's song and Juliet, longing for an end to her solitary life in death, asks for *a sea of dream*, but immediately corrects herself, *a sea of white earth*. Could the dead Juliet – or Lorca – conceive dream as a desirous but bare, white land, where nothing can fructify? And if we bear in mind that in both poems Lorca is using the word *sueño* – dream – in all its Spanish connotations – life being one of them – we see that the two first lines of Harlequin's and Juliet's poems are loaded with a polyvalence not easily perceived on the first reading.

The train of my dress through seas and sea-weeds, sings Juliet, and the Mannequin in *When Five Years Have Passed* moans: 'The train of my dress is getting lost in the sea.' In both cases the same idea of constant flight in death: Juliet because she is already dead; the Mannequin's wedding dress because it remains unborn. *And the train of my dress through time*, adds Juliet. Her remembrance, her wake lost in a time without beginning or end. 'Sea of dream', then 'A sea of time'. Contrast or fusion? Vertical and horizontal. A longing for the eternal and a life that passes, carried away by time. But again Juliet corrects herself. Time is not *sea* but a beach, a beach of constant death, end of all living. In his second quatrain the Harlequin expresses the same idea:

Time goes above dream
Sunk to the top of the hair.
Yesterday and tomorrow consume
Dark flower of mourning.

Between parentheses of death runs the fleeting today that is human life. Yet in spite of their undeniable dramatic quality those two last lines cannot compete with the sharp precision of Juliet's 'Beach of woodcutter worms'. For here, in one single short line, Lorca has crystallized two similes fairly recurrent in his work: Man-tree and woodcutter-worm-death. Let us look at a few examples. In the last act of his early historical drama *Mariana Pineda* the protagonist, waiting to be taken to the scaffold for having embroidered the Liberals' flag, describes her agony:

> *As a tree of coral*
> *My blood shakes and shivers.*

In the 'Martyrdom of St. Olalla', the flames surround the bleeding body of the Saint.

> *A thousand little trees of blood*
> *Cover all her back*
> *And oppose wet tree trunks*
> *To the lancets of the flames.*

In the sonnet 'Adam', he narrates Adam's dream of paternity:

> *A tree of blood wets the morning*
> *Where the newly delivered woman moans.*

If Man's circulatory system can be described as a tree, it is logical to refer to the generations to come as:

> *Jungle of blood of the next morning*

or to say that:

> *The hands of man have no other meaning*
> *Than to imitate the roots under the earth*

or that the woman's belly is:

> *A turmoil of roots,*

and when Lorca himself talks of his fears of losing a beloved one he says:

> *It grieves me being on this river-bank*
> *Trunk without branches but what I most regret*
> *Is not to have the flower, the pulp or the clay*
> *For the worm of my suffering.*

An identification with nature allows the parallelism Man-tree. Thus, too, worm and woodcutter become synonymous with death. This idea began to take shape in one of his adolescent prose-exercises – 'The reapers with their scythes bring death to the ears of corn', he writes in 'San Pedro de Cardeña'. But soon, after his early trials, we find in the book *Songs* this masterpiece of dramatic brevity:

They Cut Three Trees

They were three.
(Day came with its axes.)
They were two.
(Trailing silver wings.)
It was one.
It was none
(The water lay naked.)

Then later on we encounter the three woodcutters of *Blood Wedding* who, in the forest scene, act as a bridge between the real world of the lovers and the world of death represented in the play by the Old Beggar Woman and the Moon. In *Poet in New York* the theme is blended with the general denunciation of a mechanical civilization which has lost all contact with nature:

The woodcutter does not know
When the clamorous trees he cuts expire

he wrote in 'Ode to the King of Harlem', and in 'Living Sky':

The frost of the dead-eye does not reach here
nor the groaning of the tree assassinated by the caterpillar

echoing, so it seems, the primeval rites and beliefs in the soul of trees of which Frazer wrote in *The Golden Bough*.

Thus the line in Juliet's song 'Beach of woodcutter-worms' becomes a little clearer. Beach of the 'sea of time', beach crowded with men falling like trees brought down by 'woodcutter-worms', in what Lorca has described in another poem as the place in which 'we will all fall at the last banqueting-feast of hole-drilling'.

But let us return to the Harlequin's song. It would seem that Lorca was not quite satisfied with that 'Yesterday and tomorrow consume dark flower of mourning,' because he goes one better in the third quatrain, a precise and brief exposition of the fleeting nature of life:

Round the same column
Where dream and time entwine
The broken tongue of the old man
Overtakes the faint moan of the child.

Round the same column – tree, cross, man? – dream and time blend together and old-age overtakes childhood as in the strange

Titian monochrome in the National Gallery of Art in Washington in which a horse's skull pursues and almost overtakes a Cupid who, against strong winds, runs round a tree rolling a wheel.

It is difficult to see how Lorca could surpass these third and fourth quatrains, the last one alluding to the fusion of dream and time, the latter cheating the former when Man thinks himself capable of computing time, making his own life the unit of measure:

> *And if dreams feign walls*
> *In time's endless plain*
> *Time makes him believe*
> *That he is born in that moment.*

And yet what those two quatrains express with an exquisite baroque twist was already explicit in the sharp soberness of 'Beach of woodcutter-worms' followed by the line 'And dolphin of crystal through the cherry trees'. Lorca, through Juliet, perhaps sees the succession of days as a dolphin jumping over the night to illumine every morning the cherry orchards soaked in dew. The lament 'Oh, pure amianthus of the end' could perhaps be an allusion to the final end of everything (amianthus resistant to fire, to the sun of life) perhaps to eternal time or silence. If this or something similar were the meaning of these lines the exclamation 'Oh ruin/Oh solitude without arches!' would be logical and the final words 'Sea of dreams!' completes the circle. A circle in form and idea, similar in pattern to the poem sung and danced by the Harlequin in *When Five Years Have Passed*. In that sea of dream and time there will not even be for Juliet the emptiness of the three thousand arches to which she alluded at the beginning.

The symbolism of the arch is discussed later. Of the other short poems found in *The Public* something will be said when dealing with the themes and ideas which those poems illustrate.

Surrealism and Cultural Tradition

By its form *The Public* could be classified as a surrealist drama, very likely as the first important attempt to apply surrealist techniques to a theatre of living problems both on the plane of reality and of dream. The extracts so far quoted show the visual surrealism of the play. More could be mentioned. 'Propellers of minute electric fans' covered the head of the Boy in 'Roman Ruin'. The Black Horse wears 'a crest of matching colour and carries a wheel in his hands'. Two pictorial details that could be found in any work by Dalí or Max Ernst. In the last scene the Juggler says that he could, without effort, turn 'a bottle of ink into an amputated hand with fingers covered in ancient rings', or 'a navigator into a sewing needle'. Does not the first quotation approach the lyrical surrealism of René Magritte and the second Man Ray's *Homage to Lautréamont*? The flies that fell 'on the three thousand oranges' that Man 1 had prepared, belong to the world of the ants that Buñuel, at about the same time, let loose in the palms of the hands that caress the breasts of the girl in *Le Chien Andalou*. In the same way that 'girl violated by a dog' who arrives at Juliet's sepulchre 'covering herself with geraniums' belongs also to the world of Buñuel. Perhaps it should be noted that most of the pictures that the reading of *The Public* bring to mind were painted *after* 1930: after, or many years before, because the 'funnel filled with little feathers and wheels' that covers the head of the 'Fool-Shepherd', is closely connected with the 'funnel' hats that we see on some heads by Bosch and Brueghel, painters that Lorca knew well and admired.

With surrealism are equally associated the aseptic and clinical motifs that abound in this and other works of Lorca – X-ray plates, thermometers, alcanphoric oil, etc., as well as what appears to be a theatre of the absurd, truncated images, automatism, materialization of dreams, mutations of forms, and free reign of the subconscious. Yet if by surrealism we understand what André Breton, Aragon and other theoreticians of the movement understood, *The Public* has nothing to do with that literary movement and Lorca, one of the poets who has most brilliantly made use of surrealist techniques in many of his poems, will remain not only outside the movement but in open opposition to it. In 1928, in the hey-day of *avant-garde* movements, Lorca wrote to his friend Sebastián Gash, at that time a young critic and *avant-garde* writer of Catalonia: 'They – the poems that accompanied the letter – respond to my new "spiritualist" vein, emotion bared and pure, totally free from all logical control. But beware! Beware! With tremendous poetic logic. It is not surrealism. Beware! The brightest of all forms of conscience illumines them.' That 'bright conscience' is a final *no* to the surrealist movement such as Breton defined it in his famous first manifesto. A *no* neither casual nor isolated. In 1932, in answer to the question: 'What is poetry?' he wrote to his friend and fellow poet, Gerardo Diego: '. . . Neither I nor you nor any other poet knows what poetry is. Here it is, look. I have the fire in my hands. I do understand it and I can work with it perfectly well but I cannot speak about it without turning it into literature . . .' And a little further: 'Occasionally I have spoken of poetry in general and of the poetry of others; but I cannot speak of my own. Not because I am unconscious of what I am doing. Just the opposite. If it is true that I am a poet by the grace of God – or the devil – it is equally true that I am a poet by the grace of technique and effort and by the full understanding of what makes a poem.'

Neither could Lorca, in spite of the recurrent dream-theme in his work, have accepted the second important rule of Bretonian surrealism. In another letter to Gash we read: '. . . and these dreams of mine do not represent a danger for me, armed as I am with natural defences. There is danger for those who let themselves be fascinated by the great dark mirrors that poetry and madness set at the bottom of their ravines. "In Matters of Art I Walk With Feet of Lead".' And in the revealing paper 'The poetic image in Góngora' he writes: 'The state of inspiration is a state of concentration, not of creative dynamism . . . I do not believe that any great artist has worked in a state of fever. Even the mystics work when the ineffable dove of the Holy Ghost has abandoned their cells . . . One returns from inspiration as from a foreign land. The poem is the narrative of the journey.' Lorca has nothing to do with Breton's surrealism.

But if by 'surrealism' we understand the use of unorthodox techniques tending to facilitate communication between the most intimate world of the artist and the outside world, the coexistence of dream and reality, the intercommunication of different levels, the elimination of the traditional conception of time and space, *The Public* will be the first full surrealist drama and Lorca, in this play and in a major sector of his work, a singular exponent of the movement. And as this conception of surrealism embraces prominent European artists it would seem legitimate to speak of two

72

types of surrealism. The 'academic' type – norms and limitations – represented by the group exclusively directed by Breton and his friends, and the 'rebel' type – liberty and tradition – which would include the surrealists not subject to Breton. In this second type Spain is prominent. Not only because those like Dalí, Miró, Buñuel and others who belonged to the 'club' were later expelled or anathematized but because poets like Alberti, Aleixandre and the Chilean Neruda, so closely connected with the Madrid group of poets in the first half of the thirties, never participated in the movement in a recognized manner. In connection with the 'surrealist' aspects of their work, it will be difficult to speak of 'automatism of dreams without any control of reason'. What we find instead is a sounding of the consciousness, memories and dreams, glimpses of archetypes and renewal of old myths. 'Sometimes dream turns into nightmare,' at its best in visionary and prophetic poetry; but the poem is always 'the narrative of a journey'. Nothing serves better to illustrate the difference between these two types of surrealism than a comparison between Paul Éluard's *L'Amour, la poésie* (1929), Aragon's *La grande gaieté* (1929) or Breton's *Le Revolver à cheveux blancs* (1932) with *Espadas como labios* (1932) by Aleixandre, *Sobre los Angeles* (1929) by Alberti or *Poet in New York* by Lorca, written in 1929–30 though published posthumously. In the attempts at surrealist drama made by Breton and his friends there is nothing comparable to Lorca's two great experiments, *The Public* and *When Five Years Have Passed*.

What are, then, the characteristics of Lorca's surrealism? In discussing the surrealist aspect of *Poet in New York* most critics explain it by saying that surrealism 'was in the air' – which indeed was so – or else attribute it to the supposed influence of Salvador Dalí on Lorca. This latter point requires some clarification. There is no doubt that the close friendship between Lorca and Dalí was fruitful for both of them but any attempt to ascertain whose influence was greater on the other is as problematic as it is irrelevant. For those who knew both of them in Madrid at the students' *Residencia* there is no doubt as to who was the stronger personality, the more developed, the one who most encouraged all experiments, though Lorca himself preferred to remain slightly outside, as a keen observer. *A posteriori* it may seem evident that the one who was to become a leading exponent of pictorial surrealism must have exercised an inevitable influence on a poet for whom surrealism was an occasional instrument of dramatic or poetic expression. But there is nothing in what Lorca or Dalí have written about each other which could support such an assumption. If anything, the reverse was the case.[1]

Through Dalí, it is true, Lorca entered into contact with the *avant-garde* groups of Barcelona, especially with 'L'Amic de les Arts', which was well acquainted with developments in the Parisian groups. On the other hand Catalonia with all its fascinating pagan substratum, with its *joie de vivre*, was bound to attract a great sensualist such as Lorca. Barcelona and Cadaqués – summer residence of the Dalís – were for him silencers of 'black tones'. But a knowledge of that period, and a study of Lorca's work make it difficult to believe that Catalonian surrealism or Dalí's friendship were determining or important factors in Lorca's use of surrealist techniques. Most critics and historians today seem to forget the burst of intellectual activity in Spain in the twenties and the first half of the thirties. In Madrid, focus of talent from all over the country, it was particularly remarkable. If in numbers these intellectual circles in Madrid and Barcelona were smaller than similar ones in Paris, London or New York, in quality and originality they had no need to envy their neighbours. It is enough to recall artists and writers of the *avant-garde* youth of the day who were to become famous – Lorca, Dalí, Buñuel – and amongst the slightly older, not so internationally famous, one of the most original writers of the day, Ramón Gómez de la Serna, instigator of all 'isms', one of the principal influences among the young writers of the twenties.

Moreover, when speaking of Spanish surrealism one should also take into consideration the surrealist vein constant in Spanish art, letters and – some might include – way of living. In the particular case of Lorca it would be pertinent also to recall the rich, extravagant personalities who are found in all university colleges and amongst whom Lorca thrived.

[1] Among other testimonies let us quote from the jacket of the Polydor record. Privilège. LPL 1334 2Y (Poemas de Lorca y de Góngora puestos en música y cantados por Paco Ibáñez) 'illustrée par Salvador Dalí:

'. . . Au fond, je dois beaucoup de mes idées a cette espèce de masse confuse, grouillante et intégrale qui est la poésie de García Lorca . . . Mais je les ai depouillées et, comme je suis légèrement phénicien, j'ai spéculé beaucoup sur les idées qu'il jetait d'une façon confuse avec une générosité vraiment éblouissante. J'ai spéculé sur elles et je les ai systématisées, je les ai rendues intelligentes car García Lorca comme tous les grands phénomènes poétiques était très peu intelligent.'

Whatever surrealist forms we may detect in Lorca's work they certainly did not come from Paris via Barcelona. In him everything points to the visionary and prophetic tradition both Spanish and universal. He looked to Bosch, to Quevedo's *Sueños* (Dreams), to Goya's *Los sueños de la razón producen monstruos* (Reason's dreams engender monsters). Under a surrealist cloak lies an old and rich cultural tradition.

The basic components of Lorca's work are the experiences of his own life and a rich, popular and *culto*-tradition. Their many mutations should be noted for they help us to understand the true meaning of surrealist-fashioned poems, prose and dramas, and appreciate the rich variety of allusions in plot, sentence or metaphor.

With only one or two exceptions, Lorca may well be the modern Spanish poet with the greatest cultural load. This statement will no doubt shock those who accept without question the image of an intuitive poet, a spontaneous product of nature, who sang like a bird on the branch. A mere listing of names and of direct and indirect quotations found in his work would be enough to destroy the legend. That these have passed unnoticed proves that names and quotations flow with the silence and effortlessness of water. They are part of his personal vocabulary.

Some of those brilliant young Spanish poets of the twenties and the first half of the thirties may have 'studied' much harder than Lorca; some were also professors and scholars of repute. In the case of Jorge Guillén, for example, no one could fail to admire the grace, precision, irony or dramatic sense with which the intelligence of the man puts at the service of the poet the classic allusion or the scholarly quotation, but in none of these fine poets is there such total, natural absorption of what has been read or heard; and in Lorca auditory memory was as remarkable as the visual. Like so many poets before him Lorca assimilated and projected, seemingly without effort, without full awareness, the predominant ideas of his time. Sometimes he even anticipated their logical consequences. But not only names and quotations reveal the cultural load. Reading with care it is possible to detect its sources and to perceive the echoes that awaken in us truncated images, mutations of forms, disconnected sentences. Let us look at some examples to be found in *The Public*.

A little after the beginning of the play we saw how three men called on the Director to 'congratulate' him on the performance of *Romeo and Juliet, a man and a woman in love*. The desire to determine whether the two youths were really in love, and the nature of their passion, motivates the pattern of action. The action itself is centred in two performances of the famous Shakespearean tragedy. Then, 'descending' in search of truth, the Director and the men reach Juliet's sepulchre in Verona. The familiar story will suffer strange mutations, but constant echoes of words and situations prove the presence of Shakespeare's text in Lorca's mind. *Juliet lies in the sepulchre, she is dressed in a long white evening gown,* says the stage direction. And immediately Friar Laurence's words come to mind:

> *Then – as the manner of our country is –*
> *In thy best robes uncover'd on the bier,*
> *Thou shalt be borne to that same ancient vault . . .*

But the idea of making Juliet herself the one who is lying in the sepulchre instead of a statue recalls the hall in the crystalline palace where Montesinos took Don Quixote to contemplate the marble sepulchre where Durandarte was 'lying at full length, wrought not in brass, nor marble, nor carved jasper, as is usual on other tombs, but in pure flesh and on pure bone'.

The tumult of voices and swords heard by Lorca's Juliet reminds us of the deadly encounter between Romeo and Paris and of the subsidiary explanations and discussions in the crypt of the Capulets presided over by the Prince of Verona in the presence of the bodies of Romeo, Juliet and Paris.

In the last but one page of the unnumbered *cuadro* Lorca, in order not to halt the flow of his pen, scribbled between parentheses *Here the words of the Shakespearean drama,* a clear indication that he was writing without notes and without the Shakespearean text at hand. But almost certainly he was thinking of the amorous dialogue in Juliet's bed at day-break and the eternal anguish of all clandestine lovers synthesized by Shakespeare in the antonym lark-nightingale. This is confirmed when Man 3 says to Juliet a little later in that same scene: *Wait, wait. Now the nightingale is singing*. Although what is heard is in fact a car klaxon, like the klaxon on the Rugby Player's car in which he drives away the 'Juliet' of *When Five Years Have Passed*. Transposition of words and actions in a time without barriers. Yet, when everybody has gone, the scene ends with a detail of dramatic realism whose effect is to enhance the atmosphere of mystery: *Over the sound of rain the true nightingale sings.*

More coincidences could be listed. The Juliet in Shakespeare is fourteen, the boy playing Juliet in Lorca's play is fifteen, Romeo thirty-five; very likely an allusion to the boy actors who played women's parts in the Elizabethan theatre. When in Act V the Male Nurse says to the Red Nude that he is two minutes fast, the latter answers: *But the nightingale has already sung.* Lorca's Juliet says in the unnumbered scene that rats are her friends, and in the Shakespearean drama Romeo says to the Friar that he envies everything that can see his Juliet – 'every cat and dog and little mouse . . .' The White Horse which courts Juliet in her sepulchre offers her not the day, but the night, and in the subsidiary discussions on the delights of nights and days, the White Horse sums up: *Understand well one single day so as to love all nights* which again may be a reverberation, on a different level, of the nurse's advice to Juliet: 'Go, girl, seek happy nights to happy days.' Yet, in spite of the constant references to the tragedy of *Romeo and Juliet*, the theme of *The Public*, the accidental nature of love, is more closely connected with another Shakespeare play which had always haunted Lorca: *A Midsummer Night's Dream.*

'An old fairy, escaping from one of the books of the great Shakespeare, told the poet the story,' he wrote in his introduction to *The Malefice of the Butterfly*, that early, adolescent play on the world of insects written before Čapek's famous play. And then in 1935 in a letter to the sculptor Angel Ferrant, Lorca gives his friend precise instructions as to what the little heads for his puppet play *Los títeres de cachiporra* should look like. 'The character "Mosquito" is Shakespeare's Puck, half fairy, half little boy, *half insect.*' Between those distant quotations many others could be found. In 1936, at one of my last dinners with him, I was telling him and other friends of an evening performance of *A Midsummer Night's Dream* I had seen in the garden of one of the colleges of Oxford or Cambridge. Federico, who was listening with great interest, suddenly interrupted me: 'And how did they perform the scene between Titania and the ass?' I explained it, adding something about what I already thought was a negative influence of the English pantomime on the contemporary playing of the comic scenes in Shakespeare's plays.

'What a pity,' he remarked. 'That is a scene of delicate lyricism and must be performed with the utmost sincerity. The comedy is in the situation, not in the actors who must act in total seriousness. Otherwise the play is not understood.' I asked him how he interpreted the comedy. 'What Shakespeare is telling us' – were more or less his own words – 'is that love, which does not depend on the free will of the individual, is to be found at all levels with equal intensity. What is happening in that forest near Athens is what is happening to all the characters inside or outside the magic fairy world: from Theseus-Hyppolita and Titania-Oberon down to the play performed by Bottom and his companions. But the key to the play is Titania in love with an ass.' The recollection of that conversation was of help in understanding *The Public*.

In this play the first allusion to *A Midsummer Night's Dream* is indirect. Right at the beginning of the play Man 1 harasses the Director: *And if I tell you that the main character was a poisonous flower. What will you say? Answer.* But it is not until the end of the play that we fully realize all that *The Public* owes to Lorca's reading of *A Midsummer Night's Dream*. The Director says that he chose *Romeo and Juliet* to express what is happening every day throughout the world: *I could just as well have chosen Oedipus or Othello.* But the Juggler interrupts: *Had you made use of 'Diana's flower' which Shakespeare used with irony in 'A Midsummer Night's Dream' it is likely that the play could have scored a success. If love is pure hazard and Titania, Queen of the Fairies, fell in love with an ass, it would hardly surprise anybody if by the same procedure Gonzalo were to drink in a music-hall with a boy dressed in white sitting on his knees.*

Quotations or literary allusions from other sources can be detected on successive readings. With great urgency the Emperor is looking for the *one*. In the poetic prose entitled *Sol y Sombra*[1] Lorca, half-joking, sketched an aesthetic theory not unfamiliar to the attentive reader of his work. *Sol y Sombra* – the two halves into which the bull ring is divided – become symbols of the duality of the one. 'Rival elements' – he calls them – 'antagonistic halves . . . night and day embraced in the ring and inseparable', and though he does not say so openly, it is a mirror also of those other antitheses often found in his poetry: love and death; reality and dream.

---

[1] *Sun and Shadow*, Federico García Lorca. Translated by Kathleen Raine and R. M. Nadal. French translation by Marcelle Auclair. Enitharmon Press, London, 1972.

That in the work of Lorca platonic undertones can be detected should surprise no one. The problem of the one, of the unity, of the reunion of two halves, always worried him, particularly at the time when he was reading the Socratic dialogues. Of course he viewed the problem from a poet's angle. I remember an early morning conversation in the gallery of a Madrid night club just before his journey to America. Other friends had either left or were talking at other tables. 'If the one is the perfect fusion of two halves' – he was saying – 'we men are nothing but forests of halves in eternal search for the unattainable fusion. Love is nothing but the permanent longing to reach the one. Then if the one were attainable that would mean the negation of love. We die alone, as lonely halves.'

We saw how at the end of 'Roman Ruin' the Figure covered with Vine Leaves pretended to be the one the Emperor was looking for and how on shedding the vine leaves we saw a white plaster nude. Whatever doubts remain about the intention of the author, they disappear when the Centurion says to the Emperor: *It is difficult, but there you have him*, and the Figure covered with Vine Leaves cries: *He has him because he will never be able to have him*. Later on, the same Man 1 speaks of the *pure beauty of marble that glitters protecting intimate desires beneath a flawless surface*.

The preoccupation with the *one* and with the impossible union reappears from a different angle in the last stanza of 'Little Infinite Poem':

> *But two has never been a number*
> *Because it is an anguish and its own shadow,*
> *Because it is the guitar in which love despairs.*

A theme already present in the juvenile poem entitled 'Beehive':

> *We live in cells*
> *Of crystals,*
> *In beehives of air!*
> *We kiss each other*
> *Through glass.*

an idea which is connected with the total solitude of man discussed later.

Other examples of faint Hellenism can be found. One of the first sentences of the Director is that he would give all his blood to escape to Greece *so as not to leave a single dove alive in Greece*.

Helen is dressed *as a Greek*. And when in *Cuadro* V Student 2 asks for the name of the Professor of Rhetoric's wife, Student 3 answers: *Her name is Helen*. Frightened and in an aside Student 1 repeats *Selene*, that is to say moon in its double meaning of woman and death.

Just after the Emperor has murdered the child in the Ruin we read in the stage directions: *The Emperor enters drying his forehead. He takes off a pair of black gloves, then another pair of red gloves and his hands of classic beauty appear*. The literary associations that these words awaken are the little stanzas of the poet Abu-Nuas, quoted in *The Book of the Thousand and One Nights*, that Lorca knew only too well.[1] But cultural sources are by no means limited to literature. Let us look back at Act 1, to that passage when Man 1 says to the Director that he saw him one day hiding a hare – a popular symbol of speed and liberty – in the narrow confines of a brief-case, and that he also remembers the day the Director discovered the centre parting and the rose behind the ear. A cryptic sentence, especially the first part, because of the difficulty of ascertaining the value that Lorca attached to the hare. Of all contemporary Spanish poets Lorca may well have the greatest capacity to assimilate, appropriate and transform traditional symbols. In him they are part of his poetic world, intermingled with the myths he himself creates or recreates out of what he has seen on canvas or stone, heard in popular tales, read in legends. Hence their rich polyvalence, their strength and appeal but also their obscurity.

In this particular case the clue was found in the book of John Layard, *The Lady of the Hare*. In this 'study in the healing power of dreams', a Jungian psycho-therapist describes a clinical case in which the patient, a woman, had a recurrent dream of a hare. The second part of the book is an attempt to collect the huge body of material on the symbolism of this animal. In the section devoted to the study of the hare as an amorous token in ancient Greece, John Layard mentions, translating from the French, the explanation given in the *Compte-Rendu de la Commission Impériale Archéologique pour l'Année 1862* (St. Petersburg, 1863) to some drawings on Greek vases of the fifth century B.C.:

[1] Story of the poet Abu-Nuas and the three poems he improvised when the boy with whom he was in love shed the black, red and white tunics he was wearing one after the other.

(*The Book of the Thousand and One Nights*.) Translated and annotated by Richard F. Burton. Vol. 4, pp. 261–4.

We see men handling the same animal as a gift to youths, or vice versa; youths having just received one from men who in the picture appear to be occupying themselves with the gift; or paintings in which hares are hung up between men and youths, thus clearly indicating the nature of their relationship.

And this gives some sense to that passage of *The Public*. Lorca, of course, could not have known John Layard's book, but it is certain that he knew some of the many legends associating the hare with lust, fecundity, bisexualism, etc. Possibly in Spain he may have heard of that Greek offering of love; very likely in Boston he actually saw one of the Greek vases preserved in the museum. What Man 1 seems to convey is that he remembers when the Director tried to hide – in intellectualized fashion – his homosexual instinct (hare enclosed in a brief-case) and how the instinct took revenge, reappearing later on in that violent popular representation of the local Andalusian pansy: 'a rose stuck behind each ear the day he discovered the centre parting'.

Another example. In the Capulet crypt the White Horses want to sleep with Juliet and the Black Horse makes the already quoted remark: '*Who goes through whom? Oh love, love that needs to pass its light through dark heat! Oh sea, resting on twilight and flower in the arse of the dead!*' The first sentence offers little difficulty. Love as light has clear classical resonances. The 'sea resting on twilight' is a fairly clear image if projected on the sea and beach of Juliet's song and even more on the dialogue between Director and Juggler apropos the sand reflected in the blurred mirror. But what about the 'flower in the arse of the dead'? In the central panel of the famous triptych *The Garden of Delights*, to the left of what Wilhelm Fränger calls 'The Gate of Initiation', we see two naked kneeling men. One bending over, bottom up, stares with strange, intelligent passivity at the onlooker. In his arse there is a little branch with two daisy-like flowers. His companion is also kneeling but upright. His right hand holds another little branch, an exact replica of that in his companion's arse. It matters little that the latter is picking flowers from his friend's arse – as Wilhelm Fränger suggests in his *The Millennium of Hieronymus Bosch* (London 1952), or sticking flowers in it or playing a strange game. Whatever the meaning of this particular esoteric detail in the mysterious triptych, the important thing for us is that this picture was one of Lorca's favourite paintings and that this detail may have suggested

81

the plastic image we have just examined. It is tempting to assume that on the level in which *The Public* moves, any erotogenic zone is admissible. But the Black Horse refers to the 'arse of the dead', since he sees everything from the realm of death. Besides, we know that for Lorca all forms of love end in death and that in the 'void' left by forms that were dear to man, flowers, snails or thistles take possession. But this comes under another heading.

Forms—metamorphosis—void

When discussing the theme of *The Public* I felt inclined to interpret the dialogue in 'Roman Ruin' between the two Figures as a 'dialogue of impossible love, more closely connected with the Greek myths of metamorphosis than with surrealist aesthetics'. Lorquian texts justify this assumption. In that revealing essay 'The poetic image in Don Luis de Góngora' Lorca quotes lines 328–331 of 'Soledad segunda':

> *Six poplars black, by ivies six embraced,*
> *Were thyrsi of the Greek god, who was born*
> *A second time, who with vine-shoots concealed*
> *Upon his brow each horn.*[1]

This quotation is preceded by the following lines: 'In the Greek myth Bacchus undergoes three passions and deaths. First he is a he-goat with twisted horns. Because of his love for the dancer Cyssus who dies and turns into ivy, Bacchus, in order to continue the dance, transforms himself into a vine. Lastly he dies and turns himself into a fig-tree.' This may provide the key to the understanding of that strange dialogue in 'Roman Ruin'. The Figure covered with Vine Leaves – Man 1 – seems to spring from Lorca's vision of Bacchus 'who with vine-shoots concealed . . .', just as the Figure with little Bells – double of the Director – seems inspired by Cyssus. The first plays the flute, the second dances – 'dancing is the only way I have of making love to you'. To be able to continue the dance Bacchus turns himself into a fig-tree; the two figures in

---

[1] *The Solitudes of Don Luis de Góngora*. A text with translation by Edward Meryon Wilson. Cambridge. At the University Press, 1965. (p. 89.)

The Public test each other on the transformations they would be capable of undergoing for the sake of love.

Lorca's essay on Góngora has a two-fold interest. On the one hand a young, at times obscure poet of today explains the poetry of a difficult poet of the past; on the other, Lorca speaking about Góngora discloses his own attitude towards poetry, metaphors and myths; he clarifies for us aspects of *The Public* and of his later work. The poet from Granada does not find any difficulty in the syntax or vocabulary of the poet from Cordova. 'The only difficulty' – he says – 'may lie in the understanding of his mythological world. Difficult because not many people know mythology today and because Góngora does not limit himself to quoting the myth. He transforms it or gives us only one relevant detail which defines it. And it is here that his metaphors acquire an inimitable tonality. Hesiod recounts his *Theogony* with popular and religious fervour, and the subtle man from Cordova re-tells it by stylizing or inventing new myths. Here are to be found his poetic pounces, his daring transformations, his disdain for the explanatory method.' Precisely what Lorca was doing. We have already seen some examples in the texts so far quoted; we will find more when discussing the love-theme in the work of Lorca; we will find others even when looking at the short poems in *The Public*.

Let us look at one example. When Juliet rejects the White Horse's request, the latter sings:

> *Love. To Love. Love.*
> *Love of the snail, nail, nail,*
> *Who brings his horns to the sun.*
> *To love. Love. To love.*
> *Of the horse who licks*
> *The ball of salt.*

The first two lines are taken from an old Spanish children's song, a theme also used by some Spanish poets of the sixteenth and seventeenth centuries. The two last lines could mirror the 'Romeo can be a grain of salt' of the first scene. The 'mysterious horse' of the song will grow to become a very personal Lorquian myth. After a marginal comment by Juliet, the White Horse continues:

> *To love. Love. To love.*
> *Love of Ginido with the he-goat.*

83

And of the mule with the snail, nail, nail
Who brings his horns out to the sun.
To love. Love. To Love.
Of Jupiter in the stable
With the peacock
And the horse that neighs inside the Cathedral.

In the second line Lorca suppresses *serpent* – and substitutes Ginido and the he-goat; an allusion either to the metamorphosis of Bacchus or of Pan. Or did he mean to write Gnido? In this case, he may have been thinking of a sexual relationship between Venus – the flower of Gnido – and the he-goat she rides in some representations of the goddess. In lines five and six there seems to be a veiled allusion to the metamorphosis of Jupiter into a bull or a horse. In one of these Jupiter is seen making love to a peacock. Lorca makes use of the metamorphosis to illustrate the central theme of his play stated clearly by Man 1 in the first scene: *Romeo can be a grain of salt and Juliet a map*. In the last line the horse neighing in the cathedral offers us a good example of how Lorca transforms reality into myth. Thanks to Marcelle Auclair we know the essential facts. In her biography of the poet, Mme Auclair explains how the poets Salinas and Lorca prepared her visit to Cordova in the early thirties. The former was mainly concerned to put her in contact with the gongorists of Andalusia; Lorca wanted her to see the landscape and objects familiar to the seventeenth century poet: '. . . and then, Góngora apart, ask Mr. X to take you to the Artillery remount; it is a cathedral for horses'.[1] When Marcelle Auclair passed this information on to me I pressed her for further details. 'The "cathedral for horses"' – she wrote from Paris – 'appeared like this: one enters a large courtyard, and to the left – I do not remember if it was the same on the right also – was a row of little Gothic chapels; each one, a stable for one horse. Something like a church without a roof, with side chapels. Federico had advised me to go at the end of the day and, in fact, at that time they were bringing the horses out (maybe to water) and I remember the extraordinary effect of the silky light at sunset. There was one horse in particular, one horse *gris pommelé* that was a portent.' Was it Lorca himself who so nicknamed the remount of the Artillery? It matters little, for what creates the myth is not the nickname; it is that jump from 'looks like' to *is*; from *real* horses to *one* single

[1] Marcelle Auclair, *Enfances et mort de García Lorca*, Paris, 1968. (p. 206, note.)

mysterious horse whose neighing 'adorns his head' and sends taboos to flight.

The whole work of Lorca proclaims his obsession with mythological metamorphosis. In the juvenile poem 'Manantial' a voice orders the poet, seeking truth, to change himself into a tree, and instantly he describes the detail of his slow transformation:

> *With sadness and eagerness*
> *I entrust myself to the centennial black poplar-tree*
> *Like virile Daphne in panic flight*
> *From an Apollo of shadow and nostalgia.*
> *My spirit fused with the leaves*
> *And my blood turned to sap.*
> *And the source of my tears*
> *Into sticky resin.*

In another adolescent poem entitled 'Invocation to the Laurel' the same myth reappears when talking of that tree:

> *Master of kisses and orchestral magician,*
> *Formed with Daphne's rosy body*
> *And with potent sap of Apollo in your veins.*

Quotations and names from Greek mythology often appear in his work. At times Bacchus and Pan intermingle with Satan. The *cofrades*[1] with black hoods over heads and faces who accompany the images during the processions of Easter Week are seen as 'strange unicorns. From what field, from what mythological forest?' The *Ecce Homo* is defined as 'enchained Durandarte' and 'Furious Orlando'; the guitar becomes 'a golden Polyphemus' and the prickly-pear 'savage Laocoon'. In a poem of *First Songs* the oxen 'still remember the wings they once grew on their sides', and in another poem from *Songs* Cyclops and Unicorns are portrayed as symbols of the flesh's carnal rite.

In his first book of poems ancient myths are nearly always alluded to with juvenile earnestness; in *Poem of the Cante Jondo* and in *Songs*, with subtle irony. But they are always recognizable. From the *Gipsy Ballads* onwards, the allusions become more difficult. He also 'sets the myths in profile', illumined by other lights. At times with ironic twist or surrealist technique: 'Since

[1] *Cofrades*. Members of a brotherhood formed round one particular *paso*. *Paso*: literally, 'step'. Image or sculpture group usually representing a station of the cross. They are brought out of the churches for the processions of Holy Week.

you cannot turn yourself into a pigeon, it's right that you should be dead.' The same theme as in *The Public* narrated here without tragedy: 'They were a man and a woman, that is to say, a man and a little bit of earth, an elephant and a child, a child and a rush. They were two lads in a faint and a leg of nickel. They were the boatmen! Yes. They were the river Guadiana's boatmen.' The metamorphosis for love, in an effort to attain the impossible union, ends in the dramatic duel-dance in 'Roman Ruin'. The literary sources behind his interest in transformations are obvious: Ovid's *Metamorphoses* and Hesiod's *Theogony*, to mention only two books we know for certain he read and re-read. But in Lorca, as in any other true poet, the ultimate value of determining the literary sources is not so much to show what the poet has taken from the outside but to reveal what he *'carried inside'*. In the case of Lorca, cultural and popular tradition are superimposed on vital experiences and personal observations, similar to those which contributed to the birth of all metamorphosis: awareness of the periodic changes in nature and of the constant changes in all living forms from birth to death and beyond.

After *Poet in New York*, echoes of Greek metamorphosis are more difficult to perceive. They dissolve in the growing awareness of the changes that pave the way to death. Friend 2 in *When Five Years Have Passed* knows well these changes: 'But my face is mine and they are stealing it from me. I was very young and tender and used to sing and now there is a man, a respectable gentleman (*talking to the old man*) like you, walking within me with two or three masks ready . . .' More examples could be quoted.

This final stage in the evolution of this theme, as well as Lorca's obsession with death, is not the result of a temperamental necrophilia. Just the opposite. If he is obsessed with metamorphosis it is precisely because he loves form. Like all his key ideas this one can also be traced back to his very early writings. 'These flowers and these acacias are not in the atmosphere dreamt by their forms,' he writes in his adolescent prose piece 'Station Gardens', one of the literary exercises collected in his youth and published under the title *Impressions and Landscapes*. Of a fallen weathercock he says in an early poem: 'But you possess form. Be content with that.' Or when addressing himself to worms: 'Happy you, oh worms! for you possess full consciousness of yourself and forms and passions . . .' Gradually, almost without noticing it, Lorca

86

uses the concept of form in its classical definition of everything that makes a thing what it is. 'A desire for forms and limits conquers us', he says in his 'Ode to Salvador Dalí' and in 'Theory and divertissement of the *duende*'[1] tells the story of how the famous gipsy singer Niña de los Peines sang in a little tavern of Seville without tourists when a little old gipsy man had uttered the pejorative cry 'Viva Paris' ('Long live Paris') after her opening song: 'She had to strain her voice because she knew that she was being heard by people of taste who did not ask for forms but for the marrow of forms . . .'

For Lorca, lover of life, all was a question of form. But he was also aware that life is a constant shedding of dead forms in an uninterrupted march towards total death. An eternal theme. Shakespeare and Garcilaso praised in unforgettable sonnets the fleeting moment of perfect youthful beauty. But Lorca did not believe in Renaissance conventions.

In the early poems he unashamedly enjoys and praises young bodies. It is even possible to perceive a vague note of neoplatonic optimism:

> *All this echo of stars that I enshrine in my soul*
> *Will it be light that helps me to struggle with my body*
> *And does the real soul awaken in death?*

Yet in 'Ballad of the Little Square' when the children asked him: 'What does your red, thirsty mouth savour?' the poet answers: 'The taste of the bones in my big skull.' Much later, in New York, when he considers the inescapable disappearance of all living things, he will cry: 'all forms are nothing but lies.' All is undone, finished. In the poem, 'Return from a Walk' the changes take on a very personal note; Lorca sees himself 'stumbling over my own face, different every day'. At times too, changing forms are seen as costumes. 'My death agony was looking for its dress.' At times, simply as masks; others as death's masks:

DIRECTOR: If we mock the mask . . .

---

[1] *Duende.* Literally, 'hobgoblin' or 'ghost'. Is used in Andalusia, especially among *jondo* singers, dancers, guitar players and *aficionados* to describe that indefinable, rare and mysterious quality that at any given moment touches a deep chord in the performer and which is transmitted to the small group of connoisseurs round him or her. Lorca in this essay raises the *duende* to the category of an aesthetic principle applicable to all forms of art.

JULIET (*crying*): Mask.
WHITE HORSE: Form.

We shall have to wait until the 'Lament for Ignacio Sánchez Mejías' before Lorca writes with classic serenity of the disintegration of living forms:

> *We are in the presence of a vanishing corpse*
> *Which once had clear form and living nightingales*
> *And look at it now being filled with bottomless holes.*

In that human body in which the pulsation of blood sang like gay nightingales we can see now little holes appearing in what, in another poem, he called 'the last banqueting feast of hole drilling'.

To witness changes in forms that once were dear is painful. Yet the true antithesis to form is not transformation but its disappearance, the *void* left behind, the *hueco*:

> *It does not matter that every minute*
> *A new child shakes his little bunch of veins,*
> *What matters is that: void. World alone.*
> *The flow into nothingness.*

'Soul alien to my vein's void', he writes in the poem 'Your childhood in Menton' and in 'Norm and Paradise of the Negroes':

> *It is there where torsos dream under the gluttony of the grass.*
> *There corals drenched the ink's despair,*
> *The sleepers rub out their profiles under the entangled snails*
> *And only the dance's void over the last ashes remains.*

Between the familiar forms and the final void, the poet notices the gradual, constant appearance of voids:

> *It was the great meeting of dead animals*
> *Transfixed by swords of light,*
> *The eternal smile of the hippopotamus with ashen feet,*
> *And of the gazelle with an everlasting flower in his throat.*

In New York this idea becomes obsessive. It is not merely the disappearance of the living forms he once knew – the air itself is full of voids left by those who have died; and it is *filled* with the void of those still alive:

> *There is a void's pain in the empty air*
> *and in my eyes, dressed people without bodies!*

Costumes without bodies like the costumes shed by the Director and Man 2 in the unnumbered scene of *The Public*.

This idea of the *void*, to which his 'poetic logic' lead him, was also present in his early prose as we shall see when discussing the ruins theme. Soon it gathers momentum by applying, for example, the adjective *vacío* (empty) to trains, beds, cities, clouds, St. Lorenzo's overall, etc. But it strikes one most in the first three poems of the section entitled 'Introduction to Death'. In the first one there is an allusion to the painful changes of form in animals and plants. And the poet ends with a dramatic vision of his *alter ego*.

> *And I on the edge of the eaves*
> *What seraph of flames*
> *I am and search for.*

Opposition and juxtaposition: to look for and to be. In contrast to the efforts of horses, rose or lump of sugar, how easy it is for Death to wield changes:

> *But the chalky arch,*
> *How great, how invisible, how minute!*
> *Without effort.*

Chalky arch in this particular case, very likely an allusion to the arches of gateways, of cemeteries and niches.

From that other river bank or sea-shore, in order to be aware that all has gone, he begs his dead beloved, 'give me a moon-glove, the other glove lost in the grass' – empty gloves like the slow rain of rigid, white gloves at the end of *The Public*.

> *To see that all has gone,*
> *To see the voids and the dresses,*
> *Give me your glove of moon,*
> *Your other glove lost in the grass.*
> *Oh my beloved!*

In successive readings, this difficult poem shows unexpected depths, while the images of the poet-painter lose nothing of their freshness and polyvalence:

> *Impassive the row of faces*
> *Under the minute uproar of the grass.*

or

> *What a silence of supine trains!*
> *How many mummified arms in flower!*
> *What sky without exit, my love, what a sky!*

The poet looks at the dried blood on the sand in the bull-ring:

> *And the forms that look for the serpent's coil*
> *Become hard crystal and final,*

reminding us of his description of running blood in the ballad 'Brawl':

> *Spilled blood moans a mute serpent song.*

Worse even than the voids lost in the air are the concrete forms searching for their own voids, or those forms that live for thousands of years imprisoned in rocks or under layers of earth:

> *Look at these concrete forms in search of their own voids,*
> *Confused dogs and bitten apples.*
> *Look at the eagerness, the anguish of a sad fossil world*
> *Which cannot find the pitch of its first sob.*

A little further on, a possible allusion to the four rivers of paradise fades into a Goyesque etching:

> *No, not through my eyes, for now you are showing me*
> *Four rivers girding your arms,*
> *In the hard hut where the imprisoned moon*
> *Devours a sailor in front of the children.*

The second poem from 'Introduction to Death' ends with the poet seeing his own death, his own void through the air:

> *No, do not give me your void,*
> *For mine is already going through the air!*

The second part of this poem sounds like a detailed and serene premonition of the circumstances of his own death. It begins with an allusion to the horse, his favourite animal, also dead, calcinated, in a vision that in spite of the mention of the bull-ring, pertains more to Blake than to Goya:

> *With the whitest white void of a horse,*
> *Mane of ashes. Pure and folded bull-ring.*

Quickly, the details of the crime of Víznar, the ravine where Lorca was murdered at the beginning of the Spanish Civil War, unfold:

the volley at dawn, the body pierced with bullets amongst other bodies also assassinated, far from the city where the living, perhaps those who ordered his death, seem to him like dead people eating:

> *My void pierced armpits broken*
>
> *With the whitest white void of a horse*
> *Surrounded by spectators with ants in their words*
>
> *In the circus of the cold, without mutilated profile*
> *Through the broken capitals of ashen cheeks*
>
> *My void without you, city, without your dead that eat,*
> *Equestrian through my life definitely anchored.*

The poem ends in total desolation, without life after death:

> *There is no new world nor recent light*
> *Only a blue horse and a dawn.*[1]

---

[1] Any list of poems on the theme of his own death would have to start with two quotations from his very early poems:

> *Let my blood become in the fields*
> *Rose sweet river mud*
> *Wherever tired labourers*
> *Fling down their pick-axes.*
>
> (1918)

and

> *In my hour of extinct star*
> *Let my eyes be closed at dawn*
> *Hide me in a tranquil valley*
> *And while awaiting my resurrection . . .*

of the same year and the only one in which Lorca mentions his earlier belief in the resurrection of the flesh. Yet it is in *Poet in New York* and after that the theme takes on a more obsessive form:

> *Assassinated by the Heavens*
> *Between forms flowing towards the serpentine*
> *And forms seeking to become crystal . . .*
>
> 'Return from a Walk'
>
> *. . . This innocent pain of gun-powder in my eyes . . .*
>
> 'Moon and Panorama of the Insects'
>
> *. . . My isolated death with a solitary mistaken walker . . .*
> *When pure forms sank*
> *Under the cri-cri of the daisies*
> *I realized they had murdered me*
> *They searched for me in coffee-houses, cemeteries and churches*
> *But they could no longer find me.*
> *Did they not find me?*
> *No. They did not.*
>
> 'Fable and Round Dance of the Three Friends'

A blue horse is also found in the poem 'Your childhood in Menton', the meaning of which I still hope to decipher.

Form, metamorphosis, void: one of the typical patterns of Lorca's thought. With a precision only comparable to the 'Nocturnal of the Void' it is stated again by the Black Horse – death? – in Juliet's sepulchre:

> *Yes. You now know how well I behead doves. When the word 'rock' is mentioned I understand air. When air is mentioned I understand void. When void is mentioned I understand beheaded dove.*

Ruins—arches—grass

We have seen that one of the scenes in *The Public* is entitled 'Roman Ruin', that one of the props in that scene is a *fallen capital* on which sits the Figure with red Vine Leaves; that in Juliet's song the broken arch is an important element, and on the back of page 7 of the last scene Lorca drew with ink what seems to be the décor for 'Roman Ruin': two broken arches over precarious columns, one in the left corner of the proscenium, another upstage right. In the centre, a form can be seen, probably the fallen capital. It should also be remembered that the Director of the Open Air Theatre confesses to the Juggler that he failed

---

or amongst many other compositions this sonnet:

> *I know that my profile will be tranquil*
> *In the moss of a North without glare,*
> *Quicksilver of vigil, chaste mirror*
> *Where will break the pulse of my style.*

> *For if ivy and the freshness of linen*
> *Were the norm of the body I leave,*
> *My profile in the sand will be*
> *Old silence without a crocodile blush.*

> *And although my tongue of stiffened doves*
> *Will never have the taste of flame*
> *But the deserted flavour of broom,*

> *Free of constricted norms*
> *I will be in the body of the dry branch*
> *And in numberless dahlias of sorrow.*

in his experiment because the *horses, the sea, the army of grass* prevented him. In those ruins, broken arches and grass of *The Public* there are traces of a romanticism which in the case of Lorca is not only the influence of the inherent romanticism in the surrealist movement; it is a natural evolution of themes and observations already present in the poet's first writings which persists without interruption right to his posthumous poems. It is worthwhile tracing these motifs. They provide further proof of a persistence of themes and of the road followed by the poet from his first prose writings right through to *The Public, Poet in New York,* and the 'Casidas' and 'Gacelas'. In his description of the Andalusian town of Baeza we read: 'Everywhere blood-coloured ruins, arches turned into arms which would like to kiss each other, broken columns covered with hedge-mustard and ivy . . . a fountain of pagan severity, looks like the remaining body of a triumphal arch that earth has almost swallowed.' In 'Albaicín', the Moorish district of Granada, he describes 'the silent streets with grass', the 'orchards of ruined churches', 'benches half sunk, capitals and vestiges of arches covered with ears of grain and poppies'. In 'Fresdelval' he notices that 'elegant arches still stand and support the long green entanglement of ivy'. The adolescent poet does not ignore his literary sources: 'All romantic literature' – he writes in the long prose piece significantly entitled 'Ruins' – 'placed its fantastic figures amongst ruins . . . broken arches . . . enclosures carpeted with nettles and fallen capitals . . . Wherever the ruin sinks into the earth the historic tragedy is ended.' There they are, ever static, still realistic, the scenic elements of 'Roman Ruin' and of the 'theatre under the sand'.

In practically all the prose works of that first book the grass advances and occupies the place from whence life flees. Under its advance, columns, arches and capitals disappear. Thus it is hardly surprising that in the personal mythology of the poet, grass appears first as passive symbol of death, then in later works as an active agent.

Consequence becomes cause. But already in this first book there is a pointer in that direction. In the piece dedicated to Baeza, we feel his fright at the advancing grass:

The grasses are mistress of roads and paths and spread throughout the town, covering the streets, edging the houses and blotting out the footsteps of the passer-by. On the other side of this square there is a triangular house almost swallowed up by the grass. If one goes on walking the grass becomes so vigorous that it swallows the paving stones and licks the walls with greed.

The young poet lays the foundation for the advancing grass of *Poet in New York*. The recurrent themes confirm the suspicion that in his first writings we find the seeds of his later work. Those early impressions and poems are far more related to his surrealist work than to the intermediate period. In the latter they are hardly noticeable or, when present, lose their dramatic meaning: 'His dream was filled with Arab arches,' says Don Alambro in the humorous prose piece, 'The Cock', and a little later, the fine irony: 'The cardboard arch of the Corpus Christi.' Grass is seen not powerful but subdued; it withdraws before life as it advances with death: 'an air smelling of child saliva, crushed grass and Medusa's veil, announcing the constant baptism of newly born things.' Only in the dark side of the *Gipsy Ballads*, arches, grass and ruins appear as premonitions of death:

> *And murmur of old voices*
> *Resound through the broken arch*
> *Of midnight . . .*

Though here that 'broken arch' may allude to the waning moon, the 'segment of agonized silver' of the ballad 'Dead With Love'. In the 'Ballad of the Summoned Man' we read:

> *Because hemlock and nettles*
> *Will burst forth from your side*

or in 'The Martyrdom of St. Olalla':

> *Night of recumbent torsos*
> *And stars of broken noses*

or in 'Don Pedro on Horseback':

> *Don Pedro*
> *Walks under the broken arches.*

But it is in *Poet in New York*, in the posthumous poems, in *When Five Years Have Passed* and above all, in *The Public*, where ruins, arches and grass are the unavoidable companions of bad dreams. When Lorca addresses the oppressed negroes of New York he speaks to them in a prophetic tone: 'Wait . . . for hemlocks and thistles and nettles to disturb the last of the flat roofs', for the huge Stock Exchange of New York will soon turn into 'a pyramid of moss, because the jaguey plant will follow the rifles' after the war that will put an end to the civilization of steel and cement·

Grass is Death's favourite daughter.

> *Now moss and grass*
> *Open with sure fingers*
> *The flower of his skull,*

we read in 'The Lament for Ignacio'. The same fingers that Mariana Pineda foreboded in her prison-convent. Waiting to be taken to the scaffold she calls desperately for her beloved:

> *Look how close I feel*
> *Fingers of bone and moss*
> *Caressing my head . . .*

Similarly the wife in *Blood Wedding*, lamenting her dead husband, says:

> *Now, moss of night*
> *Crowns his forehead.*

In the 'Gacela of the Dead Child' the dead have 'wings of moss' and in the 'Gacela of the Dark Death' the grass torments the dead: 'I do not want to know the martyrdom of the oncoming grass.' In the brief poem entitled 'Omega', five out of the short thirteen lines consist only of the refrain 'The grass' repeated in crescendo. In 'Ruin' the identification grass-death is complete:

> *I saw the grasses coming*
> *And I threw them a little bleating lamb.*
> *The grass is coming, my son,*
> *Already their swords of saliva are heard.*
> *My hand, love, the grass!*
> *Through the broken window-panes of the house*
> *Blood lets loose her hair.*

That grass means death was suspected by the young man in *When Five Years Have Passed*. He says to the old man: 'I am going to cut all the flowers in the garden, above all that cursed rosebay that leaps over the wall and that grass which creeps out by itself at midnight.' Juliet knows it too when she says that as soon as she is caught unawares the moon 'throws handfuls of grass on my shoulders'. Among the poems published posthumously we find three under the title 'Herbalists'.

Beneath many forms of expression associated with surrealism, romantic themes indeed persist. But in the case of Lorca these themes are closely connected to an older literary tradition that he knew well. In Lorca's ruins, grass and broken arches, we perceive faint echoes of the Spanish elegies and funeral poetry. In his case a literary tradition resting, one must emphasize, on experience: ruins seen during his travels through fields and old villages of Spain, ruins always present in his native Granada, the city that most influenced him and of which Góngora says:

> *Amongst the ruins and marshes*
> *That Genil enriches and Darro bathes . . .*

The Public and *When Five Years Have Passed*

The Public, conceived in New York and nearly finished in Havana, is the key to the so-called surrealist writings of Lorca. Thus it is not difficult to see concurrences between the former and such short prose poems as 'The Massacre of the Innocents' and 'The Beheading of the Baptist', amongst others. Yet in these vignettes, crime and cruelty are treated as two of the noble arts:

> *Under a sky of soles of feet. The beheading was horrifying. But beautifully performed.*

Kafka and Buster Keaton come to mind. Details are depicted with the aseptic coldness dear to the surrealists.

> *The head of the celestial fighter was in the centre of the arena. Young lasses dyed their cheeks red and young men painted their ties in the trembling spurt of the rent jugular vein.*

Let us look at similar details in *The Public*. Gonzalo's mother says in the last scene:

> *This morning the fishermen brought me a huge moon-fish, pale, decomposed, and shouted at me: Here is your son! As a thin trickle of blood flowed ceaselessly from its mouth, the children laughed and painted the soles of their boots red . . .*

In 'The Massacre of the Innocents' we read:

Director (saliendo de debajo de la mesa) ¡Que pase!

El prestidigitador sentado cerca de la calavera de caballo silba y se abanica con gran alegría. Todo el ángulo izquierdo de la decoración se parte y aparece un cielo de nubes largas vivamente iluminadas y una lluvia lenta de guantes blancos rígidos y espaciados.

Voz (fuera)   Señor

Voz (fuera)   Que

Voz (fuera)   El público

Voz (fuera)   Que pase.

El prestidigitador agita con viveza el abanico por el aire. En la escena empiezan a caer copos de nieve

—Telón lento—

—Sábado 22 de Agosto 1930—

Last page of the play.

A drawing by Lorca published in *Una rosa para Stefan George*, a poem by the Argentinian poet Ricardo E. Molinari. The drawing is a graphic representation of several recurrent themes in Lorca. The roots and trunk of the tree are made up of the word *muerte* (death). In the base triangle: *Tierra para tu alma* (earth for your soul). Tree-top: above, *aire para tu boca* (air for your mouth). Bordering the left side, *Siempre y siempre tierra, tierra, tierra* (always and always, earth, earth, earth). Inside the left semi-circle, five times the word *cuerpo* (body). In the top circle, *y nunca* (and never); *nunca* repeated six times in the semi-circle on the right. Top of trunk and centre of the tree-top, *muerte* (death). Inside left branch, *agua para tu amor* (water for your love). Inside right branch, *fuego para tu ceniza* (fire for your ashes.)

Each dog carried a tiny foot in its mouth. The mad pianist was gathering rosy fingernails in order to build an emotionless piano, and the sheep bleated through their broken necks.

In *The Public* the masks of the Idiot Shepherd bleat and we saw how the Figure covered with little Bells said that he was *a giant, so gigantic that I can embroider a rose on the fingernail of a newly born baby.* Analogies and contrasts.

These quotations out of their context cannot, of course, give a good idea of the plasticity and musical equilibrium of those short prose poems, but they serve to prove that it is here that the more formal type of surrealism can be found. Characteristic of these proses are detachment and a subtle irony. The coldness of a surgeon in an operating theatre where sadism has no place. But what in a narrative is a graceful game, in *Poet in New York* and in *The Public* becomes drama. What was ante-chamber is now internal life, visions of a world beyond death. Once we realize the demarcation line between reality and dream has been broken, we experience at times the impact of perceiving flashes of normal life, imprisoned in a net of dreams and nightmares more lively and real than life itself.

Poet in New York and *The Public* were written about the same time. Understandable, then, the occasional similarities. Let us add two or three examples to the list that any reader acquainted with *Poet in New York* may have noted on reading the texts so far quoted.

The character Pyjama Costume, as we have seen the disguise of Man 2, has a face 'white, smooth and oval as an ostrich's egg'. And in the poem 'Return from a Walk', amongst the dead things listed we find 'a child with the white face of an egg', an idea that had appeared already in the 1928 story 'The Hen (A tale for dotty children)': the egg 'is the perfection of the mouth . . . It is the face.'

In the poem 'Interlude', from *Poet in New York*, Lorca describes the:

> *Loft where old dust accumulates on statues and moss,*
> *Boxes enshrining silences of devoured crabs.*

And in another poem from the same book:

> *I understood that my little girl was a fish.*
> *I had a daughter.*
> *I had a dead fish under the ashes of the censers.*

'Devoured crabs', to which Juliet referred in the sepulchre scene. A daughter that is a fish just as Gonzalo's mother sees her son as a moon-fish.

So far, only understandable reiterations and coincidences. Let us now look a little closer at the relation between *The Public* and the other semi-surrealist drama *When Five Years Have Passed*. Lorca finished the first drama on Saturday, 22nd August, 1930; the second, a year later, 19th August, 1931. The former may have been completed in Cuba; the latter, at least in great part, in the family country house outside Granada. Both plays were received with coldness by his friends. A lack of understanding quite comprehensible considering the difficulties of these texts and, to a lesser degree, of all the poetic work written in America. I still remember the reserve, often the half-veiled hostility with which some friends listened to his first readings of the poems of *Poet in New York*. It was necessary for Lorca to resort to his formidable gifts as a reader in order to impose his new poetic vision.

Who of those listening to him that autumn of 1930 could have forgotten Lorca's first readings of 'Office and Accusation' or 'Landscape of the Urinating Multitude', or 'Ode to the King of Harlem'?

> *With a spoon*
> *He rooted out the crocodiles' eyes*
> *And beat the monkeys' buttocks.*
> *With a spoon.*

And Lorca, who normally read his poems sitting motionless, confident that subtle interplay of voice, accent, modulation and pauses were enough to facilitate the understanding of the most difficult poem, was now frowning, raising his head, looking this way and that, brandishing an invisible spoon. Over a landscape of skyscrapers he superimposed the landscape of the African jungle and, in its centre, seated, an imposing negro was sinking his arm into the earth to tear out deep roots or to beat, from right to left, from left to right, the monkey's buttocks which escaped up tree-trunks and branches, just as at that precise moment Lorca was doing in a literary salon, small 'taverna' or garden restaurant. It was not the clearly defined metal spoon of the surrealist – it was the great wooden spoon, the spoon with a huge handle, the imposing ritual spoon carried by the chieftains of certain African tribes in ritual ceremonies. When the reading was over, he used to remain silent for a long while, absent-minded, sipping with eager concentration whisky or brandy on the rocks. One night when someone commented on the physical effort that those readings must impose on him, I heard him say: 'I have to protect these poems against incomprehension, dilettantism and benevolent smiles.' In their defence he went as far as to give public recitals in which he explained in poetic prose the background to each poem he read.

The poet was thus preparing his future public and assuring the success of a book which although finished in 1931 would not appear until 1940, four years after his death. Such slow preparation was not possible in the case of his dramatic work. The opposition encountered did not force him to abandon the aim that he was pursuing in *The Public*, but obliged him to slow down a little the initial outburst, to make some concessions. The outcome was *When Five Years Have Passed*.

Though convinced that the extant version of this play is not the final one, it is easy to realize that, even in its present form, we are in the presence of one of the most original poetical dramas in the modern theatre. Yet in relation to *The Public* it marks a step back in the evolution of Lorca's dramatic art. A summary comparison is indicated.

A Legend of Time, the sub-title of *When Five Years Have Passed*, corresponds to the internal idea of the drama, not to the plot. At the beginning of Act III, the mysterious Harlequin recites, alternating two masks of contradictory moods – exuberant gay expression in one, sleepy expression in the other – the poem that we have discussed in conjunction with Juliet's song. We saw there how in the two poems the entanglement of Dream and Time is an essential part of the whole containing them: Man's life. Outside this transitory reality time and dream lack proper existence. After the passing of that soft breeze which is man's life, there only remains silence, infinite silence.

Such reasoning carries him to another subsidiary idea also found in both plays. If time lives only in Man, inside Man, past and present abide and fuse in one another and in the multiple I's, not the never-lived I's of Unamuno, but in the multiple masks or costumes of our lives, co-existing within each one of us, as contradictory desires and passions. What was, will continue to be throughout fleeting human life.

The attentive reader will not fail to detect at certain moments of the play far-off echoes of the theory of relativity that so fascinated the specialist and general public of the period, or echoes of the time-theme in Azorín, Machado, Pirandello or Kafka. But in Lorca the eternal theme of time is welded to that of dream in its many connotations. Let us look at the theatrical devices used by Lorca in *When Five Years Have Passed*.

The drama has hardly begun when we hear a dialogue between a dead boy and a dead cat. This incident is taking place, or being alluded to, right through the play. In the second act, five years later, the Young Man, in order to explain away the embarrassment he is experiencing in the presence of his long awaited sweetheart says . . . 'in the streets I have beaten a group of boys who were stoning a cat to death'. In the first scene of Act III the Typist, speaking with the Concierge, disguised as a Carnival Mask, refers to the death of the boy as to something that happened five years ago but in the last scene of that same Act the Male and Female Servants explain to us that the Concierge is the Mother of the child that they are just going to bury. The idea that the scene in the first Act is happening all the time is further stressed by the fact that during the whole drama time is at a standstill, 'six o'clock in the afternoon', except when the Protagonist, the Young Man, dies. Then the clock strikes – twelve. The hour of truth. For Lorca the only hour.

> *The time's commercial traveller*
> *brings the herbarium of dreams.*

> I
> *Where is the Herbarium?*

> The Traveller
> *You have it in your hands.*

> I
> *My ten fingers are free.*

> The Traveller
> *Dreams dance on your hair.*

> I
> *And how many centuries have passed?*

> The Traveller
> *There is only one hour in my herbarium.*

Only one hour in *When Five Years Have Passed* and one hour in *The Public*. All seems to indicate that the Protagonist of the former also returns to his home as from a journey in which everything has been lost. In the first play, the Young Man comes back to keep his appointment with death or rather with death's angels disguised as three card players, in 'white tie and tails' and 'long ankle-length white satin cape'. In the second play the appointment is with death himself under the guise of a juggler, dressed in 'white tie and tails' with 'white satin cape down to his feet'. In both dramas the suspicion arises that the journey – the action of the play – happens only in the protagonists' minds. Before their eyes and ours the essentials of their lives seem to pass by, with the detailed 'slowness' and distortion of a dream or a nightmare that last only brief seconds.

Both are 'surrealist' dramas, but in *The Public* there is not the slightest concession to conventional logic. The curtain rises, three horses enter, and from this moment to the fall of the last curtain nothing breaks the atmosphere that has been established. The characters from real life taking part in the drama – Centurion, Women, Students – come from *outside* but their intervention does not affect the prevailing atmosphere. Quite the reverse: the contrast emphasizes it. In *When Five Years Have Passed* it is the whole play that steps out of its world to enter into a truly realistic scene. The Servant of the Bride belongs to the great gallery of Lorquian servants; the Father is the twin of the Uncle in *Doña Rosita*. Both are ironically treated romantic characters and amateur scientists, one is an expert on eclipses, the other on roses. The Bride herself speaks to the Young Man as *Yerma* would have spoken to her husband had she known Victor; as Adela, half naked, her dress stuck with hay, speaks after having experienced the weight of The Roman's body. The realistic sketches in *When Five Years Have Passed*, though perfect in themselves, interrupt without intensifying the natural flow of the work: the anguish of the dream world in which the Young Man moves.

To make a little more acceptable what was then a daring experiment, Lorca often resorts in the second play to the magic of his verse. Very seldom does his understanding of the child and his tenderness towards animals reach such delicate shades as in the scene between the Dead Cat and the Dead Boy; seldom has he portrayed with greater urgency and intensity the longing for maternity than in the dialogue between the Mannequin in the Wedding-dress and the Young Man; never has he given to folkloric elements richer tonalities and variations than in the trio Harlequin-Clown-Girl. The whole drama has a poetic character of exceptional quality and yet, compared with the dramatic starkness of *The Public*, *When Five Years Have Passed* is a step backwards. Inevitably one compares the lyrical Dead Cat to the ferocious horses; the romantic-surrealist Mannequin to the Emperor in search of the One; the decor in the Bride's room – ironical *art nouveau* – to the windows that are X-ray plates, the gigantic blades seen in huge close-up, the bed-cross, and the rain of rigid, well-spaced white gloves. Various scenes in *When Five Years Have Passed* seem at times illumined with a moonlight somewhat similar to the atmosphere in certain of Maeterlinck's plays. *The Public*, all the way through, is a projection towards the future. In both plays but even more so in the latter, behind the daring plot and form, myths and themes belonging to an old cultural tradition are being renovated.

It is only natural that in *When Five Years Have Passed*, following so closely on *The Public*, we should meet characters that resemble each other, similar sentences, situations that are alike, identical stage directions. Let us point to some examples that could be added to those which any reader of Lorca may already have noticed:

The servants in both plays are similar: the same *suavity*, the similar placing of themselves outside the actions.

In *When Five Years Have Passed*, the Dead Cat and the Dead Child want to *emerge from* death; the Young Man wants to *emerge from* the forest of Death and in *The Public* Gonzalo's Mother wants to *emerge from* the Director's room where the Juggler is.

In the former play Friend 2 says that he is afraid of falling *into the well down which we all will fall*, and in the unnumbered *cuadro* in *The Public*, when the Director fights with Man 1, Man 3 says to Man 2: *We can push them and they will fall into the well*.

The wrestling between the Young Man and Friend 1 in the first scene of *When Five Years Have Passed* seems a gay version of the fight between the Director and Man 1 in *The Public*. In the forest scene, in the former play, Harlequin and Clown make their exit *without turning their backs, on tip-toe, marking a dance step*.

The Male Nurse and the robbers of *The Public* also disappear dancing *marking a ballet step without turning their backs*.

In both plays, Lorca makes use of a folding screen: in *When Five Years Have Passed* to cover up, in *The Public* to reveal. Both plays end with the voices and echoes of the voices of the dead off stage.

The two plays are dramas about men, while *The House of Bernarda Alba* is about women. And just as in the latter everything turns round the invisible yet ever present Pepe, 'The Roman', in *The Public* the only person who triumphs is the woman, rarely seen on the stage. The Bride and the Secretary of *When Five Years Have Passed* – the one the Young Man seems to love and the one who really loves him – triumph over him, and it is the Mannequin in the Wedding Dress who makes the Young Man aware of his coming death. With the exception of Man 1, all the characters taking part in *The Public*, in spite of their homosexual relationships, are constantly vanquished by Helen, the woman; and are at times, and without wishing it, attracted by her.

The Young Man of *When Five Years Have Passed*, the most Hamlet-like figure in Lorca's drama, thinks he loves the girl with all the vigour allowed him by his hesitant nature and his constant dilemma, of being or not being in time and dream. This Young Man is somewhat feminine without being effeminate. The protagonist of *The Public*, married and with children, can love another man, and one of his costumes or personalities is the Guillermina 'of the horses', but at every stage he behaves as a man, antithesis of the effeminate or feminine. With virile decisiveness he goes in search of the last truth, with virile stoicism he faces death. He and his friends – or may they not be his doubles? – discuss their homosexual relationships with a frankness and a courage not yet seen on the western stage. But in themselves all these points matter little. What matters is that in the disentangling of the theme, ideas and symbols in this difficult manuscript there emerges a poet of a totally unexpected dimension. This almost certainly first draft of the unpublished drama *The Public*, throws new light on the whole work of Lorca, especially on *Poet in New York* and on the 'Casidas' and 'Gacelas'. It illumines with completely new light, and explains, the polyfaceted, all-important love and death themes in the work of the poet, themes to which we must now direct our attention.

PART II

LOVE, DEATH,
HORSES, THEATRE

I

LOVE IN THE WORK OF GARCÍA LORCA

> *For already have I been a boy and a girl, a bush and a bird and a dumb sea-fish.*
>
> EMPEDOCLES.

No student or occasional reader of Lorca could fail to notice that love and death are the two main themes in his poetry repeated with as much obsessive insistence as variety. Yet the characteristic, evolution and cross-currents of the themes have not been properly studied. It is imperative to discuss and clarify these points, for love and death – beginning and end – condition and to some extent explain a work of great thematic and symbolic richness frequently difficult to understand.

In the work of Lorca, love is not so much a theme as a vital attitude, the main focal point and axis of his human and artistic personality. This is true not only in the characters who appear on the stage or in his poems but in his brotherly feelings towards his rich bestiarium, in his love that also embraces trees, plants, blades of grass or mere elements. Even the inanimate things made by man – railway tracks, gloves, lenses – are treated with a love which in spite of its occasional surrealist cloak belongs more to the world of a Vermeer than to that of a Dalí. It would be fitting to apply to Lorca what he himself said of Fray Luis of Granada: 'Like all good men of Granada he is a master in the art of looking . . . he looks, and feels amorously attracted by the object.' His work 'is not a work of patience but of time; not a work of labour, but of pure virtue and love.'

Hatred, the hatred capable of personification, does not enter

Lorca's work. I have not found a single line transmitting hidden rage, resentment or envy. True, frequently one encounters protest, at times violently Jacobin, against social injustices, against moral conventions, against a religion in which 'behind the statues there is no love'. What moves his protest – naive in *Impressions and Landscapes*, lyrical in *Book of Poems*, fierce and prophetic in *Poet in New York* – is not a political creed, a religious faith, or even a definitely ethical conscience. What moves him is love towards all victims of life and society; women tormented by too long waiting or social taboo; negroes and mulattos in the New York of 1929 and 1930; homosexuals persecuted by society or by their own consciences. With true pantheistic feeling he is moved by the suffering of millions of animals daily sacrificed to provide man's food, by the pain of 'handcuffed roses', by the way worms are crushed under the wheels of cars and man under the wheel of life, both with the same indifference.

He goes even further. He takes his love 'to the other bank', to the 'other half', the half represented by man, animals and vegetation already dead but suffering an agonizing life in death. And death itself – supposed antithesis of love and life – his own death, his violent death, so often foreseen in his writings, is constantly alluded to in his poems without fear or hate, as if the poet had half seen a false antithesis. The artist knew – whatever the personal fears that Lorca as a man may have had – that it is death who brings *los toques de bordón* – the plucking of the brass guitar string – to his work, the black tones announcing the presence of the *duende*. Forever aware of her constant company, Lorca speaks to Death, courts her, flees from her only to call her again. 'Death, his beloved,' to quote the poet, Antonio Machado.

All the work of Lorca reflects this amorous attitude. In the introduction to the book of his adolescent years we read already:

Love and mercy and respect towards everybody will lead us to the ideal kingdom.

From that moment on love is his only ethic. In the introduction to his other youthful work, the play entitled *The Malefice of the Butterfly*, love is also the central axis in the insect's world:

Love passed from father to children as an old and exquisite jewel which the first insect received from God's hands.

And a few lines later we hear the first cry of his cosmic love, a cry which will go on resounding until its final explosion in *Poet in New York*:

> *Very soon the kingdom of animals and plants will come; man has forgotten his Creator, and animal and plant are very near His light. Poet, tell man that love is born with equal intensity at all levels of life: that the same rhythm of the leaf rocked in the air is in the distant star, and that the same words uttered by the fountain between the trees are repeated by the sea with equal tone. Tell man to be humble. Everything is equal in Nature!*

A few years later Lorca would perhaps have laughed at the imperfection of its form, never at its content. In 1922, in discussing the 'melancholy pathos of the *Cante Jondo*' he wrote:

> *So irresistible is its melancholy, and so sharp its emotive strength that it draws from each one of us true Andalusians tears that cleanse the spirit, carrying it to the inflamed lemon grove of love.*

That *lemon grove* is Lorca's inner and true centre, detectable in all his work.

We see this attitude clearly expressed in the opening words of his lecture on *Cante Jondo*, read in the Madrid *Residencia* where he himself had stayed for so many winters.

> *In a simple way, with the register that in my poetic voice has no flaming faggots, nor bunches of hemlock, nor sheep that turn suddenly into knives of irony . . .*

And in 1935, in the Barcelona Athenaeum:

> *My love for others, my deep love for and inter-penetration with the people . . .*

When he believes there is in others a similar capacity for love he praises it as something far above all other qualities. Thus when introducing Pablo Neruda to a Madrid audience he stresses that:

> *He lacks the two elements with which so many fake poets have lived: hatred and irony.*

In his youthful poem 'Autumn Rhythm' he asks himself about man's destiny and hears the worms complaining like the dust on the road, and the trees and the stars. Then the poet cries out:

> *Asking for what belongs to man: Boundless Love.*

> *Without terror and without fear of death,*
> *Frosted with love and lyricism.*

Another cry that persists throughout all his work right to his mature 'Double Poem of Eden's Lake':

> *. . . I do not want world or dream, divine voice,*
> *I want my liberty, my human love*
> *In the darkest corner of the breeze that nobody wants.*
> *My human love!*

In 1926, in a letter to the poet Jorge Guillén, Lorca writes:

> *. . . The true poetry which is love, effort and renunciation . . . I can only tell you that I hate the organ, the lyre and the flute. I love the human voice. Just the human voice humbled by love.*

Of all those human voices the one preferred by the poet is that of the little child:

> *All of us who feel that the child is nature's first spectacle, we who believe that there is no flower, 'number' or silence comparable to him . . .*

Lorca's preference for the purest, asexual form of love is unmistakable. When in moments of depression the poet wants to escape from his obsession with time and fleeting life, to run away from dream, beauty and the desires of the flesh, he does not seek comfort or shelter in any church, morality or grown-up friends: he goes for comfort and security to the company of the poor children who play on the outskirts of little villages, children who *see* tigers and thieves, who always observe little dead animals with fresh eyes:

> *I wanted to go down to the bulrush bank. Under the yellow tile roofs. On the outskirts of the little villages, where tigers eat children. At such times I am far away from the poet who looks at the clock, who struggles with the statue, who struggles with dream, who struggles with anatomy: I have escaped from my friends and gone with that boy who eats the unripe fruit and watches the ants devouring the bird crushed by the motor-car.*

That main focal point, that serene and unchangeable inner centre, is ruffled by erotic gusts at its periphery. When eros or lust intervene, Lorca's poem becomes an impassioned love-song pouring out 'crowns of gaiety' or cries of despair due to the early or recent termination of passion or to the proximity of death.

Eros demands the total surrender of his victims. This aspect of the love-theme fascinates Lorca, who views it from every possible angle. Whether love occurs between persons of opposite or of the same sex makes no difference. In this sense, *The Public* is not unique but a link in a chain in which heterosexual and homosexual love intermingle. For the author both are forms of the same rite, accidental expressions of the same phenomenon.

A silence, perhaps more senseless than hypocritical, hushed for many years this duality of the love-theme; incomprehensible silence, since Lorca himself does not hide it but proclaims and defends it. The inevitably exaggerated reaction has appeared in the last few years. After not mentioning what Lorca himself was not afraid of putting into writing, we have gone to the other extreme of reading that when Lorca mentions a woman in an amorous poem, she, of course, is a substitute for the opposite sex; and that when he deals in his plays with the universal conflicts of women recognized as such in all times, countries and societies, he is 'projecting' a so-called personal problem. The obsessive preoccupation in favour of or against homosexuality and the application of psychoanalytic techniques to literary criticism – a tempting but dangerous practice – can create curious distortions. The reaction is understandable, but it is perhaps pertinent to state from the outset that there is nothing in the work of Lorca to justify or support such suggestions. A number of unnoticed 'Albertines' may be hidden in the work of Spanish and European poets and writers never accused of homosexuality. But no 'Albertine' can be found in the work of Lorca. In homage to the beauty of a gipsy lad, he draws the portrait of 'Antoñito el Camborio' or of 'St. Gabriel'. In defence of the legitimacy of homosexual love, he writes the 'Ode to Walt Whitman' or *The Public*; in 'Your Childhood in Menton' or 'Fable and Round Dance of the Three Friends' it is an unorthodox passion that he sings. The contortions of some critics look then somewhat comic in trying to prove that 'The Unfaithful Wife' or the Estrella of the poem 'Summer Madrigal' or the clear feminine forms that Lorca delineates with such unbridled voluptuousness are nothing but masculine disguises. A detailed analysis of each one of these and other similar poems will show a literary honesty on the part of the author not always equalled by his critics.

Before examining this dual aspect of love it should be stressed that the whole subject is treated by Lorca with the same virility and daring which characterizes all his work, sometimes brutally challenging but never decadent. The fire consuming him – search for the one, for a boundless love embracing everything, and everybody – may have telluric roots, *duende* or Socratic daimon; the one thing totally lacking is contact with the more or less *maudit* literary salons.

Eros: Surrender or Frustration

The first thing to note is that for Lorca erotic love is, above all, a vital force, a Dionysiac urge impossible to resist whatever its disguise. This is the central theme of *The Public*, but it is in two plays from his rural trilogy that this attitude is most clearly expressed. Leonardo in *Blood Wedding* says to the bride in the forest scene after their elopement from the wedding feast:

> *But I am not to blame.*
> *The blame is on the earth*
> *And on the fragrance that spurts forth*
> *From your breasts and your tresses.*

And the Bride cries out in despair to the Mother in the last scene:

> *For I ran away with the other, yes I did! You yourself would have done the same. I did not want to. Your son was my goal . . . but the other's arm dragged me like a huge wave in a heavy sea, like the headshake of a mule, and it would have dragged me always, always, always, even if I'd been old and all your son's children had grabbed me by the hair –*

In *The House of Bernarda Alba*, Adela, when believing herself triumphant over her mother and sisters, challenges Martirio:

> *After the taste of his mouth I can no longer stand the horror of these roofs. I'll become what he will . . . and I'll put on the crown of thorns worn by the mistresses of married men.*

Even the tender and romantic *Mariana Pineda* in his early historical drama murmurs in the first vignette of the play:

> *And this heart, where does it lead me*
> *That even my own children I forget?*

Sexual instinct, telluric voice, Eros demands the surrender of the flesh, triumphantly imposes his will and breaks taboos, rules and social conventions, even at the cost of those serving him. And when nothing stands in his way, after a long or slow flowering, this love ends, as everything in life, with the sadness of death and oblivion:

> *Tomorrow loves will become rocks and Time*
> *A breeze that arrives sleeping through the branches.*

or

> *What shall I do? Set in order the landscapes,*
> *Set in order loves that later become photographs,*
> *That later are bits of wood*
> *And mouthfuls of blood?*

But for Lorca there is something worse than the violent or gradual end of an amorous passion, something that he denounces constantly either with violent protest or with bitter smile: the resistance to or refusal of love that ends in frustration, in the pain of the still-born:

> *Because it is much better to cry for a living man who stabs us, than to cry for this phantom sitting year after year on my heart,*

says Yerma, thinking of the son that is not to come. These are almost the words used by the Ama in the final act of *Doña Rosita*:

> *But what is happening to my Rosita is the worst. It's to desire and not to find the body; it's to cry and not know for whom one is crying . . . it's an open wound incessantly bleeding a little trickle of blood . . .*

An idea also expressed with perfect clarity by the Mannequin in the Wedding Dress in *When Five Years Have Passed*:

> *I sing*
> *The death I never had.*
> *Pain of veil without use,*
> *With lament of silk and feather.*

For Lorca, worse even than death itself is the hollowness of an empty coffin.

Frustrated Love in Women

Many years ago I pointed out that frustrated love was a recurrent theme in the work of the poet.[1] Since then, and especially in recent years, many critics have dwelt on this aspect of the love-theme only to find some explanation which is easy and logical from the Freudian or Jungian point of view. Frustrated love: the projection of a personal problem of the author. But is that so? Let us examine more closely what could be termed Lorca's philosophy of love.

An awareness of the problem of frustrated love – whatever the causes may be – coupled with a condemnation of attempts to resist the fulfilling of the carnal ritual demanded by love is to be found throughout the whole work of the poet. We see it already in his juvenile book *Impressions and Landscapes*. In that naive, defective, sometimes trivial early book, all the main themes of the author's later works are to be found, together with excellent examples of a new way of looking at things and people.

In the prose-exercise entitled 'La Cartuja' Lorca describes how suddenly the famous Spanish Carthusian monastery appears 'with all its funeral vestments' on that spot where 'the brimming river gives the impression of dryness'. The young poet stops before the famous altar-piece, in front of 'the frightening vision of the Christ carved by Siloe', in front of 'the Eternal Father with pride and fearful gesture', in front of 'the marble blaze' which is the sepulchre of Juan I and his wife. And he continues in this romantic vein to project on to this painting the tragedy he is unearthing:

How overwhelming the silence! Everybody sees the Carthusian silence as peace and calm. I feel only anxiety, restlessness, a formidable passion beating like a huge heart throughout these cloisters.

He gives a twist to the quotation from St. Paul which heads his prose-piece ('For he that soweth to his flesh shall of the flesh reap corruption; but he that soweth to the Spirit shall of the Spirit reap life everlasting.' Galatians 6.8). In some cells he perceives the scent of quinces, in others the smell of sufferings and passions half

---

[1] *Poems: F. García Lorca, with English Translations by Stephen Spender and J. L. Gili. Selection and Introduction by R. M. Nadal.* The Dolphin, London, 1939.

suffocated. 'Satan prays in the centre of this solitude. The silence of the Cartuja is painful.'

He feels the desire to shout at them 'that there is sun, moon, women, music . . . to awaken them that they may do good to their souls, which are in the tenebrae of prayer . . .' And a little later:

What a huge nightmare for these men who flee from the temptations of the flesh and enter silence and solitude that are the greatest aphrodisiacs of all . . .

He hints at the same theme in the pages dedicated to the Monastery of Silos, but more strongly still in 'Another Convent', writing this time of nuns.

What they want to forget becomes present in their souls . . . Within the compass of the church there beats a great emotional failure . . . The heart triumphs over everything . . . The crystalline fountains of far-off lips often flow in the chaste imaginations of the nuns . . .

The poet has started along the road that will take him to the ballad of 'The Gipsy Nun', and finally to *Doña Rosita, the Spinster*; the long gallery of women consumed in useless waiting, of women who in convents and clean provincial homes hide away the intimate failure of their lives, the perpetual conflict between their virgin imaginations and the passing of life; a gallery too of unsatisfied married women.

In that first book we find plenty of examples. In the prose-piece 'San Pedro de Cardeña' the figure he remembers is not the famous Cid, but his wife:

The amorous figure of Jimena . . . still seems to be waiting for the knight, who loves wars more than her heart, and she will always wait, like Don Quixotes for their Dulcineas without perceiving the frightening reality.

In those lands of Castille, the young poet sees 'the history of that strong love . . . all the melancholy of El Cid's wife', Jimena, 'heartsick and tearful woman . . . the most feminine and subjugating note in all Spanish ballads'. And when he quotes from memory it is from Jimena's lament:

> *King of my soul and of these lands, Count.*
> *Why are you leaving? Where are you going? Where?*

In another piece, 'Holy Week in Granada', he remembers the

religious festivities of his childhood before tourism became a national industry:

> *Then it was a Holy Week of lace, of flying canaries . . . of soft and melancholic air, as if the day had been sleeping on the opulent bosoms of the Granada spinsters, who walk on Maundy Thursday full of longing for the visiting army officer, professor or judge who will take them to other places.*

It is rare to find a description of a Spanish town in which there is no allusion to the poor waiting women.

Between these first vignettes and the great female creations of his drama, the theme appears ceaselessly. In the first book of poems, among other compositions, in the 'Elegy to Doña Juana, the Mad':

> *Princess in love without being loved.*
>
> . . . .
>
> *You never had the nest, nor the suffering madrigal,*
> *Nor the troubadour's faraway sobbing lute.*
> *Your troubadour was a lad with silver scales*
> *And the trumpet's echo his enamoured accent.*
> *And yet for love you were shaped.*

In history as well as in legend, the poet is attracted by these women waiting for a love that never comes, or that does not satisfy. Above all he observes the reality of the provincial world round him. The poem entitled 'Elegy', with the sub-title 'Granada', dated 1918, is a clear antecedent of the drama *Doña Rosita* of 1935. It is a long lament for the spinsters of his native Granada:

> *As an incensory full of desires,*
> *You pass by in the luminous and clear afternoon*
> *With your darkened flesh of faded tuberose*
> *And powerful sex in your gaze.*

He sees 'in the Dionysiac cup' of her belly 'the spider that weaves the barren veil' . . . in her hands 'the skein of your illusions dead for ever', and in her soul, motherly love dreaming of far-off secret visions of cradles in an atmosphere of silent dissimulation, 'murmuring with her lips the blue of lullabies'. And as epitaph:

> *No-one will kiss your thighs of fire.*

In this poem we find also the main and most obvious reason for the persistence of the theme in the poet's work: a protest against the human grief, secret and shameful, of the provincial spinster. That Granadine 'Elegy' is in reality the elegy to all the Andalusian spinsters:

> *No-one fecundates you, Andalusian martyr . . .*
> *Virgin in grief . . .*
> *Mirror to Andalusia*
> *Suffering gigantic passions in silence . . .*
> *You fade away in the autumn mist, virgin*
> *Like Ines, Cecilia and the sweet Clara,*
> *Being a bacchante who would have danced . . .*

And it ends with the sharp dichotomy of the old spinster:

> *What depth of sadness you must carry in your soul,*
> *Feeling in your now tired and exhausted breast*
> *The passion of a girl just enamoured.*

In *Songs*, his second great book of poems, where everything undergoes a delicate, subtle stylization, the 'marvellous butterfly dust' to which Roy Campbell referred, the theme is half seen in the little poem 'The Unmarried Woman at Mass':

> *Lulled by the incense,*
> *Half asleep . . .*
> *Bull's eyes gazed at you.*
> *Your rosary raindrops.*
> *With that dress of black silk,*
> *Don't move, Virginia.*
> *Give the dark melons of your breasts*
> *To the murmur of the Mass.*

Not less stylized the theme appears in the ballad 'The Gipsy Nun', whom the poet presents embroidering winter gilliflowers when:

> *She would like to embroider*
> *Flowers of her fantasy.*
> *What a sunflower! What a magnolia*
> *Of spangles and ribbons!*
> *What saffrons and what moons,*
> *In the Mass altar-cloth.*

And then the protest of imperfectly subdued instincts:

> *Through the nun's eyes*
> *Gallop two horsemen.*

> *A final dumb murmur*
> *Loosens her shirt.*
> *Oh! What a rising plain*
> *With twenty suns above.*
> *What upright rivers*
> *Half seen by her fantasy!*

Together with other elements this theme of frustrated love, of the anxiety of waiting, runs through the 'Ballad of the Black Sorrow' and in the 'Somnambulistic Ballad'. The Soledad Montoya of the first – sister of the Ophelian Gipsy of the second – climbs down the mountain where she has been alone the whole night wrestling with her exuberant and lonely beauty. Metaphors are not difficult to understand:

> *Yellow copper her flesh*
> *Smelling of horse and shadow.*
> *Her breasts, smoked anvils,*
> *Moan round songs.*

The poet asks her where she comes from:

> *I come in search of what I search,*
> *My joy and my own self.*

And when Lorca says:

> *You cry lemon juice*
> *Bitter with waiting and bitter of mouth* . . .

Soledad Montoya confesses:

> *What grief! My flesh and clothing*
> *Are turning to jet.*
> *Oh my shirts of linen,*
> *Oh my poppy-like thighs.*

After the *Gipsy Ballads* it is no longer the lyrical treatment of this aspect of the love-theme but the dramatic side that attracts the author. His Bride, Yerma, Rosita, Bernarda Alba and her Daughters, belong to the theatre; women dragged along by their respective obsessions or consumed in waiting. Outwardly they are created in the image and after the likeness of the women Lorca saw and knew intimately in the villages of his childhood, and later in villages and cities throughout Spain. The insistence on this theme, far from being proof of a personal problem, points to the awareness of a human and social problem by no means limited to the rural zones of the Peninsula or to a more or less far-off yesterday, but still present today in all western countries even if confined to the secrecy of the confessional or the psychoanalyst's couch.

Such people and such problems attracted the artist on account of their dramatic potentialities; they attracted the rebel in Lorca because they activated his protest against human and religious laws that created such miseries; they attracted the young dramatist because they allowed him to study rural tragedy, starting from a reality that he knew only too well. But Lorca's ultimate intention was the study of characters consumed and dominated by a passion.

It would be possible to argue that his personal sympathies lie with the rebels, with Leonardo and the Bride in *Blood Wedding*, with the Girl who in *Yerma* proclaims freedom of love or with the youngest daughter of Bernarda Alba, Adela, whose defiant gesture of breaking her mother's stick could be interpreted as a symbol of the triumphant rebellion of the coming generation. However, there is nothing in that trilogy to support the assertion that there is a thesis in the traditional sense or a message in the modern one. One feels that the concern of the dramatist is to penetrate the inner secrets of those feminine souls, to perceive the delicate shades or the violent explosions of passion or maternal instinct, or the most piercing cry of frustrated lives. He recreates, poetically and dramatically, happenings of everyday life, magnifies his characters with a technique similar to the film close-up and projects them upon an objective reality. Poetry and realism, humour and gaiety side by side with tragedy. And thus we see moving on the stage those obsessed, almost mythical characters: Mother, Bride, Yerma, Bernarda Alba and her daughters. All giants due to the close-up focus, but accompanied, heightened in their tragedy by all those other women, also of flesh and blood, who live in Lorca's drama: servants, neighbours, sisters-in-law, washer-women. Like Cervantes and Galdós, like Tirso, Lope de Vega and Clarín, like Shakespeare, Ibsen and Chekhov, like all great dramatists, Lorca is a deep connoisseur of women, almost a soothsayer of woman's mind. Could one suggest that in Lorca, as in all these, the 'anima' mentioned by Jung manifests itself at times with remarkable clarity? Already in 1919 Lorca wrote in an early poem:

> *Venus is the inner recess*
> *Of man's soul.*

In dealing with men, Lorca, as we will see later, can give an ironic twist to the theme of frustration. Never in the case of women. His understanding of female psychology prevents him from doing so. One could object, however, that in nearly all his tragedies it is precisely the women who come to relieve the tension of the drama with typical Andalusian wit and humour, nearly always bordering on the sexual theme. It is, for example, the Servant in *Blood Wedding* who, dressing the Bride in the courtyard of her father's house, comments:

> *Happy you who are going to embrace a man, and kiss him and feel the weight of his body!*

And when the Bride protests, the Servant insists:

> *But my child! What is a wedding? A wedding is that and nothing else. Is it the sweets? Is it the bunches of flowers? No. It is a shining bed and a man and a woman.*

It is the Girl 2 in *Yerma*, happy without children, who tells the poor obsessed Yerma:

> *. . . one is really married before going to the church . . . What need is there for my husband to be my husband? Because what we do now we did before.*

Or the other servant, Poncia, who recounts to the Daughters of Bernarda Alba, already on heat, how Evaristo, 'the Colín', the one who was going to become her husband, approached her window for the first time:

> *It was very dark. I saw him approaching and on reaching the window he said 'Good evening!' 'Good evening,' said I, and for half an hour we remained there without uttering one word. The sweat ran down my body. Then Evaristo came nearer, so near that it seemed he was going to get through the window bars and said in a deep, low voice, 'Come, let me feel you.'*

However, all this implies wisdom after the event, seeing the theme through the back door as it were, a counterpoint that accentuates the intensity of the drama. It is as if Lorca suddenly pulled the spectator into everyday life, back from the distortion of some huge optical illusion. But his protagonists live in the restless grandeur of a world with only one idea, an alienation that will inevitably lead to the 'with a knife, with a little knife' in *Blood Wedding*, to Yerma's words 'I've killed my son, I myself have killed my son', or to the slow swing of the courageous Adela's body.

The Case of Doña Rosita

Nothing illustrates better his inability to treat the theme of frustrated love in women ironically than the play *Doña Rosita*. Let us look a little closer at the structure of this work. Its full title – *Doña Rosita the Spinster, or the Language of Flowers*, points to a stylized dramatization of the youthful poem 'Elegy' to which we have already referred. All seems to indicate that Lorca's first idea must have been to write a period piece with an ironic twist: a comedy of the middle-class within the provincial frame of Granada at the end of the century. This impression is confirmed by the way in which the author introduces his characters. Some could belong to a subtle farce of the second half of the 19th century (the Uncle, a green-house botanist, 'cultivator of roses', as Mr. X scornfully calls him); others bear some relation to the *genre* characters of the conventional Andalusian middle-class so much exploited by the brothers Quintero (the Aunt and, at the beginning, Rosita herself). Then comes a typical Lorquian character, the Servant, linked like all the others in his plays to the great tradition of male and female servants in Spanish literature. The plot itself – the young woman left 'to dress images' after waiting many years for the fiancé who left for America promising to return and marry her – had, looking at it from 1935, an unmistakable ironic undertone; indeed all the first act is constructed in that vein although at times the poet, almost unconsciously, betrays the dramatist. Two examples from the first act. Rosita and her three exuberant young friends return home. The conversation takes the form of a gay, quick ballad satirizing the *chi-chi* language of the period, except when Rosita refers to her friend's breasts:

> *Whose hands steal perfumes*
> *From their two round flowers?*

or evokes Granada's atmosphere:

> *The cathedral has set free the bells*
> *And the breeze has taken them up.*
>
> *Night comes loaded*
> *With hills of shadow.*

The second and better example is in the farewell dialogue between Rosita and her Cousin. The author revels in the description of the setting for this scene of delicate period prettiness.

The stage is empty. A Czerny study is heard on a far-off piano. The Cousin enters and on reaching the centre of the stage stops at the entry of Rosita, from the opposite side. The two stand still staring at each other. The Cousin advances, throws his arm round her waist. She leans her head on his shoulder.

And Rosita begins:

> *Why did your treacherous eyes*
> *Melt with mine?*

To Rosita's first stanza, the Cousin answers with the one beginning:

> *Oh! Cousin, my dearest treasure!*
> *Nightingale in the snow . . .*

As if the words were not enough to make his intentions clear, the author underlines it in the stage direction preceding that stanza: 'The Cousin takes her to a *vis-à-vis* and they sit together.' An obvious lyrical parody on the romantic duos in dramas and even more in operas. The Cousins sit on the romantic sofa. We expect from one moment to another to hear the two voices join together in a final duet. But suddenly the tone changes, and the connoisseur of Granada speaks in subtleties.

COUSIN: *When my horse slowly eats*
> *Stems sprinkled with dew.*
> *When the river's haze*
> *Blurs the wall of the wind.*
> *When violent summer*
> *Turns crimson the plain*
> *And frost leaves on me*
> *Needles of morning star . . .*

To which Rosita answers:

> *I long to see you arriving*
> *One afternoon in Granada*
> *With all its light salted*
> *By the sea's nostalgia . . .*

Nevertheless the general tone of that first act is one of a gay period piece constantly bordering on the farcical. The poet smiles benevolently at these vignettes of the past. He observes them through inverted opera glasses: diaphaneity, remoteness, objectivity and, as a consequence, a reduction in the size of persons and passions.

The same tone persists through most of the second act. There is a parade of visitors coming to compliment Rosita on her birthday: Mr. X, a maniac for progress and for the first cars that could hurl themselves 'at the fantastic speed of thirty km. per hour'; the Señoritas de Ayala making cruel fun of the three spinsters of a declining middle-class family who in answer to their mother's question, 'Egg for supper or chair in the promenade', do not hesitate to answer simultaneously 'Chair, chair!' But there are two moments in this act when the mockery disappears and Lorca begins to reveal the human grief and drama that is unfolding. The first is when Rosita, whose mother has been encouraging her to go out and amuse herself, explains the inner motive of her voluntary sequestration:

> *In the street I perceive how time passes and I don't want to lose my illusions. They have already built a new house in the little square. I do not want to become aware of the passing of time.*

And a little later, in a way that would have pleased the Pirandello of *Cosi é se vi pare*—Right you are! (If you think so):

> *. . . my roots are very deep, very firmly planted in my feeling. If I did not see people, I would believe that he left only one week ago . . .*

The second instance is when the Nurse tells the Aunt how Rosita insisted on passing in front of a circus again and again because she saw in one of the artists a great resemblance to her Cousin:

AUNT: And was there any real resemblance?

NURSE: He was handsome as a novice coming to sing his first mass, but your nephew might well envy that figure, that mother-of-pearl neck, that moustache. There was not the slightest resemblance . . . What happened is that Rosita fancied the acrobat, as I fancied him and as you would have done. But she imputes everything to the other.

These are hints of the theme which in the third act will be placed squarely in the centre of the stage from curtain-rise to its slow coming down over Rosita's empty house, where a gust of wind throws the windows open and the lace curtains flutter.

What has happened to produce such a radical change? Lorca has righted the opera glasses and on seeing his protagonist at close quarters he, and we, are facing a Doña Rosita whose martyrdom of an old virgin in love has assumed gigantic proportions. The fashions may well be those of 1900 or 1910 but in this last act the farce has been shed even by Don Martín, a poor teacher at a neighbouring school, another farcical character turned dramatic.

Doña Rosita begins as a gay period comedy and ends in a void that cannot even be termed drama. The fact that Doña Rosita leaves the house alive increases the tension. The void left when Aunt, Nurse and Rosita leave the stage is not greater than that carried by Rosita within her. Behind frills and ribbons, puffed sleeves and crinoline skirts, lies an aching heart. The amiable comedy has turned into desolate drama, the slow passing of a life consumed in useless waiting. The flying curtains and the deserted 'carmen'[1] evoke in us those dramas where everything depends on a delicate recreation of atmosphere, an art in which Chekhov is undisputed master. But in Lorca the atmosphere, however perfect, is only the background. Over it we see the delicate silhouette of Rosita fading away, already old, but still feeling in her exhausted breast 'the passion of a newly enamoured girl'.

Frustrated Love in Men

When Lorca decided to apply farcical treatment to the old theme of imagination versus reality, the example he chooses is that of a young and beautiful woman married to an old man. Two themes dear to Cervantes intermingle and overlap. *The Prodigious Cobbler's Wife*, *The Love of Don Perlimplín and Belisa in his garden*, and even his puppet pieces, show how their author sees the theme of frustrated love in men.

It is evident that men do not feel paternity, if they feel it at all, to a degree comparable to women's experience of the maternal instinct. The frustration will be felt on a different level and with a variety of motivations: temperance in maturity (The Cobbler); impotence in old age (Perlimplín); temperamental coldness (Yerma's

[1] *Carmen.* Typical country house of Granada with orchard and garden.

husband); lack of real attraction for women (Young Man in *When Five Years Have Passed*). The first two are treated in more or less violent farce, a technique never used in the case of women. And yet neither the typically Andalusian Cobbler, nor Don Perlimplín, in which various literary associations can be detected – the 'Commedia dell' Arte', Cervantes' exemplary novel *The Jealous Estremaduran*, *Le Cocu Magnifique* and *Cyrano de Bergerac* – are grotesque figures. There is, of course, plenty of fun in the situations, in the popular expressions used and in the form in which the plot and action appear to the subsidiary characters. But neither the Cobbler, to whom the Mayor wants to give lessons in conventional manhood, nor Don Perlimplín (peacefully asleep on his wedding night while from the five balconies of his room, hang five stairs up which have climbed Belisa's five lovers, representing the five races of the earth) lose for one instant their human dignity. The author does not condemn the fantasy of the Cobbler's wife nor the exuberant and lustful Belisa. In the gaiety surrounding the former there is no mockery of the Cobbler, and the hidden drama of Don Perlimplín, summed up in the simile of thirst and water, is treated with such delicate lyricism and understanding that what began as a farce, ends in grave tragi-comedy.

Frustrated love in men, whatever the reasons, can produce dramatic situations, but these will run on a different level from those in women. Maternal instinct will be lacking. Yerma poses the key question to the old Woman – 'What am I going to think when he leaves me in bed lying with sad eyes staring at the ceiling while he turns to one side and goes to sleep? Must I lie there thinking of him or of what may come out shining from my breast?'; this is indeed the graphic expression of an obsessed woman, but in a minor key, at times hardly perceptible, it is the question asked by most women really in love and, as a consequence, aware of maternal instinct. It is the question that no man ever asks himself.

Lorca, who has created so many feminine characters to be added to that notable gallery of women in Spanish novels and plays, never succeeded in giving life to a single male figure of similar magnitude. As subsidiary characters Lorca's men have human veracity, but are seen obliquely, without *chiaroscuro*, with perhaps the only exception of Leonardo in *Blood Wedding* – though not fully developed – and Don Perlimplín. In contrast, the Mother in

Blood Wedding, Yerma, Bernarda Alba and her daughters, Doña Rosita and the Cobbler's Wife are, in addition to being paradigms of different types of obsession, women of flesh and blood.

Not his men. In *The Prodigious Cobbler's Wife* Lorca creates the funny and human Cobbler, as a counterpoint to his fanciful wife. The problem, from the husband's point of view, is the problem of a quiet, mature man, not impotent but unable to satisfy fully the appetites and needs of his imaginative wife. When Lorca faces squarely the problem of frustrated love in men his characters become stylized and lose reality. They are intellectualized or symbolical beings. The grief that transpires is more cerebral, perhaps richer in shades, though imprecise in motivation. In farce it is the 18th-century-like figure of Don Perlimplín, one of the most delicate figures in Lorca's drama, the one with greatest range, who evolves furthest within the narrow frame of the farce. On his wedding night he peeps through the keyhole and discovers his impotence on seeing the beautiful body of his naked wife, Belisa, as a 'dark nightmare'; a grandiose body of a woman 'that I could never decipher'.

The end of this erotic tale brings to mind the end of Cervantes' short novel *The Jealous Extremaduran*, the same sublimation of the old cuckold through an act of heroic self-sacrifice. Carrizales, the protagonist in the Cervantes' novel, disposes in his will, dictated when he recovers from a faint on seeing his misfortune, that Leonora, his wife, should contract marriage with the seducer who stole his honour, a subtle form of an exemplary punishment. Don Perlimplín punishes his lustful wife by helping her to direct all her powerful sensuality towards the fictitious character he himself has created, the Pygmalion of his own dream.

In its dramatic form we have already seen the theme of frustrated love in men when discussing the mysterious Young Man of *When Five Years Have Passed*, sexually timid or impotent, who postpones for five years the marriage with his young and beautiful fiancée in order to enjoy the dream of a possession that he will never have.

The recurrent theme of frustrated love in women, and to a lesser degree in men, important though it may be, is not so all-embracing as some critics would have us believe. It is only an aspect of the central love-theme in the work of the poet. Impotence or sexual deviation – which are the obsessions of those critics – certainly do not occur in the conception or development of *Blood Wedding*, drama of feuds and of destiny. Neither do they enter into the theme of *The House of Bernarda Alba*, although the steely coldness with which the mother imposes her moral code creates the problem in her daughters, but only as a by-product of her wrongs. On the other hand the frustration of Yerma is not due to the fact that when the husband makes love to her she thinks he is doing so out of duty, or because she notices 'his waist is cold', but to the fact that those rapid, brief encounters do not bring her the long awaited child. In Lorca's dramas the theme of frustrated love only appears in *Doña Rosita the Spinster* and *Don Perlimplín*; and perhaps in a subtle way in *When Five Years Have Passed*.

On the other hand, in contrast to that theme, there are its antipodes: the joyous encounter of bodies in love, the enjoyment of love and beauty, fountains of life and gaiety. The poet sings his song and delights in love and sensuous descriptions of beautiful young people of both sexes, in details at times veiled, at times realistic, of the rite of the flesh. Whether the rite be 'by coral vein or celestial nude' matters little to the author.

The love-theme in all its manifestations has, on the other hand, depths of thought and feeling not always easy to perceive on a first reading. With the theme of love Lorca intermingles nearly always – especially in *Book of Poems*, *Poet in New York*, and in his 'Casidas' and 'Gacelas' – another theme equally recurrent. If life, just as erotic love, is nothing but 'a footprint in water', a 'broken mirror', a 'breeze that comes sleepily through the branches'; if love generates life and life ends in death, Lorca, in spite of his boundless love of life and horror of death, ends by seeing a correlation that makes these antitheticals inseparable. Hence his declared refusal to procreate himself, to enter into a play whose deceit he thinks he knows. The Dance of Love becomes for him only the other side of the Dance of Death.

Thus two apparent opposites live together in the work of the poet from his early writings. One could trace the graph of the two themes of Love and Death, the curves that fuse and cross each other. But however much one line may predominate over the other in any particular piece of writing, the opposite is never totally absent.

'Ars Amandi'

In *Impressions and Landscapes* one can already see flashes of that sensuality which still relied timidly on imagination more than on memory, but constituted such a characteristic feature in Lorca's later work. In 'August Noon' the author delights in a description which is like a transposition of a picture by Poussin, or Cézanne's *Baigneuses*:

> *Women from the village bathe in the river. They shout with pleasure, feeling the freshness of the water licking their bellies and breasts. The local lads hide like fauns in the thickets to see them naked. All nature desires a gigantic copulation. The bees buzz monotonously. On seeing a girl coming out of the water, naked, her breasts firm, twining her hair as the others in fun throw water at her belly, the young men stumble among the alder trees.*

In his early *Book of Poems* Lorca writes about sensuous love with complete freedom. It is a book of farewell to his world of childhood and adolescence, full of first experiences and confessions. In the poem entitled 'Song to Honey' – 'Sweet as woman's belly' – he establishes a simile between the golden liquid and poetry – 'man's honey' – flowing 'from a honeycomb with wax made from memories by the bee of the inner self' or, as he wrote some years later: 'We have to probe and explore our inner intimacy and secrets . . .' From that honeycomb flows the best of his amorous poetry. The autobiographical element is the constant denominator in his poetry, from his adolescent experiences, often recalled in the form of children's songs, to the masterly 'Sonnets of Dark Love'. It is autobiographical in the sense that each love poem stems from an actual experience, though the poetic imagination transforms it with a logic completely divorced from reason. After his visit to New York these transformations were to become so radical that only with an intimate knowledge of the author's life and work would it be possible to detect their sources.

With that joyful freshness of the first period he discloses in *Book of Poems* the two fundamental constituent elements of his early poetry – lust and dream:

> *And my heart opened*
> *Like a flower under the sky,*

> *Petals of lust*
> *Stamens of dream.*

The autobiographical element does not mean, of course, that the author is incapable of imagining situations he himself has not experienced, yet it is as well to repeat that in most of his poems the 'lyrical bee' of the poet sucks from memories:

> *Join your mouth to mine,*
> *Oh! Estrella, the gipsy one,*
> *Under the sunny gold of noon*
> *I will bite the apple.*

That 'Summer Madrigal', written in the Vega of Zujaira, is the confession of a first sexual experience:

> *Why did you give yourself to me, tanned light?*
> *Why filled with love*
> *Did you give me the lily whiteness*
> *Of your sex and the tremor of your breasts?*

The poet, not without astonishment, asks why he was the preferred one instead of some country peasant lad with 'sweaty thighs . . . slow in love and beautiful'? He fears it may be due to compassion and in a clear biographical note, almost as an aside, alludes to his slight physical defect: 'Oh my clumsy walk!'

'Danaide of pleasure you are to me,' he cries a little further on; Lorca seldom alludes to a myth without knowing to what he is alluding, and since the young woman he conceals beneath the Cervantine pseudonym of 'Estrella, the gipsy one,' apparently does not want to kill him, the epithet can only refer to the marriage of the daughters of Danaus to the sons of Egypt.

There is a thematic relation between that early 'Madrigal' and the more mature ballad of 'The Unfaithful Wife'. Nothing illustrates better the speed with which Lorca masters poetic expression than the way he narrates a similar story. In the early poem the shy sensuality has obvious sentimental undertones; in the ballad it is gay, and manly. In contrast to 'Over the Meadow, her hair stretched solemnly as a cloak of shadow', the sharp 'Under her mat of hair/ I scooped a hole in the river mud'; in contrast to 'paint for me with your bleeding lips/ a heaven of love', the 'that night I ran/ without bridles or spurs'. In contrast to the unexpected drama of 'in a depth of purple flesh the star of pain', the vital gaiety of 'her thighs escape me/ like startled fish'.

What prevails in the poetry of Lorca until the appearance of *Poet in New York* is a concept of love, remembrance or desire, as a carnal rite. He does not silence or hide it. Love, desire, lust, are one and the same:

> *Besides, Satan loves me much,*
> *He was my companion*
> *In an examination*
> *Of lust, and the rascal*
> *Will look for Margarita*
> *– He has promised her to me –*
> . . . .
> *So that I may tear off*
> *Her pure thighs.*

Had Lorca completed the normal span of his life, he might well be alive today and his 'he-goat' would have slowed down its run. The love-theme could have reached the depth and serene maturity already foreshadowed in the 'Casidas' and 'Gacelas'. But what we have is a poet who, particularly in his first books, sees not only love but himself also as a prisoner of uncontrollable forces:

> *I was riding on*
> *A he-goat.*
> *Grandfather talked to me*
> *And said:*
> *'That's your way.'*
> *'It's that,' shouted my shadow,*
> *Disguised as a beggar.*
> *'It's that gold one,' cried my dress.*
> *A big swan winked at me*
> *Saying: 'Come with me!'*
> *And a serpent bit*
> *My pilgrim's sackcloth.*

This type of vision or dream, the internal conflict it discloses, the use of symbols and myths – he-goat, dress, swan, serpent – still on only one plane, still without the later polyvalent quality that allows multiple interpretations, place this poem, as well as many others in that first book, much nearer to *Poet in New York* than to *Songs*; or to the *Gipsy Ballads*, books in which the theme of love takes on a far more erotic and joyful tone.

In the book *Songs* the love-theme is treated with irony through-out the set of poems grouped under the title 'Eros With Walk-ing Stick'. The little poem 'A fright in the dining-room' is an exquisite, short lyrical 'still' of a moment without words. Nothing happens yet everything is possible, it is a moment on which everything hangs in ecstatic hesitation.

We seem to be looking into a clean Andalusian dining-room during a well-shaded summer-siesta. The poet is drowsing in a rocking-chair and we see advancing towards him a young servant girl carrying at the height of her small breasts fresh apples in a great *fajalauza* plate. The poet stretching out a hand to take an apple and the girl's hidden fright caused by his gesture floats in the air, making him realize all too suddenly the heat of the sen-suous afternoon – a jump from the intimate into the cosmic:

> *Your colour was rosy,*
> *But you turned to lemon.*
> *What intention did you see in my hand*
> *That almost threatened you?*
> *I wanted the green apples*
> *Not the rosy ones . . .*
> *Lemon one*
> *(Afternoon, that sleepy crane*
> > *stamped his other leg down to earth.)*

Poet-painter, Lorca delights in descriptions where the drunken-ness of light, colour and feminine forms bring to mind the inter-iors of Bonnard. On seeing the red silk dress worn by the woman disguised as Lucía Martínez – black eyes in the soft velvet white-ness of her face – the poet writes:

> *Red silk in the shade.*
> *Your thighs, like the afternoon,*
> *Go from light to shadow.*
> *Hidden gems of jet*
> *Darken your magnolia . . .*
> *I come to wear away your mouth.*

In 'Interior', another brief song in the series, Lorca says to the Andalusian Carmen that he wants to be neither poet, nor gallant; he wants 'Sheets in which you may faint!' The changing perfume of the naked body of the tireless Aphrodite blinds the poet with passion:

> *You do not know sleep*
> *Nor the splendour of the day.*
> *As ink-fish*
> *Naked you blind with perfumed ink.*

When the poet praises the sensuous Lolita we find expressions such as 'aniseed of your white thighs', and in the little poem which describes the sumptuous Leonarda of Málaga – 'pontifical flesh in white dress' – leaning on the railings of her villa facing the sea:

> *Exposed to tramways and ships.*
> *The black torsos of sea-bathers darken*
> *The sea-shore. Oscillating*
> *– Shell and lotus –*
> *Come your buttocks*
> *Of Ceres in marble rhetoric.*

These descriptions of female forms, visible under clinging fabric, reminiscent of the *drap mouillé* in sculpture, abound in the poetry of Lorca. A gipsy is dancing:

> *Her skirt of moiré trembles*
> *Between her copper thighs.*

Beneath the black silk of her dress he sees the hard breasts of Soledad Montoya:

> *Sooty anvils, her breasts*
> *Moan round songs.*

In 'St. Miguel's Ballad' some *manolas*[1] approach eating sunflower seeds:

> *Their buttocks big and hidden*
> *As copper planets*

If from these markedly visual images we focus on the sense of touch we find a similar sensuality expressed in precise, unexpected comparisons. The great success of 'The Unfaithful Wife' has over-popularized a ballad which in its day was a daring gesture. Yet any man who has caressed a woman's breast will recognize the sensory transposition:

> *And suddenly they open to me*
> *Like a bunch of hyacinths.*

[1] *Manolas.* Originally the popular, witty, gaily dressed young women of eighteenth-and nineteenth-century Madrid. Later came to mean a lady well-dressed in a conspicuous, popular fashion and of easy manners.

Or the other experience summed up by the man-wind pursuing Preciosa:

> *Open in my ancient fingers*
> *The blue rose of your belly.*

The nervous agitation, the fire that one body gives off when in contact with another, is contrasted with the coldness in the back when lying on sand, grass or river mud:

> *Her thighs escaped me*
> *Like startled fishes,*
> *Half of them full of fire*
> *Half of them full of cold.*

Even when describing the martyrdom of St. Olalla, the poet uses female forms as still life of a surrealist clarity:

> *The Consul carries in silver dish*
> *Olalla's sooty breasts.*

Or:

> *Her sex trembles entangled*
> *Like a bird in the brambles.*

Gaiety of life prevails in the amorous or erotic poetry of Lorca, written before his journey to New York. On the periphery are already the 'black tones', but in the centre is a feast of colour and human forms, mainly feminine, described with sensual delight. Those female forms become the canon of perfection. Thus, a lemon grove is 'Nest of yellow breasts', or 'breasts that suckle the sea-breeze'; the pomegranate is described as 'Venus' flesh-sister . . . light of life . . . the female of fruits'.

In the *Gipsy Ballads* we find also descriptions of handsome youths worthy of figuring next to his women and of taking part in the sensuous gaiety of life. Already in the first ballad he draws a quick sketch of a group of gipsy lads advancing slowly along a road that passes through an olive grove:

> *Through the olive grove they came,*
> *Bronze and dream, the gipsy lads.*
> *Uplifted their heads,*
> *Half-closed their eyes.*

The tardy walk, the colour of the skin, the haughty, disdainful gesture, all is briefly alluded to, though the word 'dream' partially removes them from reality.

In the third ballad Lorca offers us one of his typical close-ups:

> *The afternoon mad with fig-trees*
> *And warm murmurs*
> *Falls fainting on the wounded*
> *Thighs of the riders.*

The adjective 'wounded' could be interpreted in its literal sense – wounded in the brawl he has just described – or metaphorically – wounded by the rays of the setting sun. In either case the sensuous delight is clear.

In the ballad 'St. Gabriel' and still more in the two about the arrest and death of Antoñito el Camborio, we find a full-size masculine portrait. 'St. Gabriel' is one of the three ballads dedicated to the three archangels representing the three main Andalusian towns: Seville, Cordova and Granada, whose individuality in the lyrical map of Andalusia Lorca was so keen to establish. If Rafael is the patron Saint of Cordova, if in Granada there is special veneration for St. Miguel, Lorca gives St. Gabriel, the messenger of good news, the giver of life, to Seville 'the city to be alive in' (*para vivir*):

> *A lad slender as a reed,*
> *Broad shoulders, thin waist,*
> *Skin of nocturnal apple,*
> *Big eyes and sad mouth . . .*

Lorca takes delight in the description of the physical beauty of his gipsy – St. Gabriel. Neither dove nor crowned emperor nor guiding star can be compared to him. He sees him of such beauty that:

> *When he bows his head*
> *Over his chest of jade*
> *Night seeks plains*
> *In which to kneel.*

But it should be remembered that Lorca is not portraying here a real character but a personification of an ideal asexual beauty in the shape of a gipsy Annunciation based on clear pictorial models: Botticelli, Fra Angelico, Filippo Lippi, painters whom he admired. An Annunciation in motion. A Botticellian angel – 'Big eyes, sad mouth' – in the body of a gipsy lad of today, goes through the streets of Seville in search of the gipsy virgin Anunciación

Reyes; naughtiness and tenderness in wise poetic play. In the reconstruction of the Biblical myth, Lorca dissolves one plane into another, and the interpolation of dream and reality gives to the whole scene an atemporal character. 'The guitars play by themselves', and the poet warns his archangel, a double of the one revered in the church:

> *Saint Gabriel, the child cries*
> *In his mother's womb.*
> *Don't forget that the gipsies*
> *Presented you with your dress.*

The virgin is described as 'Well mooned (soft and olive skin) and poorly dressed'. Speaks to the archangel: 'Here you have me/ with three nails of delight', and St. Gabriel underlines the allusion to the Passion:

> *Your child will have in his chest*
> *A beauty spot and three wounds.*

In this ballad, as well as in the one entitled 'The Civil Guard' and 'Don Pedro on Horseback', Lorca was anticipating the 'a-temporal' atmosphere he would perfect in *When Five Years Have Passed*, and still further, in *The Public*.

Of quite another order are the ballads dedicated to Antoñito el Camborio, the best male creation in the *Gipsy Ballads*. The poet, apparently using an actual incident, draws a type whose first distinctive feature is an extraordinary beauty: 'tawny of green moon, voice of manly carnation', 'skin kneaded of olive and jasmine'. In the first ballad 'Antoñito el Camborio', the indolent gipsy throws lemons into the river for fun, just to see the water turning gold. The gipsy is arrested by the Civil Guard, without any resistance or resort to knife.

In the second ballad we see the gipsy in a desperate fight against his four cousins:

> *He dug into their boots*
> *Wild-boar's fangs.*
> *During the fight he made jumps*
> *Of slippery dolphin.*

Then follows a dialogue between the dying gipsy and his creator, echoes no doubt of Unamuno and Pirandello. Then the last gush of blood and the falling of the head to one side:

> *And he died in profile.*
> *Living coin that never will*
> *Be repeated.*

These ballads may well have been based on actual facts but the transformation suffered by the model is such that the characters become creatures of pure imagination. This dying gipsy is first cousin of the Amargo, the protagonist of the poetic prose of that name. Both are indolent, both walk alone a solitary road in the unavoidable company of death. And when the poet describes the dead gipsy lad, certain Florentine pictures come again to mind:

> *A swaggering angel*
> *Sets the gipsy's head on a cushion.*
> *Others with tired blush*
> *Light an oil lamp.*

These gipsy youths are the counterpart of the angels in Giovanni Bellini's *Pietà*, or in Filippo Lippi's *Crucifixion* or in Botticelli's famous medallion. The hues of their faces may have changed, but the 'big eyes and sad mouth' and the compositions are almost identical.

A poet who could portray with such gay sensuality the juvenile beauty of his heroes or heroines could not fail in poems and dramas to sing the union of bodies, the carnal rite, the whole gamut from soft caress to forbidden kiss. The ballad of 'The Unfaithful Wife' has distracted attention from the best of Lorca's hardly-known amorous or erotic poetry, ranging from the juvenile 'Summer Madrigal' to the posthumous 'Sonnets of Dark Love'. Let us look at some examples:

> *Nobody knew that you tormented*
> *A humming-bird of love between your teeth.*

Góngora would have envied this description of the tongue as an imprisoned humming-bird.

The effort made by Vladimir Nabokov to describe Lolita's delight in the secret kisses he gives her – the same kisses to which so many poets from Solomon to Quevedo and Pierre Loti have referred – becomes easy for Lorca:

> *Nobody understood the perfume*
> *Of the dark magnolia of your belly.*

or

> *I tore my veins,*
> *Tiger and dove, on your waist*
> *In a duel of bites and white lilies.*

We find equal delight in the description of all forms of caress and in the mere contact of bodies:

> *They love each other beyond all the museums. Right hand with left hand. Left hand with right hand. Right foot with right foot. Left foot with cloud. Hair with sole of the feet. Sole of the feet with left cheek. Left thigh with left forearm. Closed eyes with open fingernails. Waist with nape of the neck and with beach . . .*

Often the waist is associated with expressions of voluptuous ardour, as in 'Waist of restless sand', in the poem 'Your Childhood in Menton'.

And when at last dream conquers love, the poet feels the quiet regular breath of the beloved as the pungent perfume of a rose:

> *I fear to lose the marble wonder of your statue eyes*
> *And the solitary rose of your breathing that pricks my cheek at night.*

In one hundred lines Lorca narrates the Biblical incest of Thamar and Amnon: the fatal visit, the dialogue between brother and sister, the act of rape. The ultimate consequence of the drama is portrayed as in a Persian miniature and the physical and psychological reactions attained by an interplay of antitheses: burning heat and shades or freshness of liquids; outside the torrid summer that calcinates the earth and opens crevices ('the earth offers herself covered with healed wounds'); inside the cool water in earthenware jars ('well's oppressed lymph /silence from the jar spurts forth').

Water and fire, Thamar and Amnon, remedy and disease. Thamar sings 'To the compass of cold tambourines', her nakedness 'demands snowflakes from her belly' and 'hail from her shoulders'. She sings and around her feet there are 'five frozen doves'. This is how Amnon sees his sister while he suffers the fever that consumes him, making him feel the coolness of the sheets as 'ivy of a shudder'. The presence of his sister in the tent excites his imagination. In his sister's breasts there are 'two fishes calling me'; and in a beautiful sensory transportation he speaks of his sister's rosy fingernails as 'murmur of enshrined roses'. Amnon pretends submission to his sister: 'My threads of blood/ weave flounces over your skirt', like one more colour on the colourful tunic worn by the Israelite virgins. On contact with her brother the feeling of burning and restlessness becomes hers:

> *Let me be my brother.*
> *Your kisses on my shoulders*
> *Are wasps and little winds*
> *In double swarm of flutes.*

And when Amnon forces his sister's virginity, Lorca shows us Thamar's blood in yet another of his characteristic close-ups:

> *Warm corals draw*
> *Streams on fair map.*

And, as often, the word blood brings with it the antithesis red-white:

> *Round Thamar*
> *Gipsy virgins scream*
> *While others gather the drops*
> *Of her sacrificed flower.*
> *White handkerchiefs reddened*
> *In locked alcoves.*

No doubt Lorca knew Tirso's *Thamar and Amnon* and old Spanish ballads on the famous incest, but his direct model is of course Samuel, Book II.

We have already seen how the irresistible attraction of the sexes leads to the dialogue between Leonardo and the Bride in the forest scene of *Blood Wedding*. 'All this scene is violent, loaded with great sensuality', says the stage direction, as if the meaning of the words were not clear enough proof that we are witnessing one of the most erotic scenes in Spanish drama. 'I love you, I love you', Novia cries out in an outburst of passion, throwing herself into Leonardo's arms. And after a last attempt at resistance, the confession of utter surrender:

> *Oh! what a lament, what fire*
> *Is creeping up my head!*

(again the fire symbol):

> *I look at you*
> *And your beauty burns me.*

And Leonardo:

> *Fire and fire consume each other.*
> *The same small flame*
> *Kills two joint ears of corn.*
>
> *What nails of moon are fusing*
> *My hips and your waist.*

She wanted to escape from fire but could not. Similar is Leonardo's experience:

> *And when I saw you from afar*
> *I threw sand into my eyes.*
> *But I mounted the horse*
> *And the horse came to your door.*

For the rest we know that neither he nor she is to blame, only the earth and 'the perfume that comes from your breasts and your tresses'. Moon and death alone – the latter disguised as an old beggar woman – will be able to stop the consummation of the rite thus begun.

Even in those plays where the central theme is amorous frustration, the glorification of the flesh emphasizes the conflict. Yerma, the married woman without children, sees her obsession accentuated by the exuberant fertility all around her:

> *Because I am insulted, insulted and humiliated to the last, seeing the corn begin to turn, the fountains that never cease to give water, or the sheep to give birth to hundreds of little lambs, and the bitches too, and it seems as if the whole countryside rises up to show me its tender offspring while here I feel, instead of the mouth of my child, two blows of a hammer.*

In the drama there is also a hidden denunciation of the social conventions which are the real cause of the betrayal of the instinct of the flesh. Victor, the shepherd, was the man for Yerma, but she married Juan, a richer man, because 'my father gave him to me and I accepted him'. But this Juan is the man whom the pagan old woman holds responsible for Yerma's sterility:

> *Your husband is the one to blame. Do you hear me? I would bet my two hands. Neither his father nor his grandfather, nor his great grandfather behaved as men of good breed. They had to call in heaven and earth to get a son. They're made of saliva. But not your people . . .*

Right through the play Lorca maintains the contrast barren-fruitful in a crescendo that culminates in the final explosion preceding the end of the play. In the final scene, outside the hermitage where the 'cuckold's pilgrimage' takes place, the women who accompany Yerma pass in procession, barefoot. They pray to the Saint, echoing Yerma's desperate prayer:

> *Oh Lord, open your rose-tree*
> *Over my withered flesh.*

> *Open your rosebud on my flesh*
> *Though it may have a thousand thorns.*

They enter the hermitage and at the same moment the Male and Female Masks rush on to the stage with a Bacchic dance and song:

> *If you come on this pilgrimage*
> *To pray for the opening of your womb*

> *Go alone behind those walls*
> *Where the fig-trees are dense*
> *And support my body of earth*
> *Until dawn's white moan.*

> *Seven times she moaned.*
> *Nine she raised herself up,*
> *Fifteen times jasmines*
> *Were joined with oranges . . .*

As the Dionysian rhythm of the dance is lost in the distance the erotic poem dissolves in the prayer of Yerma and her companions coming out of the hermitage:

MALE FIGURE: Let the dance burn
              And with it the shining body
              Of the beautiful married woman
(*Exit dancing and laughing with accompaniment of handclapping. Singing offstage.*)

THE PROCESSION: Heaven has gardens
                With rose-trees of gaiety.
                Between rose-tree and rose-tree
                The rose of wonder.

Like so many authors before and after Cervantes, Lorca, as we have already seen, was attracted to the theme of the old man married to a young woman. He examines it from different angles. With gaiety and comedy in his guignolesque *Títeres de Cachiporra* or in his puppet play; or uses it as an ideal setting for the clash between reality and dream in *The Prodigious Cobbler's Wife*; with earnestness hidden behind the playful tone of 'commedia dell' arte' in that splendid erotic fable *The Love of Don Perlimplín and Belisa in his garden*. Common to all is the contrast sterile–fertile, the sadness of frustrated love versus the gaiety of life and normal encounter between the sexes. That is to say, the Cristobita of the *Títeres* versus the impassioned and young Cocoliche; the Cristóbal of the *Retablillo*, versus Currito or the Poet; the quite good-hearted Cobbler, as against the harsh and comic lessons of manhood given by the local Mayor. Lastly, in opposition to the 18th-century-like figure of Don Perlimplín, the five whistled signals on his wedding night, and the enervating and repetitive song of Belisa:

> Love, oh love!
> Between my closed thighs
> The sun swims like a fish.

In *When Five Years Have Passed* we find a condemnation of the refusal to answer to the call of love. The Bride's Wedding Dress laments the fruitless waiting:

> Thread by thread and one by one,
> My silks have,
> Longing for the warmth of wedding.
> And my chemise asks
> Where are the warm hands
> That press on my waist.

And then it accuses the young man of his bride's elopement with a rugby player:

> You could have been for me
> A colt of lead and foam,
> The air broken in the bridle
> The sea tied on the rump.
> You could have been a neigh
> And you are a sleepy backwater.

The accusation is not only due to sexual dissatisfaction, but to the frustration of the maternal instinct. The Mannequin produces, as a last appeal to the Young Man's virility, 'a little dress stolen from the sewing basket', an offspring which for the Mannequin, for Yerma and for most of Lorca's women is the natural consequence of all normal relations between man and woman.

Norm of Yesterday

> He too, he too! Stained fingers
> point to the shores of your
> dreams . . .
>
> *Ode to Walt Whitman.*

Lorca looks at love in all its forms, examines it from all angles, and identifies himself with all its victims. His capacity for human love knows no limit. There is love, mixed with tenderness and respect, for small children; in his scale of values pure friendship comes next after the strongest family ties, and to his grief at the death of a friend we owe one of the most imposing elegies in the Spanish language; recondite corners of sexual instinct are explored not only in man–woman relationships but also in the love between persons of the same sex. In this sense *The Public* is only a link – though a most important one – in the long chain of love themes.

It seems that in erotic love he was fully conscious of a dichotomy, on occasions accepted as natural, with undisguised gaiety. One detects how at times he is dominated by one, then by the other. At times he places both forms of love in the balance. In the poem 'Nocturnal Song of the Andalusian Sailors' he uses as refrain for the two first stanzas the lines: 'Oh, girl, girl /how many ships in the port of Málaga?' and for the following two 'Oh lad, lad /the waves carry my horse away,' finally linking both vocatives together in the last two stanzas, 'Oh girl, oh lad / what a good little road . . .' This is of course mere poetic play, but it is a form that recurs in other poems, the light of a philosophy of love expounded in all seriousness in the 'Ode to Walt Whitman':

> *Man can, if he so wishes, direct his love*
> *Through vein of coral or celestial nude.*
> *Tomorrow loves will be rocks, and Time*
> *A breeze that comes sleepy through branches.*

That is to say man can direct his desire towards woman or towards man. (I take 'through vein of coral' to be an allusion to the myth of the birth of Aphrodite; 'celestial nude' as an allusion to Apollo, the god not very fortunate with women, the god who knew the love of ephebes.) The form of amorous passion matters little to Lorca; what does matter is its consummation, because love dies quickly and man's life, and time itself, are like a gentle 'breeze' flowing quietly through the tree branches. Once this attitude is understood it is possible to read afresh poems whose meaning was previously incomprehensible. For example, the two *décimas*[1] – which with unmistakable cryptic intention he entitled 'Norms':

I

Norm of yesterday found
Upon my present night;
Adolescent radiance
Which challenges the snow.
My two vigilant pupils
Do not want to give you entry
Bronzed by a moon in suspense
And the heart wide open;
But my love looks for the orchard
Where your style never dies.

II

Norm of breast and waist
Under the suspended branch;
Ancient and newly born
Virtue of spring.
Already my nude wished to be
Dahlia of your destiny,
Bee, murmur or wine
Of your number and madness;
But my love is seeking pure
Madness of breeze and trill.

In the first 'Norm' the poet speaks of love for the adolescent. In hours of despair or dismay – 'present night' – (faint echo of St. John of the Cross) the author discovers the love for the adolescent in ancient Greece and calls it 'Norm of Yesterday', renewed beauty in constant opposition to old age, 'snow'. The

[1] Spanish stanza consisting of ten lines of eight syllables.

poet would like to resist the temptation of the newly-discovered norm of which he has caught a glimpse. (He describes his own pupils 'bronzed by a moon in suspense', a metaphor full of Lorquian resonances.) But the wound received opens the heart of the poet for its acceptance and in spite of not wanting to give it shelter he looks for the place where the norm of that ancient love 'never dies'.

The second 'Norm' speaks of woman. In the first two lines there is a subtle allusion to Botticelli's *Birth of Venus*, to the beautiful forms of a female nude. The poet would wish his own body to become the flower of her destiny, or murmur of bee (symbol of love), or wine, that is to say proximity, and delight at the contact of bodies; but, as in the previous *décima*, the poet's love follows a path alien to his will in search of a 'pure madness of breeze and trill': preference for Norm 1? Love in search of the 'one'? In any case the two 'Norms' are a serene avowal of a dichotomy and of a preference, at least at the time of writing, for the first 'Norm'. Let us trace in his work the encounter with that 'norm of yesterday' and the search for the orchard where its type never dies.

In his first book, *Impressions and Landscapes*, it would be difficult to point with relative certainty to the presence of Norm I, but we can see it clearly stated in the interesting prologue to his earlier first play *The Malefice of the Butterfly*. Here, the as yet unskilled hands drew haltingly what were to become the general lines of practically all his themes, not excluding the one under review: 'Poet, tell man that love springs forth with equal intensity on all levels of life . . . Everything is equal in nature.'

In his first book of poems, next to compositions recalling his early loves – 'the first kiss to savour of kiss', 'the girl with tresses who looked straight at you', or his first sexual experiences with women – there are others which could hide some secret beneath cryptic sentences and imprecise allusions. In one poem the poet sees 'how lilies became dry in contact with my voice'; in another he tells of the 'ancient noon of my lips . . . the ancient noon of my glances' and confesses that 'a hallucination milks my looks. I see the word love crumbled'. At times, too, he alludes to his hidden love: 'I tell in the night the sadness of my unknown love', or 'I, alone, with my unknown love', or confesses real or imagined sins: 'a grave sadness stains my lips with sins'. In another poem he asks the nearly-shed cover of his heart: 'Shall I hang thee from the walls of my sentimental museum next to the frigid and dark sleeping lilies of my sins?' and in another: '. . . today I meditate disturbed, facing my heart's turbid fountain'. It would be unwise to attach too much importance to this outburst of lyrical adolescent sadness. But the preoccupation it betrays will persist and become more intense.

In the book of poems entitled *Songs* all the themes become stylized in the form of poetic *divertissement* so characteristic of most of these compositions. The theme of homosexual love may lie beneath the playful poem entitled 'Ribereñas (accompanied by bells)':

> *They say that your face is*
> *(balalín)*
> *Like the full moon*
> *(balalán)*
>
> *But your eyes . . . Ah!*
> *(balalín)*
> *. . . Sorry, that ring under your eye*
> *(balalán)*
> *And that golden rose*
> *(balalín)*
> *And that . . . I can't, that . . .*
> *(balalán)*
> *The bells beat*
> *Their hard hoop-skirt.*
> *Oh, your hidden delight . . . your . . .*
> *(balalín*
>   *lin*
>   *lin . . .)*
> *Excuse me.*

Or in the gay, harmless Andalusian mockery entitled 'Song of the Little Pansy', a scene in which the pleasant, the cranky and the lyrical intermingle. Poem in two tempos: a statement of fact is immediately followed by a marginal ironic commentary with a rhythmical alteration at the end:

> *The little pansy combs his hair*
> *In his silken dressing-gown.*
> *At their back windows*
> *The neighbours smile.*

The little pansy sets aright
The ringlets on his head.
In the patios parrots are screaming,
Fountains of planets.
The little pansy adorns himself
With a shameless jasmine.
The afternoon becomes alien
With combs and climbers.
Scandal trembled
Striped like a zebra.
The little pansies from the South
Sing on their flat roofs.

Of course all this is poetic virtuosity. That this was the initial intention of the author is clearly shown in the title and in the dedication of the section to which both poems belong: 'Divertissements: Dedicated to Luis Buñuel's head. *En Grand plain.*' Yet there are in this book some brief songs or poems that with unexpected drama and intensity sum up Lorca's attitude towards the theme under discussion. In them he exposes to the 'guillotine of the wind' 'the eyeless head of all my desires'. Above all we find in two songs of the section entitled 'Trasmundo' an uncommon example of formal repetition, not only in the same book but in the same section:

<table>
<tr><td>'Scene'</td><td>'Betrothal'</td></tr>
<tr><td>High Towers.</td><td>Throw that ring</td></tr>
<tr><td>Long Rivers.</td><td>Into the water.</td></tr>
<tr><td>'Fairy' – Take the wedding ring</td><td>(The shadow rests his fingers</td></tr>
<tr><td>Which belonged to your forefathers.</td><td>On my shoulders.)</td></tr>
<tr><td>Under the earth one hundred hands</td><td>Throw that ring away. I am</td></tr>
<tr><td>Are missing it.</td><td>More than one hundred years old. Silence.</td></tr>
<tr><td>'I' – I shall feel in my hands</td><td>Ask me nothing!</td></tr>
<tr><td>An immense flower of fingers</td><td></td></tr>
<tr><td>And the symbol of the ring</td><td></td></tr>
<tr><td>I do not want it.</td><td></td></tr>
<tr><td>High Towers.</td><td>Throw that ring</td></tr>
<tr><td>Long Rivers.</td><td>Into the water.</td></tr>
</table>

In the first song all the poet's ancestors expect him to perpetuate his name, but he refuses because he does not want to feel on his hands the fingers of all his ancestors, or the fingers of his potential successors. Willingly the poet establishes himself as the last of a clan. The short dialogue is framed in a simple fairy-tale landscape with the river standing possibly for life, in the old Spanish literary tradition.

In the second version the fingers resting upon the poet's shoulders belong to the shadow of his ancestors or to his possible descendants. The conclusion in both poems is identical. Fairy or shadow, the poet refuses to take part in the dance to which he is invited. In 'Betrothal' the command 'throw that ring into the water' brings to mind the early poem 'Sad Ballad':

> *And I lost the ring of my happiness*
> *On crossing the imaginary stream*

which besides alluding to a children's folk song, anticipates the lament of the Bride Mannequin in *When Five Years Have Passed*:

> *My ring, sir, my ring of old gold.*
> *It sunk through the sands of the mirror.*

In both compositions we find the same firm refusal to perpetuate his name in his own children, an idea well reasoned and explained in his later 'Ode to Walt Whitman':

> *Because it is right that man seek not his delight*
> *In the forest of blood of next morning.*
> *Heaven has beaches where life can be avoided*
> *And there are bodies that should not be repeated at dawn.*

It is fitting, he says, that a man should forfeit a relationship which results in the procreation of the species – 'forest of blood of next morning' – because for those who reject or do not feel paternity, life offers alternatives where that aim is totally excluded.

In discussing the poem sung by Juliet in *The Public* it was already pointed out how that 'forest of blood of next morning' refers to the coming generations. Lorca, on thinking of the multitude of children to be born – fruits of love – and the flow of so much blood through so many veins, transfers his image to the vegetable kingdom, as he has done in other poems. Here the idea is an elaboration, conscious or not, of what he had already pointed to in the obscure, difficult and beautiful sonnet 'Adam'. Let us look at it more closely in connection with the theme of homosexual love:

> *A tree of blood wets the morning*
> *Where the newly delivered woman moans.*

147

> *The voice leaves crystals in the wound*
> *And a diagram of bones on the window-pane.*
> *But the dawning light defines and attains*
> *White goals of a fable that forgets*
> *The tumult of veins fleeing*
> *Towards the turbid freshness of the apple.*
> *In the fever of clay Adam dreams*
> *Of a child who approaches galloping*
> *Through the double beat of his cheeks.*
> *But another dark Adam is dreaming*
> *Of neuter moon of stone without seed*
> *Where the child of light is self-consuming.*

That tree, whose multiplication will give rise to the 'forest', could be either the first man's son, or the son of any man, as well as other images that the tree brings to mind.

'The voice' I take as referring to the tree, that is to say to the child who comforts the mother but sets 'a diagram of bones on the window-pane'. This brings to mind the stage direction in the first scene of *The Public*: 'The window-panes are X-ray plates.' In both cases the image points to the presence of death; in the sonnet, from the very moment of birth, an idea which the Harlequin in the third act of *When Five Years Have Passed* expresses with remarkable precision:

> *The broken tongue of the old*
> *Overtakes the faint moan of the child.*

The light of a new day 'defines and attains' the dream of possible realizations of the newly born, 'fable', without being aware that he who is born thinking himself advancing, in reality flees 'towards the turbid freshness of the apple', towards love that spells death. (Further on we shall see how often the apple has in Lorca the double symbolical value of love and death.)

Adam, in his joy of life-clay fever, forgets his fragile existence and dreams of his child born from his own blood, but within himself another Adam is dreaming with the superimposition of sterile elements 'where the child of light' who was already galloping would burn himself out without being born. Another example of the conscious duality of the theme of love in his work is stated here with an intention resembling the simile of the mirror: living ants – grains of sand – used by the Juggler in the last act of *The Public*.

Let us now look at the 'Ode to Walt Whitman', after the 'Lament for Ignacio Sánchez Mejías', Lorca's longest poem (137 lines), one of his most inspired, daring and original both in thought and exposition. It is moreover a key poem in the understanding of the theme we are discussing since in it Lorca clearly states, with a courage and a clarity unheard of in Spanish letters, his attitude as man and artist towards homosexual love.

The *Ode* begins with two tempos, two planes or two voices: exposition and marginal comment. In stanzas 1, 3 and 5 the poet describes his vision of New York, a city of work and activity, a city in which man sustains a constant struggle with industry, a city in which everything is sold or bought, in which clouds and barges pass by over the roof-tops or under the bridges as 'herds of bison pushed by the wind', a city in which even the appearance of the moon suggests to the poet the industrial pulleys, where the memories of its inhabitants are limited and encircled by the huge needles of the skyscrapers and where – thinking no doubt of the 'bums' who sleep and die on the Bowery – 'coffins will take away those who do not work'.

In stanzas 2, 4 and 6 are the comment and the contrast with that reality: 'But no-one slept' – in the sense of dream – no-one loved the imagination, the natural life in fields or beaches, nor – in contrast to the wheel of industry – the wheel of the dance. In such a New York, 'city of slime, wire and death', living with its back to country and life, the poet asks himself who would be capable of speaking the truth of the ear of corn, the visible – for the majority the invisible – truths such as 'the terrible dreams of your stained anemones'. For Lorca such a voice was Walt Whitman, 'the caresser of life wherever flowing'. He sees him as the Homer of America, old man 'beautiful as a mist', with 'thighs of virginal Apollo' moaning like 'a bird with its sex pierced by a needle', an image that immediately brings to mind certain surrealist pictures and the legend that a deep wound makes the nightingale sing better, used by Oscar Wilde in *The Nightingale and the Rose*.

Lorca describes Whitman as 'enemy of the satyr, enemy of vine', natural, anti-'maudit' but 'lover of bodies beneath rough clothes', an allusion, no doubt, to Whitman's association with 'powerful, uneducated persons' such as young boatmen or coach-drivers. Recalling perhaps Whitman's courageous behaviour during the American Civil War, Lorca sees him, whatever his sexual inclinations, as the prototype of the virile man; therefore it enrages him that American 'pansies', or the 'pansies' of any land, should count Walt Whitman as one of them; as though any similarity were possible between a man looking for a love that 'could be like a river, bull and dream capable of uniting wheel and water' and the debased search by the 'pansies' of all lands. A large part of the poem is devoted to establishing a distinction between the homosexual by nature, the man in search of the 'one', or a boundless total love, and the corrupt homosexual, 'woman's slave'. Between those two types of love there is for Lorca an even greater disparity than between a deep man-woman love and the bawdy sexual encounters in the brothels frequented by soldiers and carters.

As the poem advances the tone heightens. Then come the alexandrines already quoted ('Because it is just that man should not seek his delight . . .'), followed by the lamentation promoted by the state of the world in the thirties, perhaps by a premonition of what was going to happen a few years later, first in Spain and then in the whole world:

> *Agony, agony, dream, ferment and dream.*
> *This is the world, my friend, agony, agony.*
> *The dead rot beneath the town clocks,*
> *War passes by crying with a million grey rats,*
> *Rich men give to their mistresses*
> *Little illuminated dying ones*
> *And life is neither noble, nor good nor sacred.*

Such a pessimistic attitude leads inevitably to the major declaration contained in the four alexandrines previously quoted – 'man can, if so he wishes, drive his desire through vein of coral . . .' In consequence Lorca does not attack those he labels 'pure', but in an uncompromising way condemns corruptors and decadents. Between the former group and the latter he draws a sharp line to the bitter end. On one side 'The love that gives away crowns of gaiety', on the other 'drops of dirty death with bitter venom'; on the one hand the 'confused, the pure, the aesthete, those pointed at, the suppliants of love', on the other 'the pansies' that are 'flesh for whip, boot or bite of the tamers', 'woman's slaves', 'bitches of their boudoirs'.

The 'Ode to Walt Whitman' is dated 15th June, 1930, when Lorca must have been writing *The Public*. The theme of homosexual love – latent throughout all his work prior to his journey to America – becomes obsessive at the time of his stay in New York. It is present, among others, in the poem 'Your Childhood in Menton' and in the strange 'Fable and Round Dance of the Three Friends'.

After his return from New York the theme of homosexual love starts to recede. A year later, in 1931, he finishes *When Five Years Have Passed* whose protagonist, of undetermined origin, at times similar to the men in *The Public*, tries but fails to find in a woman the outlet for his longing for love and dream. Then come the rural tragedies and *Doña Rosita*. The passions that motivated these dramas derive from normal sexual relations.

In its double flow the theme of love reappeared in the 'Casidas' and 'Gacelas' of the *Diván del Tamarit*. Whereas some of the *Sonnets of Dark Love*, but not all, may allude to love for boys several 'Gacelas' are clearly addressed to a girl. And yet most of these posthumous poems seem rather to be inspired by an all-embracing love. Such are the 'Gacelas' of 'Unexpected Love', of 'Terrible Presence', of 'Desperate Love', of 'Market at Dawn'. Although in all these poems love is the central theme, it takes on diverse characteristics, flows through other channels, often fused or confused with the death theme. A prototype of this tendency is 'Casida of the Recumbent Woman':

> To see you naked is to remember the earth.
> The smooth earth free of horses.
> The earth without a blade of grass, pure form
> Closed to the future; silver confine.
>
> To see you naked is to understand the longing
> Of the rain searching for a faint form,
> Or the fever of the sea of immense face
> Which cannot find the light of its own cheek.
>
> Blood will resound in bedrooms
> And will come with resplendent sword,
> But you will not know where hides
> The toad's heart or the violet.
>
> Your belly is a struggle of roots,
> Your lips a boundless dawn,
> Underneath the warm roses of the bed
> Moan the dead awaiting their turn.

The first stanza offers no great difficulty. The poet compares the naked body of a woman, obviously a young virgin, with the earth in a hypothetical state of perfect virginity, without animal, flower or fruit, that is to say 'pure' and as a consequence 'closed to the future'.

In the second one he equates the desire which the female nude awakens in man to the longing of the rain to feed or contribute to the germination of trees and plants. The telluric content of these two lines is found also in other poems. More difficult to understand are the third and fourth lines referring to the cosmic force of a sea looking restlessly for something unattainable.

The third stanza is an allusion to the inevitable encounter between the sexes – with once again the sword as a phallic symbol – and to woman unable to distinguish the heart of vulgar desire from real love.

The last stanza echoes, sums up and answers the three previous ones. To the first one corresponds the line 'Your belly is a struggle of roots'. To the second the line 'Your lips are a boundless dawn', and to the third 'under the warm roses of the bed' – allusion to the rosy face and breasts as well as to the embroidered roses on the bed-cover of the newly-married. The closing line is his synthesis of the consequence of carnal union: 'The dead moan awaiting their turn.'

To see death as the only and true fruit of love or love as death's enticement is a recurrent note in the work of the poet. The final union of those two apparently antithetical ideas obsessed Lorca from his first writings. Nothing could illustrate better the ground covered by the poet than a comparison of the sharpness of that line – very likely dating from 1935 – with the naive expressions of the young writer. But neither does any poem better illustrate the early presence of his own themes. In 1919 he wrote in the *Malefice of the Butterfly*:

> And the truth is that Death takes on the disguise of Love! How very often the skeleton, carrier of the scythe that we see depicted in religious or prayer books, takes the form of a woman to deceive us and to open for us the gates of her shadows. It seems that the child Cupid very often sleeps in the empty cavities of her skull.

From the 'How often' of that prologue to the definite statement of the 'Casida' lies a long road marked half way by the two short poems on the ring-theme to which we have already referred. Before them what predominates is the 'Die we must', awakened in contact with the call of the flesh. When in the 'Ballad of the Little Square' the children ask the poet 'What do you feel in your red and thirsty mouth?', the poet answers, like someone from a Ribera *chiaroscuro*: 'The taste of the bones in my great skull.' In the poems written after *Songs* that taste of skull will also be on the lips he kisses or even in the caressing of a newly born child:

> *There is no night that on giving a kiss*
> *I did not feel the smile of people without faces.*
> *There is no-one who, on touching a newly born child,*
> *Forgets the motionless skull of the horses.*

The final equation love=death, or death=love, is what gives to Lorca's amorous poetry after the book *Songs* such an unmistakable and grave intensity. The mastery of form gives a classical beauty to poems which at first sight might look like surrealist mannerisms. That equation, it must be added, owes nothing to the duality of the love-theme. Neither does the homosexual love-theme give rise to any hatred or despising of woman, victim of the same destiny as man.

By its very nature therefore love will thus be inseparable from death, obverse and reverse of the same coin, without possible escape, as depicted in the strange symbolism of the final scene of *The Public*. In *Poet in New York* the fusion of what is for him false antithesis gathers momentum.

However, in most of the 'Gacelas' and 'Casidas' the theme of Love in all its forms is already transcended, because the poet sees himself alone with death. As if in the knowledge of his future tragedy, he does not now ask for love of woman or of lad. Contemplating his forthcoming hour of transit the only thing he begs is for a wounded hand to hold a wing of his own death. This 'Casida of the Impossible Hand' is one of Lorca's most desolate poems:

> *I want nothing more than a hand,*
> *A wounded hand, if possible.*
> *I want nothing more than a hand*
> *Even if I pass a thousand nights without a bed.*

It would be a pale chalk lily,
It would be a dove tied to my heart,
It would be the guardian who on the night of my transit
Would prevent the moon from coming in.

I only want that hand
For the daily ointments and the white sheet of my agony.
I only want that hand
To hold a wing of my death.

All the rest passes.
Already nameless blush, perpetual star.
The rest is the other thing; sad wind,
While the leaves flee in flocks.

II

DEATH IN THE WORK OF GARCÍA LORCA[1]

> *For I am not a man, or poet, or leaf*
> *But a wounded pulse sounding things of the otherside.*
> **DOUBLE POEM OF EDEN LAKE.**

Death, like love, is a constant theme in the work of Lorca. With romantic undertones it appears in revealing adolescent writings. With slow rhythm in the youthful *Book of Poems*; in humorous vein:

> *On the solitary hill*
> *A village cemetery*
> *Looks like a field sown*
> *With seed skulls . . .*

and in dramatic mood when suddenly a solitary swallow produces the same ominous effect as the flock of crows in one of Van Gogh's last pictures:

> *How many sons has Death?*
> *They all dwell on my chest!*
>
> *A swallow comes*
> *From far away!*

In the book *Songs* the theme takes on an almost Chinese stylization in short poems such as 'Hunter':

> *High pine grove!*
> *Four doves circle the air.*

[1] This completely new chapter, which did not appear in the first Spanish edition, formed the subject matter of two of the four Norman Maccoll Lectures given by the author at the University of Cambridge during the Academic year 1972/3.

Four doves
Fly and circle.
They bear
Four wounded shadows.

Low pine grove!
Four doves spread on the ground.

In the book *Poem of the Cante Jondo* the death-theme is full of Andalusian maxims, as in for example this gipsy's Death Lament:

. . . .

I came with eyes into this world
And I depart eyeless.
Lord of the Great Sorrow!
Then
An oil lamp and a blanket
On the floor.

I wanted to reach the place
Reached by the saintly.
And I have, my Lord!
But then,
An oil lamp and a blanket
On the floor . . .

From those early books onwards death appears with an ever-increasing urgency. It is a character in *Blood Wedding* and *When Five Years Have Passed*; it haunts many of the *Gipsy Ballads*; furiously beats the tom-tom in *Poet in New York* and reaches its climax in *Lament for Ignacio Sánchez Mejías*, an elegy not only for a bull-fighter friend but for death itself. In nearly all the 'Casidas', in practically all the last sonnets and posthumous poems the theme revolves round the poet's own death. Love and life are already seen as from 'the other side'. Such a thematic obsession turns an important section of his work into a song on the frontier of death, silence and oblivion. Why such insistence? Certainly not because of temperamental necrophilia.

'A box of joy'

The contagious gaiety that radiated from the man, often referred to – sometimes misinterpreted – by all who knew him, alternated with moments of deep depression or sadness of which only his closest friends were fully aware. Joy derived from avidly absorbing life through his five senses, depressions sprang from a constant awareness of the presence of sorrow and death. But life came first and into life he threw himself without reserve. Naively he confesses this in those first prose exercises to which one must constantly return:

> ... *And to pass through life in such a manner that when we reach the door of the 'solitary path' we may sip the last drop of all the existing emotions: virtue, sin, purity, blackness . . . One has to be religious and irreverent . . . See everything, feel everything. In eternity we shall gather the prize for having no horizons.*

His work bears witness that he remained true to such a programme. It is confirmed also by the statements he made during his life. In 1929, on giving thanks for a toast offered to him and to his interpreter, the actress Margarita Xirgu, Lorca improvised:

> *Now, more than ever do I need the silence and the spiritual depth of the atmosphere of Granada in order to survive the constant duel I maintain with my heart and with poetry. With my heart to free it from a destructive passion and from the deceitful shadow of the world casting its sterile sun. With poetry so as to be able to create in spite of her defence of her virginity, the living, true poem where beauty and horror and the inexpressible and the repugnant live and clash with each other in the midst of a deeply burning joy.*

And joy emanates from all his work; though of course with greater intensity, before the journey to New York. But it does not altogether vanish after the American experience, not even when he had glimpses of the coming storm.

'It was summer, 1926. I was in Granada and I owned a box of joy,' he wrote in 1933. But the box of joy was there before and after that summer of 1926. From the introduction to his first book of poems all his work shows a semi-religious, joyous communication with nature, sheer joy in poems grouped in the book *Songs* under the title 'Songs for Children', 'Eros with Walking-Stick', and 'Love'. Even in *Poet in New York* love and death dance in 'Two Waltzes' and on his arrival in Havana he wrote his very gay *Son Negro* (a Cuban song and dance).

Amongst his posthumous compositions it is surprising to find such optimistic poems as 'Gacela of the Early Morning Market' and 'Casida of the Bunch of Flowers'. Even the theme of his own death wears an air of delicate rigadoon in the 'Casida of the Dark Doves':

> *Through the laurel branches*
> *Two dark doves pass by.*
> *The one was the sun,*
> *Moon was the other.*
> *'Little neighbour', I said,*
> *'Where does my sepulchre lie?'*
> *'In my tail', said the sun.*
> *'In my throat', said the moon.*
> *And I who was walking*
> *With the earth up to my waist*
> *Saw two eagles of snow*
> *And a naked girl.*
> *The one was the other*
> *And the girl was neither.*
> *'Little eagles', I said,*
> *'Where does my sepulchre lie?'*
> *'In my tail', said the sun.*
> *'In my throat', said the moon.*
> *Through the laurel branches*
> *I saw two naked doves.*
> *The one was the other*
> *And the two were neither.*

Gaiety in the work is a reflection of his vital joy. 'You and I', he wrote in 1926 to his friend the poet Jorge Guillén, 'are poets. Poets! For our own joy.' Not only in his letters to a fellow poet for whom life was also a jubilant prodigy, but also to another writer, the sad, earnest and intelligent Colombian Jorge Zalamea. 'I need all the gaiety God bestowed upon me, now that I am surrounded by so many conflicts.' And a few lines later: 'All day I am possessed by the poetic activity of a factory, and in the evening I throw myself into what is man's due, a full-blooded Andalusian's due, the bacchic feast of flesh and laughter.' Even when writing the poems of New York and preparing *The Public*, Lorca writes to a friend: 'Now I am in New York, a city of unsuspected gaiety. I am serene and happy.' Three years later, in an interview with a Spanish newspaper: 'Yes, I am always happy. I have had a very long childhood and from this prolonged childhood I have kept this joy, my inexhaustible optimism.' And in 1935 he confesses to another journalist: '. . . Then I already had this laughter. Better, this laughter of today is my laughter of yesterday, the laughter of my childhood and of my days roaming in the fields, my country laughter that I will always protect, always, always, until I die.'

Then what are the reasons for his obsession with death? Before all else, background and upbringing.

Theory and divertissement of the 'duende'

Lorca himself refers to them in his essay on the 'duende': 'a candid lesson on the hidden spirit of sorrowful Spain', one of the poet's most penetrating and revealing essays. Let us look at some of the passages which are relevant to our theme:

> *Spain is at all times moved by the 'duende', as a country with millennia of music and dance behind her . . . as a land of death, as a country open to death. Everywhere death is an end. It arrives and the curtains are drawn. Not in Spain. In Spain the curtain goes up. A dead person in Spain is more alive when dead than anywhere in the world. His profile hurts like the razor's edge. The pun about death and its silent contemplation is familiar to all Spaniards.*

In support of these general statements, ironic or otherwise, Lorca quotes examples from Spanish literature and the arts, from Quevedo's *Dream of the Skulls* to the Sybillas' song and dance in the cathedrals of Mallorca and Toledo. From Joseph Valdivieso's Dance of Death to 'the numberless rites for Good Friday which, together with that most cultured feast of the bull, constitute the popular triumph of Spanish death', everything in Spain reminds him of death. In the long list of quotations, both erudite and popular, we come across some unexpected associations: 'The carving knife and the wheel of the cart, the razor blade and the shepherd's prickly beard, the peeled moon and the flies, the damp kitchen cupboards and the church images wrapped in lace, the quicklime and the wounding line of wide eaves and glass verandahs have in Spain tiny blades of death which put us in mind of the stilled breath of our own passing.' Lastly he defines the Spanish as a people made of 'contemplators of death, with Jeremiac verses on the rough side, with fragrant cypresses on the smooth'.

This manner of expression is personal. The actual fact observed comes from diverse and deep sources and applies to most Spaniards to a greater or lesser degree. Why then does death appear in the poet's work with urgency, with a strength equalled only in the work of Unamuno? In both cases the cause seems to be the loss of faith in an after-life. It is an obvious conclusion. For the real believer, whatever his creed, death is a liberation. We see it in the *Book of the Dead*, in the funerary rites of China and Japan, in the pyres overlooking the Ganges, in the escape from prison of the Neoplatonists, in the gaiety of Mohammedan warriors, or crusaders, galloping against pikes and harquebuses, in St. Teresa's 'I die because I do not die.' Even for those who agree to pass through life trying to understand the world around them, death alone can disclose its own mystery. Socrates' reputed answer to Simmias just before drinking the hemlock is an example that even in Spain has found past and present followers. But Lorca, like Unamuno, is left only with death 'the true inspiring genius, the muse of philosophy'.

'There is no night that on giving a kiss /I did not feel the smile of people without faces.' In these two lines from the 'Gacela of the Flight' there is something more than an extreme example of how the joy of life, highlighted by the constant presence and knowledge of death, can lead to a macabre *sic transit gloria sexi*. The triangle life – love – death is as old as literature itself. In all the Spanish authors quoted by Lorca, as in most European writers and artists of the same period, elegy, sonnet or canvas, always give an intimidating but comforting lesson: oncoming death, last judgement and everlasting life. Not in Lorca. In Lorca, as in Unamuno, faith has disappeared, though not the longing for life here and in the hereafter. It is a problem without solution. In Unamuno it is a fully conscious one, intellectually formulated with relative consolation in the agony of doubt. In Lorca, man of passion and instincts, his thinking is poetic and as such chequered with apparent contradictions. Without conscious formulation the drama is present in all his work as a living reality, as a sentiment of every hour and of every act of living; a drama which the very pleasure of a full life makes even more poignant. For life can be beautiful and love its finest flower, but life leads to death and beyond death the poet sees nothing.

Religious thought in the work of García Lorca

The point of departure will be a truism. Lorca, like the immense majority of Spaniards of his time, was brought up as a Catholic. His work proves it. But like many baptised Christians, his adult life developed outside the control of the Church. I do not remember ever having seen him fulfilling one of the religious obligations of the Church, or giving any indication that he practised his religion. True, I never saw him making fun of those who did practise, unless, like so many Catholics, he did so when it was a question of the ritualistic behaviour of priests and old 'beatas'.[1]

All his friends knew about his interest in the processions of Holy Week and the rites of the Catholic cult. But his enthusiasms, at least those I witnessed, did not betray religious faith but artistic delight, dramatic emotion, followed in the case of the rite of tenebrae by the questions that invariably came to his lips when the theme of death cropped up in any conversation: 'After the passing, what do you think will happen? Will the dead feel they are dead or will there be a life of the dead?' Of course, against this personal recollection other testimonies, no less authentic, may portray a quite different image. The man, one has to remember, was as many-faceted as the artist. Therefore, Lorca's religious thought must be studied in his work, available to all.

First let us look at those writings where theme or title are specifically connected with religion. We can exclude the three archangels of the *Gipsy Ballads* – poetic fantasy in which both

[1] Among his most famous 'sketches' were his 'Sermons of Passion' and his 'Mass at Dawn' in which Lorca himself was at the same time old priest, naughty acolyte, hissing 'beata' and creaking door.

popular and cultured smile at the legends from three Andalusian towns; 'The Massacre of the Innocents', 'The Beheading of the Baptist', 'St. Lucy and St. Lazarus' – surrealist prose writings in which the artist places himself outside all beliefs. The compositions touching religious themes are 'Ode to the Blessed Sacrament', 'Nativity by the Hudson', 'Birth of Christ', 'Moon and Panorama of the Insects', 'Crucifixion' and the beginning of a poem apparently never finished, which is published here for the first time.

The 'Ode to the Blessed Sacrament' is the only poem – 'Christs', 1917, is the only prose piece – in which the author seems to make an effort to write within the dogma. Yet, when the first two parts were published in 1928, they produced a strong reaction among most Catholics and a temporary cooling off in his long-standing friendship with Manuel de Falla, to whom Lorca had dedicated his 'Ode'. To a certain extent the indignation was understandable. Daring surrealist imagery and unconventional attitudes were bound to shock the average Spanish Catholic who would have been equally shocked by sculptures, paintings and stained glass windows which today adorn churches such as Notre Dame de Toute Grace in the Plateau d'Assy in Haute Savoie, or even the new Coventry Cathedral. In fact, what was shocking in the 'Ode' was the outer vestment, not the ideas which in any case, orthodox or otherwise, were not easy to understand:

> *Stone of solitude where grass moans*
>   (allusion, I believe, to the stone of the sepulchre)
> *Where dark water loses its three accents*
>   (where life ends and with it its three voices: world, devil, flesh)
> *Raise your column of tuberose under snow*
>   (reference to the pure whiteness of the Host and to the moment of
>   the elevation)
> *Above the roaming world of wheels and phalli.*

If my reading is accepted, death, the fear of total death, is what creates and elevates the Host, the body of Jesus, thus killing death. This is why in the two first lines of the last stanza of 'World', the second part of the 'Ode', Lorca says:

> *World, there you have an end to your forsakenness,*
> *To your perennial horror of bottomless holes.*

In that eulogy of the Blessed Sacrament, not one of Lorca's best compositions but worthy of careful attention, we have an example of metaphors and similes in the service of a religious theme.

He sees God in the offertory pulsating and naked like a child pursued by 'seven young bulls' – the seven deadly sins – the Host as 'little tambourine of flour', 'God in saddlecloth', 'concise form of ineffable murmur', 'snow encompassed by icebergs of music', 'crackling flame', 'meeting point and union of century and moment'. Precision and beauty, yes, but emotion or inspiration is not sustained. The Ode gives the effect, just like his youthful 'Ode to Salvador Dalí', of a work in which intellect and the cold asepsis of surrealism take the upper hand. However, the ode to Dalí is a polished, finished composition while the religious ode remained unfinished in spite of the fact that all the known sections were written before 1928.[1] Yet this is the only poem in which Lorca tried to write from within the Catholic orthodoxy, without forfeiting however, his poetic freedom. In the other poems mentioned above, the author, as we shall see later, places himself and all the symbols of religion outside the rules of the Church. This of course does not preclude, especially in his first period, exclamations, sentences, lines and even stanzas reminding us of the religious atmosphere of his upbringing in the same way as we are aware of the religious background to say André Gide or James Joyce. Thus in the poem 'Morning', of 1918, in praise of water, we read 'What is the Holy Baptism but God turned into water?' In other poems from that early book, honey 'is Christ's world', the ear of corn 'Christ materialized in life and death'; a few examples that with the more stylized 'Ode to the Blessed Sacrament' give us an indication of what the religious poetry of Lorca could have been if faith had not forsaken him. But the forsakenness is always there.

Impressions and Landscapes, 1917. His first book of prose. The young writer, as we have already pointed out, attacks the hypocrisy he believes to be hidden in religious houses and protests against the debasement of the cult. The artist speaks:

> *St. Cosmas and St. Damian; two stupid-faced dolls. All the faith of this village was deposited in these badly made dolls . . . all the vision of the beyond in this wretched village looked only to these ridiculous forms.*

[1] On going to press I hear that Lorca's heirs are soon to release the last two missing parts, finished, so it seems, in New York. If that is so, I feel confident that they will not depart from the general trend under discussion.

This is one instance of the many that could be quoted from this book to show how the religious is subordinated to the aesthetic. Yet, when he takes up a specific point of religion the future poet comments without reserve. Of his visit to a famous Carthusian monastery he concludes that the example given by the monks is one of 'great cowardice' because:

> *What God do they seek? Certainly not Jesus . . . If these men dreamt of the doctrine of Christ they would not follow the path of penitence but that of charity . . . of love towards each other . . .*

Describing visits to other convents he confessed that he always entered those precincts 'with religious illusion', for man searches for something spiritual or full of beauty to 'unload his soul of its main sorrow . . . Impossible happiness'. In Burgos he saw the empty sepulchres of Philip the Fair and wrote:

> *We are appalled by our tremendous vanity especially when seeing that all will end . . . because both the world and eternity are only infinite dreams.*

Let us remember this significant statement and the idea of seeing Jesus as symbol of love and charity rather than of eternal life. This will help us to trace the course of the evolution of Lorca's religious thought, an evolution firm and clear in spite of the inevitable meanderings of his poetic thinking. Let us look for a moment at *The Malefice of the Butterfly*, his second work. Curriana, one of the insect characters, tells how a swallow has warned her that all the stars will be extinguished because 'God is asleep' and a little later, Currianito asks: 'What if Saint Currianito did not exist?'

Throughout his first period Lorca puts into the mouth of small animals the ideas that obsessed him at the time. *Book of Poems* abounds in examples like the poem 'Encounters of an Adventurous Snail'. We find a frog who does not believe in God but pretends to do so because of the comfort the belief brings to her children, a theme that Unamuno was later to treat seriously in his famous novel *St. Manuel the Good*. The theme was in the air. One frog asks another:

> *'Do you believe in eternal life?'*
> *'Not I'*, says sadly
> *The wounded, blind frog.*
> *'Why then did we tell*

> The snail to believe?'
> Says the blind frog.
> 'It fills me with emotion
> To hear how my children
> Call for God
> In the pond!'

The idea is repeated in the same book when the poet comments on another consoling remark, this time by a paper bird:

> Though you don't believe you say you do
> Lest the children know
> That there are shadows behind the stars
> And a shadow on your castle.

Sometimes the religious preoccupation takes on an ironic twist. In 'Song to the Moon' the satellite is advised to protest against the tyranny of Yehovah, 'the old man of the seven days':

> Who leads you
> Down a path
> Always the same
> While he enjoys himself
> In the company
> Of his mistress . . .
> Doña Death.

Occasionally the mood is pensive: 'Each stone says:/ God is far away'. In despair at not finding the God he is searching for, the poet cries in 'Prologue':

> Keep your boring blue sky to yourself,
> And the rigadoon of the stars
> And your infinity.

Many of those early poems are loaded with questions:

> Oh God!
> I came with the seed of questions,
> I sowed and it did not flower . . .

Sometimes the questions become irreverent:

> Do you sink us in the shadow
> Of the abyss?
> Are you deaf? Are you blind?
> Does your spirit squint
> And do you see the human soul
> With light and shade inverted?

These and similar questions lead to a clear statement:

> *My heart sees its ideal far away*
> *And asks,*
> *My God!*
> *But my God, to whom?*
> *Who is my God?*

Only in *Poet in New York* and later works will we see Lorca speaking in so definite and insistent a manner. Yet the evolution of his religious thought filters through the intermediary period.

In the book *Cante Jondo* Jesus and the Virgin are Andalusian, Easter 'pasos', folk motifs and nothing more. In this book the drama is provided not by the figures of the Passion but in some other short sketches. For example in that personification of death as mistress of the 'Bel Dançar' that awakens so many associations:

> *Along a path*
> *Goes death crowned*
> *With withered orange blossom.*
> *She sings and sings*
> *A song*
> *On her white guitar*
> *And sings, sings, sings.*

In the book *Songs* it is precisely the absence of all religious ideas that strikes the reader in poems such as those included under the general title of 'Trasmundo' (The Beyond) or in little songs in which death without God sums up the destiny of everything that is born. In this group we find the already quoted 'Hunter' and 'They Cut Three Trees'.

Even in the rural trilogy there are undertones of lingering religious doubt. In the last scene of *Blood Wedding* the Mother, 'without a single son to raise to her lips', cries before the beginning of the brief litany leading to the 'knife prayer': 'But no. No churchyard: no churchyard! Couch of earth, bed which will shelter them, dangling them through the sky.'

In *Yerma*, the Old Woman, who with the male and female masks underlines the contrast between the pagan way of life and Christian morality which is the root of the drama, says in Act III: 'Here – in the Saint's fair – barren wives come to know new men and then the Saint performs the miracle.' Before, in Act I, when the Old Woman's moments of reticence dishearten the poor child-less Yerma – 'Then, God help me! – the Old Woman replies quickly: 'I never have liked God. When are you going to realize he does not exist? Though there should be a God, just a tiny one . . .'

In *The House of Bernarda Alba,* the two servants make fun of the offstage rigmarole of their master's funeral. The 'requiem' which follows, led by Bernarda and reluctantly echoed by the neighbours, is like an empty rite without real belief.

To a certain extent *Poet in New York* could be described as a mirror of death where themes, motifs, people and memories suffer violent transformations before dissolving into nothingness. Religious rites and beliefs do not escape the general rule. Let us look briefly at the religious poems mentioned above. What did the poet see in that 1929 'Nativity by the Hudson'? In addition to the scream of the worm, to which we have already referred, a beheaded soldier and four sailors struggle with the world – an allusion to St. John the Baptist and to the four evangelists? – without becoming aware of the solitude of the world, 'the solitary world in a solitary sky'. The believers go on singing alleluia:

> *Alleluia, empty sky!*
> *It's all the same, all the same, alleluia!*
> *All the same . . .*

It's all the same because for the poet, facing sheer death, Church and hymns have no importance: 'All that matters is this: Void. Deserted world. Outflow.' The poem ends with a sad human cry: 'Oh edge of my love, oh wounding edge!'

The poem 'Birth of Christ' is a game of transpositions. It begins by describing what looks like a Christmas crib with 'a shepherd asking to suck' (a possible allusion to the Holy Child?) and with a little earthenware Jesus with broken fingers. Around this crib what happens is just the opposite of what we see in the famous Botticelli Nativity in London's National Gallery. Instead of demons hurriedly escaping underground we see the coming of 'ants and the frozen feet . . .' and 'the devils' bellies resounding through the valleys', and hear 'wolves and toads singing in the green fire'. Then, suddenly, the Child, not that of the crib, but rather one modelled on Gómez Manrique's 15th-century Nativity play:

> *Cries and looks with a number three on his forehead,*
> *Saint Joseph sees in the hay three thorns of brass,*
> *The napkins exhale a murmur of desert*
> *With stringless zithers and decapitated voices.*

The last two lines are clear allusions to the forty days in the desert and to the massacre of the innocents. The poem ends with a semi-realist vision of the Nativity in New York as seen by a Catholic Andalusian:

> *Idiot priests and feather cherubs*
> *Followed Luther round the high street-corners.*

The poem 'Crucifixion', one of the most esoteric in the book, offers special interest. No doubt on account of ecclesiastical censorship this poem appears in the collected works of Lorca, published in Madrid, under the title 'At Last the Moon could Come to a Halt'. A detailed analysis would be out of place here; I will limit myself to its typical distortions and its proximity to the world of *The Public* where we have already encountered a strange crucifixion. In the poem, the blood, obviously the blood of Christ though there is not a mention of Jesus, 'came down from the mountain and the angels were looking for it/but the chalices were of wind and in the end it filled shoes.' In the last scene of *The Public*, Gonzalo's mother tells the Director and the Juggler that the village children used her moonfish-son's blood to paint their boots red. In 'Crucifixion' a tailor who 'specialized in purple' showed 'the three holy women' a skull on the window pane, bringing to mind the X-ray window-panes in the first scene of *The Public* and the window in the sonnet 'Adam'. In 'Crucifixion' we encounter cows, horses' phalli being burnt by the moon, and a live girl for whom nobody cares. In *The Public* we saw similar allusions and a real Juliet gagged under the stalls, forgotten by all.

From youthful *Book of Poems* to mature *Poet in New York*. What in the former were questions, rhetorical or otherwise, his first rejections, became in the latter that strange, difficult visionary world of apparently negative value; Goyesque dreams and nightmare in which disintegration, but disintegration no less moralistic than that of the painter, seems to triumph. A detailed knowledge of those years and of the poet's personal problems which preceded and in part determined his journey to America, could help to clarify some of the constituent elements and the logic of many so-called 'unconnected metaphors' and truncated images. However, the 'Ode to Walt Whitman' bears witness to how, even in *Poet in New York*, Lorca was capable of expressing with clarity and relative serenity his considered attitude towards homosexual love. The crystallization of the much deeper obsession with death will have to wait for yet another five years.

The 'Lament'

On seeing the body of a friend lying in state, when alive he was 'a river of lions', what can the poet say, to whom can he turn?

> *I want to be shown the exit*
> *For this captain bound by death.*

The *Lament for Ignacio Sánchez Mejías*, unanimously acclaimed as Lorca's best long poem, is for many people among the best elegies in the Spanish language. Much has already been written about this poem, mostly elaborations of what Angel del Río said in 1941, but a scrupulous annotation is still needed to unravel obscurities as yet unexplained. From the Iberian stone bulls of Guisando, 'half corpse half stone' (the granite perforated by the action of time also takes part in that 'Great feast of hole drilling' to which we have already referred), down to the lines:

> *He did not shut his eyes*
> *When he saw the horns near,*
> *But the terrible mothers*
> *Raised their heads . . .*

Which seems to me an echo, very likely unconscious, of the scene where Mephistopheles gives Dr. Faustus the key that will take him to the dwelling place of the Mothers, whose mention fills the Doctor with awe.[1] This is not the moment however to discuss the

[1] As on previous occasions I owe this Lorquian source to a conversation very vivid in my memory. In 1928 I would often discuss Dr. Faustus with Jorge Zalamea. One night Lorca, who on previous occasions had listened to our conversation in silence, surprised both of us with an impassioned, fascinating and most personal interpretation of some passages from the drama. So much so that some thirty years later, Jorge Zalamea, then preparing a work on Lorca, wrote to me to ask whether I remembered the conversation with Lorca on that occasion. What I still remember very distinctly

Elegy in detail, but only to consider it in relation to the theme under discussion.

The *Lament for Ignacio Sánchez Mejías* may or may not be one of the greatest Spanish elegies but it is certainly the most desolate. Lorca was not forgetting of course that death is, in the words of Quevedo, 'unavoidable and inherited, law but not punishment'. The desolation of his lament comes from elsewhere. Even Quevedo's stoicism is of a Christian type, operating on seventeenth-century readers well imbued with the idea of the resurrection of the flesh. Quevedo's lesson, like the lesson of all elegies in the western world of that period, is an orthodox one. It is legitimate to lament the death of king or nobleman, father or friend and to remember, as in 15th-century Jorge Manrique's 'Stanzas on the death of his father', details of the deceased's life in the world in which he moved, the rich jewels which adorned the ladies, or the delicate velvet clogs which encased their feet; but ultimately the sole purpose of this is to emphasize that 'this world is only a path whereby to attain the other, sorrowless dwelling'. The only reason for being in this world is to 'conquer that one for which we are waiting'; behind the mournful lamentations and the black palls shines the bright candle of eternal life.

Not so in the *Lament*. Here Lorca attains mastery of his form. He dissolves one plane into another. He can lead us from a visionary world – 'grey bullring of dreams', 'white poplars on the

---

is that the passage about the key that grows on Mephistopheles' hand (Part II, Act I, Scene 5), was one that Lorca interpreted and discussed with most enthusiasm. Though Goethe does not mention the number of Mothers moving round the mysterious tripod, for Lorca there were only three. The three Parcae, 'The Trinity of Death', he called them. He placed them in 'the last centres' – *'últimos centros'*. When they raise their heads they announce, crying, the death of whoever looks at them: 'at the same time, son and victim' – Lorca said – 'for they are the terrible mothers who give life and bring death'. It is easy to see what Lorca added or transformed from Goethe's text, but it is difficult to ascertain how much comes from other readings or from poetic invention. Without excluding other possible resonances which those lines from the 'Lament' may awaken in other readers, – virtue of the poetic word – Lorca's comments on Goethe's *Faust* not only explain one of the levels on which the metaphor certainly moves, but they deepen the meaning of the four lines that follow the previous ones quoted above:

> *And through cattle ranch*
> *Came an air of secret voices,*
> *Shouting to celestial bulls*
> *Stewards of pale mist.*

That is to say, from the depths of the Mother's 'abyss' to the heavenly bull of the zodiac.

barreras', 'old cow of the world', in which we see Ignacio moving in an ominous *ralenti* – 'Ignacio climbs the steps carrying his death on his shoulders' – to the world of reality where we meet the bull-fighter we knew: 'A touch of Andalusian Rome gilded his head.' But nine lines later, 'How tremendous with his last banderillas of tenebrae!' And what was a perfect realistic portrait dissolves again into death's endless dream, into blood almost personified, running, stumbling, sliding until it forms 'a pond of agony near the *Guadalquivir of the stars*'.

Ignacio's death is total death, without exit or hope. From the lines 'the rest was death and only death' in 'Spilt blood' to the almost Biblical stanza[1]

> *Neither the bull nor the fig-tree knows you*
> *Nor the horses or ants in your house*
> *The child and the afternoon do not know you*
> *Because you are dead for ever.*
>
> *Because you are dead for ever*
> *As are all the earth's dead*
> *Forgotten in a pile*
> *Of extinguished dogs.*

No. For this 'Captain bound by death' just as for all the dead of this earth, the elegy does not allow the slightest comfort or hope.

What remains of the author's Catholic upbringing? Certainly the external side of the liturgy – litany in the first part of the Lament – and several allusions to Christian ceremony and legends. He refuses to see Ignacio's blood spilt because there is no chalice to collect it, like the one held by Raphael's angels round the Cross, no officiating priest, nor the swallows which, according to Spanish tradition, pulled out the thorns from Christ's crown. The only relief, if relief it can be called, is that Death too will die, not in the resurrection of the flesh, but in silence and oblivion. This idea of Lorca's explains the recurrent motif in all his elegiac compositions: to go, to dissolve into nothingness, without trying to prolong a precarious life of the dead. 'Forget me and forget the vain world', he writes in the sonnet to a young friend and poet; 'sleep in

---

[1] As the cloud is consumed and vanisheth away; so he that goeth down to the grave shall come up no more.
He shall return no more to his house, neither shall his place know him any more.
                                                                    Job. VII, 9-10.

oblivion of your old life', he says in an epitaph on the composer Albéniz and in the *Lament*:

> *Go, Ignacio, do not feel the hot bellowing of the bull.*
> *Sleep, fly away, rest. The sea also dies.*

Life in death

Having lost his faith in eternal life, we see the poet taking temporary shelter in a nightmarish life of the dead, in a strange world beyond the grave. He has none of the romantic taste for the macabre; but we do find traces of the visionary tradition which he certainly knew well: Isaiah and Jeremiah, St. John the Divine and St. John of the Cross, Quevedo's 'Dreams' and the Cervantes of the 'Cave of Montesinos', Goya and Blake, Bosch and Patinir, the Comte de Lautréamont and Kafka.

'Sounding things from the other side.' In various poems it looks as if Lorca goes in search of Death, courts her, hoping to rob her of her secret. He tries again and again. 'A wall of bad dreams separates me from the dead,' he says in one poem; in others he would already seem to have forced the barrier, for a moment writing from 'the other shore'. Another old cultural tradition revives in Lorca as it did – to limit ourselves to two of his most brilliant Spanish contemporaries – in Valle Inclán and Ramón Gómez de la Serna. They also tried to imagine what life would be like as seen from death. Through one of his characters, Don Estrafalario, Valle Inclán explains the aesthetics of the 'esperpento':[1]

> *Sublimation of pain and laughter, as it must be in the conversations of the dead when they retell stories of the living . . . I would like to see this world in the perspective of the other shore.*

Ramón Gómez de la Serna, in his first period of non-belief,

---

[1] Ramón del Valle Inclán, one of the most original Spanish writers of the period, coined the word 'esperpento' to define his particular type of farce. In these, conventional values and the moral code of the day suffers a violent, satirical and marionette-like twist. They are written 'in a harsh, dry, racy style of extraordinary vigour and cruelty', as Gerald Brenan puts it. But underneath runs deep human compassion.

when he declared that 'man doesn't want to realize that he lives on the margin of creation', confesses:

All depends on my looking at you as the dead look at the dead; I live in an eternal twilight of death, I smell flowers as a corpse does . . .

and again:

One has to see life in a process of constant decomposition . . . that things lose that excessive content of divinity.

However, both in Valle Inclán and in Ramón Gómez de la Serna the centre of interest, the object observed, continues to be on this side of the river. Lorca looks at the other side. At first with juvenile irony:

> *Now, on the far-off hill*
> *The dead will play cards,*
> *It is so sad*
> *Life in the cemetery!*

That semi-humorous tone is only to be found in the first period. Then the prevailing attitude is the one in *When Five Years Have Passed* which comes through in the scene between the Dead Child and the Dead Cat when the former laments: 'No. The angels did not come'; or in the confusion suffered by both Boy and Cat at not being able to find the way out; or in that mysterious hand which drags them out of their precarious living Death with the same indifferent agility with which the poker-players cut the invisible strings still holding the Young Man to the reality of his games room, or with which the Juggler in *The Public* causes Gonzalo's mother to vanish.

The theme of life in death reaches its climax at the time of the poet's stay in America, that is to say in *The Public, When Five Years Have Passed* and *Poet in New York*. From the latter book one could quote as good examples 'Submerged Church' – 'but the dead are stronger and know how to devour morsels of sky' –; 'Landscape of the Urinating Multitude' – 'Because there is a world of the dead with definite sailors who will peep through the arches and will freeze you from behind the trees'; – 'City Without Sleep' – 'There is one corpse in the most far-off cemetery/ who has been moaning for the last three years because . . ./ and the child they buried this morning was crying so much that . . .' In effect this theme forms the whole content of poems such as 'Ruin', 'Jewish Cemetery',

'Introduction to Death', and much later 'Gacela of the Dark Death'.

Yet, as in certain Chinese beliefs or, more recently, in *One Hundred Years of Solitude*, that life of the dead is equally transitory. Death also dies. About the same time, or perhaps a little later, Jean Giraudoux in *Intermezzo* (1933), reaches similar conclusions. '*La vie des morts sans dents*', '*eux aussi, ils meurent*', '*La fin de la mort*', etc.[1] In Lorca, however, this life in death is only one connotation of 'the other side', a region in which dream, memories and the countless animals, big and small, that live in his work intermingle. From the horse of 'sculptural sapientia' to the 'tiny worms that are forgotten', Lorca treats everything with equal Franciscan brotherhood; the little child, the drunkards who step over him, the 'mute creatures passing beneath the arches', the 'green sponge'.

Life of the dead, the other side, the other systems; intermediary zone between being and nothingness. But at the hour of truth, when the Young Man of *When Five Years Have Passed* returns to his house to play the final game with death's emissaries, or when the Director of *The Public* returns to his room for the final conversation with Death, the attitude of both characters has a noble serenity in which there is not the slightest allusion to an after-life. Just the opposite: 'It disgusts me to see a dying man draw a door on the wall with his finger and quietly go to sleep,' says the Director shortly before his death. We have already indicated that there are in the Director many characteristics of Lorca himself, but it can always be argued that after all the Director is a creation, not the author, that the attitude of the former does not necessarily reflect the beliefs of the latter. The fact remains however that none of his characters call upon God at the moment of death. But there is something still more revealing. As we have seen, from time to time throughout his life Lorca wrote poems which seem to foresee his own tragic end. God and the hereafter never come into them with the exception of the allusion to the resurrection of the flesh in the early poem 'The Rose's Prayer', mentioned in a note in *Analysis*.

Having lost faith in eternal life, what remains of the poet's

[1] W. B. Yeats represents the opposite view. Theosophy, Occultism and Neoplatonism ratified him in his belief in the immortality of the soul. See Kathleen Raine: *Yeats, the Tarot and The Golden Dawn*, Dolmen Press. Dublin, 1972 and *Death in Life and Life in Death. Cú Chulainn Comforted and News from the Delphic Oracle*, ibid., 1974.

Catholic upbringing? Love and charity become a part of himself rather than a standard of conduct. Reading his work attentively we witness a subtle logic, a possibly unconscious evolution of his religious thought which could be summarized thus; if Jesus is not the son of God, if his death does not kill death, the drama of Golgotha will no longer be the symbol of redemption, of the liberation of the Spirit, of the resurrection of the flesh and eternal life. Yet, precisely on account of this the figure of Christ is, if anything, most unexpectedly enhanced. If, for preaching a religion of love to all men, as against the tribal obedience to the Mosaic law, Jesus dies on the cross as if he were the son of God, being only the son of man, Jesus becomes for Lorca an even greater symbol of love, of supreme sacrifice for love.

In the early prose piece 'Christs' (1917), Lorca already under-lines the human side of Jesus, his fear of pain and death, his human love. Lorca laments that people fear and take pity on Christ 'not on account of the shoreless sea of his soul' (this is the first time he uses an expression which, with variants, is found later in his work) 'but on account of the terrible sufferings of his body'. And a little later:

> *When thinking of Jesus on the cross people never remember Jesus on the Mount of Olives, with the bitter fear of the tremendous, nor are they amazed at the Jesus of the last supper overcome by human love.*

Soon God and Love will be one and the same. In his lecture on *The Duende*, he describes St. Teresa as the perfect *enduendada*:

> *For being one of those very rare creatures whose 'duende' (not her angel, for an angel never attacks) pierces her with an arrow, wanting to kill her for having robbed him of his last secret, that subtle bridge linking the five senses with that centre in living flesh, in living cloud, in living sea, of Love liberated from Time.*

In a letter to Carlos Morla the poet comments:

> *All religions have and have had the same map. The radiance of life is for him who carries a little pail of tears, not for him who carries a dream of diamonds.*

Love and Charity: religion without God and without churches. This idea crops up in the most unexpected places. He writes about the *Cante Jondo*:

> *The couplets have a common denominator: Love and Death . . . but love and*

death seen through the Sybil . . . Our people raise their arms in a Cross,
looking up at the stars, and wait helplessly for the sign of the Saviour . . . The
poem either states a deep emotional problem, without possible reality, or
resolves it with Death, who is the question of questions.

Love is Lorca's religion, but a love which is not limited to human beings. In a letter to the Catalan critic Sebastián Gash, in which he discusses problems of aesthetics, he jumps suddenly to that familiar world of the poet, 'the other half', and sharply points out the weaknesses of the Christian faith. The idea of a God for whom only man is ultimately worthy of attention:

> *If craziness is alive, it is true; if the theorem is dead it is a lie. Does it not*
> *fill you with anguish, the idea of a sea with all its fishes bound with a little*
> *chain to just one unconscious centre-point? I do not discuss the dogma, but I do*
> *not want to see the point where the dogma ends.*

Fishes and worms, trees, plants and vegetables, living a life and death without consciousness, without heaven or recompense in a hereafter, amidst the indifference of men and God: the dogma fails. This idea, already formulated with clear naivety in his introduction to *The Malefice of the Butterfly*, explains and justifies the very rich bestiary we find in the poet's work, as well as the part played by animals and plants in *Poet in New York* and other poems.

An attempt to go beyond that point where dogma ends seems to inspire the other two 'religious' poems that remain to be looked at. Both belong to the period of his stay in New York, though rightly not included in the posthumous edition of *Poet in New York*. One is 'Moon and Panorama of the Insects'. (The poet asks the Virgin for help.) It looks like a half-thought-out draft probably left aside to be corrected or changed. It adds little to what we have already seen but is a further confirmation of the tendency now under discussion. From the 'quasi-serioso' beginning:

> *I ask the divine Mother of God,*
> *Celestial Queen of all creation,*
> *To give me the pure light of the little creatures*
> *With only one letter in their vocabulary . . .*

right to the 'finale jocoso':

> *You, always dreaded Mother, whale of the skies.*
> *You, always joking Mother. Neighbour of the borrowed parsley . . .*

the whole poem is an identification with and defence of worms, insects, fishes and onions:

> *There is no one to cry because he understands*
> *The millions of little dead crowding the market,*
> *That Chinese multitude of decapitated onions*
> *And that splendid yellow sun of old flattened fishes.*

Lastly we have the fragment of a poem here published for the first time. I found it amongst the pages of *The Public*, on a loose sheet, written in pencil but on different paper. I feel almost certain it bears no relation to the drama. It is rather the answer of the Virgin to the previous poem. The title brings to mind poems of the thirteenth-century Spanish poet Berceo, and of old mystery plays. Candour of a primitive, idiom of *Poet in New York*:

> *The Most Holy Virgin Speaks.*
>
> *If I take off my giraffes' eyes*
> *I put on the crocodile ones.*
> *Because I am the Virgin Mary.*
>
> *The flies see a cloud of pepper dust.*
> *But they are not the Virgin Mary.*
> *I see the crimes committed by the leaves,*
> *The wasp's piercing pride,*
> *The indifferent donkey mad with double moon*
> *And the stable where the planet eats its little offspring.*
> *Because I am the Virgin Mary*
>
> *Solitude lives nailed to the mud.*

Unfinished this speech by the Virgin, unfinished the previous poem, interrupted the 'Ode to the Blessed Sacrament'. The poet seems unable to keep alive inspiration about a purely religious theme. Perhaps he is prevented by the clash of his very personal concept of religion with the prevailing political and social stand of the Church. For when he writes about the conflict itself the outcome is the impressive 'Ode from the Tower of the Chrysler Building'. The poet's most Jacobin *cri de coeur*.

Mercilessly he slashes the Pope and warns him of the evils his conduct will bring upon his church:

> *Upon the great cupola*
> *That military men anointed with their tongues*
> *Where a man urinates over a dazzling dove.*

The violence of the attack has nothing of professional anti-clericalism. True, the poet must have been influenced by the traditional association in Spain of the Church with the Army, the rich and the powerful, its attachment to material wealth, the images bedecked in costly jewels, the pomp and ostentation that in the world of 1929 surrounded the spectacle of the Church. What moved his pen was the treason he saw not only to his own ideal of a God of love and charity but the disillusionment of those multitudes for whom the Christian symbols of love and humility could still have brought inner calm and relief. The poet laments: 'There is no longer anyone to divide up the bread and the wine.' And not satisfied with the faint murmuring from Rome before the hunger of multitudes, before the injustices, the oppressions and threats of yet another world war, the poet addresses himself to the Pope:

> *The man who despises the dove should speak out*
> *And inject himself with leprosy*
> *And cry with such terrible tears*
> *That they dissolve his rings and diamond telephones.*
> *But the man dressed in white*
> *Ignores the mystery of the ear of corn*
> *Ignores the moan of the woman giving birth,*
> *Ignores Christ and His gift of water*
> *Ignores the coin burning the kiss of prodigy*
> *And gives the lamb's blood to the stupid beak of the pheasant.*

It is of no consequence that priests teach children the doctrine of Christ, or that the Pope fills his mouth with the word 'love' when love, far from being 'underneath the Christian images', takes shelter with the poor, the suffering and the lonely. The ode ends with a vision in which the poet sees millions of the oppressed and persecuted shouting and offering their breasts to the bullets of their oppressors until 'the prisons of oil and music burst open':

> *Because we want our daily bread*
> *Alder-tree flower and perennial shedding tenderness*
> *Because we want to see fulfilled the will of the Earth*
> *That gives its fruits to all.*

Social awareness

In Lorca the protest against social injustice, against man's exploitation by man, against cruelty to nature, is a consequence of his religious attitude. On several occasions I heard him say that if one believes in God there can be no fear of death, but that if one believes that death is total death and no more, who, he asks, would not revolt against social injustice? How quell the cry of protest? If eternal life, if the promised heaven are no more than another form of dream, Lorca demands at least bread, love and charity here and now:

> I am and always have been on the side of the poor, I will always be on the side of those who have nothing, and even the tranquillity of nothingness is denied to them ... If I were to be presented with a pair of scales, my own suffering on one side, and on the other Justice for all, I would come down with all my strength for the latter.

This often quoted declaration to an interviewer, and others less well known, tends to give us the impression of a poet suddenly aware in those last years of his life of a social reality, of a precipitated *prise de conscience* in the turbulent period that preceded the outburst of the Spanish Civil War. Yet that clear statement is only the best known example of an uninterrupted line of thinking already present in his earliest writings. Let us recall some of the things which attracted the attention of the adolescent writer. It is 1917: We are in a filthy old inn of Castille, 'as bad as any in Spain', a modern Swinburne would have added, before the tourist invasion and luxurious hotels of today:

> They also pass by those women who are like a sheaf of twine, with sore eyes ... who walk with the air of victims to be treated at the provincial capital ... 'Had she been rich' – comments one referring to her sister – 'the doctor would already have cured her ... but the poor! ... the poor ... !'

Elsewhere he comments on the decorations of cloisters and churches, suddenly turning to the artist who carved the stone:

> They were men of the people and as a consequence oppressed by the church and nobility ... but when their callous hands took up pencil and chisel they did so with rage and fury against those who enslaved them.

And a cry of protest, here describing a Galician orphanage:

Perhaps, one day, this building, taking pity on its hungry inmates and on such grave social injustices, will crumble down over one of those municipal welfare committees, where so many bandits in morning coats are to be found, and crushing them will make one of those beautiful omelettes so much needed in Spain. An orphanage raises in the heart an immense desire to cry and a formidable longing for equality . . .

An attitude at that time frequent, of course, amongst the youth of all lands. But the remarkable thing in Lorca – son of a wealthy land-owner – is that such an attitude persists and becomes more intense with each personal and literary success, the motivation being both human and artistic. Take Granada in 1923: for Epiphany, day of presents for Spanish children, Lorca, in collaboration with Manuel de Falla, arranged at his family home a special party for the children of friends. The poet recalls it ten years later in Buenos Aires:

. . . and there took place the first performance in Spain of 'A Soldier's Tale' by Stravinsky. I still remember, amongst the curls and ribbons worn by the children of rich families, the smiling faces of the children who sold newspapers on the street, who were invited by the poet to join the company.

Other anecdotes could be told, but it is more important to stress that social conscience runs through his whole work. It appears even in the most unexpected places. For example, when discussing Spanish lullabies:

It is those poor women who carry this melancholy bread to the house of the rich. The child of rich people receives the lullaby from the poor woman, who gives him, together with her pure country milk, the marrow of the nation. These wet-nurses, the maids and other more humble servants, have for a long time been performing the most important task of bringing the old ballads, songs and folk tales to the homes of the aristocrats and the upper middle class. The rich children know of Gerineldo, of Don Bernardo, of Thamar, of the Lovers of Teruel, thanks to these most admirable wet-nurses who came down from the mountains or along our rivers to give us the first lesson of Spanish history, to brand on our flesh the rough mark of the Iberian: 'Alone thou art and alone willst thou live'.

Country people are to him depositories of a rich cultural tradition. For the Spanish aristocracy, for the other ruling classes, he only felt, with few exceptions, indifference or contempt. In Cuba, when introducing his lecture on 'El Duende' he remembered the lecture room of his old Madrid 'Residencia de Estudiantes':

> *I have heard in that refined hall, which the old Spanish aristocracy frequented in order to counteract the frivolity they had learned on French beaches . . .*

In 1934, speaking to another journalist about La Barraca, the Student Theatre he founded and directed with such remarkable success, he contrasted the enthusiasms of humble people from hamlets and villages with the indifference of the rich:

> *They don't even realise what is going on. Neither do they know the great Spanish Theatre. And they call themselves Catholics, and Monarchists, and feel complacent. Where I prefer to perform is in the squares of small villages. Suddenly I notice a villager in wonder on hearing one of Lope de Vega's characters reciting a ballad and, unable to control himself, exclaims: 'How well he expresses himself!'*

It is perhaps pertinent to underline that in none of Lorca's utterances of a social character is political ideology 'handed out' as though from any political party. In contrast with other European and American poets of his generation, Lorca, solely on account of his personal and literary ethics, never belonged to any political party. He was fully convinced that poetry can only breathe when free. Let us look at one example from his lecture on the lullabies:

> *A complete faith in poetry is needed. It is fundamental to reject with violence any temptation to become committed.*[1]

In all Lorca's published work I have only noticed two direct allusions to the politics of the day. Both are in the guignolesque farce *Retablillo de Don Cristóbal* and both are humorous.

Furthermore, when in 1927 the dictatorship of Primo de Rivera was already on the wane, instead of cashing in on the popular image of a Mariana Pineda, heroine of freedom and nothing more, Lorca humanizes his romantic Marianita. Freedom's heroine, yes, but champion of human love and of a longing for the infinite:

> *I have fulfilled my duty as a poet by contrasting a Mariana alive, Christian,*

[1] I remember one particular afternoon in the summer of 1935, on the terrace of a Madrid café. Some of his friends, already 'committed', were half-jokingly, half-seriously challenging him to define himself politically. 'I?' he reiterated, 'I am an anarchist, libertarian communist, pagan Catholic, traditionalist and monarchist supporter of Don Duarte of Portugal.'

resplendent with heroism, with the cold Mariana dressed in foreign clothes, free-thinker on a pedestal.

It is precisely Lorca's moral and political independence that gives character and strength, emotion and drama to this aspect of his poetry not to be found in the work of other first class poets already 'committed'.

In *Poet in New York*, Lorca's 'fury', reaches a prophetic, sustained note. But fury which is love.[1]

In 1932, in his still unpublished introduction to *Poet in New York*, he wrote:

Wall Street, because of its cruelty and coldness, is the most impressive. Rivers of gold come here from all over the world, and death comes too.

From the Tower of Chrysler Building, in 1929 the tallest in the city, the poet sees at his feet the great city adoring Moloch and the Golden Calf and writes his accusing cry against the Pope. Then he walks the streets of low Manhattan where the skyscrapers turn them into 'ravines of chalk' during the day, 'ravines resisting the attack of the moon' by night. For him none more characteristic than Wall Street which on reaching Broadway runs into the churchyard of the sooty little Trinity Church where death lies in wait 'in the corners of terror'. Through there he saw Joseph Valdivieso's death dancing under the disguise of a giant African head-mask while the Director of the Bank was observing the 'manometer that measures the cruel silence of the coins', unaware that 'from the sphinx to the safe vaults there is a tense thread running through the hearts of all poor children'. Who are those who dance with death? 'Not the dead, of that I am certain.' 'They are the others,' the rich, the exploiters, the fake prophets, those who live with their backs to nature:

> *. . . The drunkards of silver, the cold men,*
> *Those looking for the worm under the landscape of the stairs,*
> *Those drinking in the Bank the tears of a dead girl.*

Like an enraged, exterminating angel, the poet accuses:

> *O savage America! Oh shameless! Oh savage!*

[1] It is not without significance that the first poems of the book open with this quotation from his fellow poet Luis Cernuda: 'Fury colour of love, love colour of oblivion'.

for it permits the dance of death 'between hurricanes of gold and the moaning of unemployed workers'. In prophetic vein he addresses all those who keep company with or help death in her hunt for victims. It is Lorca's *dies irae*:

> *Let not the Pope dance!*
> *No, let the Pope not dance!*
> *Nor the King,*
> *Nor the blue-teeth millionaire,*
> *Nor the dry ballerinas of the cathedrals,*
> *Nor shipbuilders, emeralds, madmen, or sodomites.*
> *Only that giant head-mask!*
> *For now the cobras will whistle through the top floors,*
> *For now the stock exchange will be a pyramid of moss,*
> *Lianas will come behind the guns,*
> *Soon, soon, very soon.*
> *Oh, Wall Street!*

In a way this poem sums up two tendencies present in all Lorca's work and most acutely in *Poet in New York*: protest against the injustices that man commits against man, animal and plant; protest against life's injustices. All is projected against that landscape of chalk, cement and steel of the great metropolis.

The rest is silence

Christianity and paganism, faith and doubt; desire to believe and impossibility of believing; simultaneity of bearings. Perhaps that was Lorca's compass as a man, but not as a poet. His work, that constantly testifies to his Christian upbringing, seems to show a clear evolution of his religious thought, to present a more logical pattern than one would expect. From the 'box of joy' to the *Lament for Ignacio Sánchez Mejías*, from the gay farce and the jubilant joy of the senses to the world of *Poet in New York*, there is a clear path, an inner connection within what at first looks like contradictory coexistence. At the end of the path, when Lorca faces death, his standpoint is unmistakable. He looks at the cold reality: 'white sheet', 'a pail of quicklime', 'whitewashed wall' . . . but wall without exit.

'The rest was death and only death.' Of the passing of Ignacio through life, only 'the memory of a sad breeze through the olive groves' remains, and of his own life, of the life of the poet, 'the other thing' of the 'Casida of the Impossible Hand': 'Sad wind, while the leaves take flight in flocks.'

To this finality is the poet led by his obsession with death and the evolution of his religious thought. No resurrection, no eternal life, and after the passing, silence: 'Everything in the world has broken. Only silence remains.' Silence, the 'death cloak' of his youth and a little later 'formidable ring where stars collided with the twelve floating black numbers', a silence which in yet another poem, is a spring that:

> *In the eternal night*
> *Before God and Time*
> *Flowed quietly.*

III

THE HORSE IN THE WORK OF GARCÍA LORCA

From the first Babylonian representations, from the first mention in the Zend-Avesta, and above all ever since the Greeks considered the horse a worthy companion of the gods and, in winged form, a symbol of poetic genius, down to the horses in Picasso, de Chirico and Marino Marini, the noble steed has formed a constant theme in art and literature, an essential element in numerous legends in the folk-lore of Asia and Europe. In modern literature as well as in representational art we have witnessed the renewal of the old theme. In a letter to the Comtesse de Noailles, quoted by Maurois, Proust wrote: '. . . dans l'homme le plus méchant il y a un pauvre cheval innocent qui peine . . .' In D. H. Lawrence and Synge we find horses frequently associated with sexual or vital vigour. In Edwin Muir they become symbols of the vertiginous race of man through life: 'It cannot be/these animals know their riders,/mark the change when one makes way for another . . .'; in the Spanish poet, Cernuda, the instincts are like reinless horses '. . . bodies under the branches' shade, as flowers/or fleeing in a gallop of enraged horses', while Jorge Guillén limits himself to defining the animal with classic sobriety: 'Horse, most happy beauty.'

An essay on twentieth century literature will no doubt prove that no other contemporary poet or novelist makes use of this animal with the insistence and variety found in Lorca. In the vast bestiary of his work the horse, reality or myth, stands out above all other animals. We hear it galloping through ballads and plays, neighing in imaginary cathedrals, kicking the stable walls and the heart of Bernarda Alba's daughters; we see it caracoling in fairs

185

and Andalusian *cortijos*[1] or rearing up on its hind legs 'inside' the eyes of a child; we witness the decomposition of its forms through the walls and skies of New York; we listen to its dialogue with Juliet in the tomb of Verona, and know that it will be drowned in the sea at the end of its vertiginous flight.

Why this preference of the poet? First through having spent the important years of childhood and adolescence in direct contact with nature, periodically renewed until his death. In the two first decades of this century the Andalusian countryside was still so far away from modern mechanized agriculture that the horse must have appeared to the child-poet as it did thousands of years ago to the generations that forged the horse legends: as a prodigy of energy and beauty, constant companion of man in good and bad fortune. As a child he learned what the horse meant in Andalusian life, and as a child too he learned how to see the animal at close quarters – hence his many graphic comparisons:

> *While the sky shines*
> *Like a colt's rump.*

And when later he remembers the galloping sound of a horse he will express it in metaphors where hearing is the keenest sense:

> *The rider approached*
> *Beating the plain's drum.*

or

> *And when the four hooves*
> *Were four resonances . . .*

at other times the metaphors are predominantly visual:

> *And though your horse place*
> *Four moons on the stones . . .*

or

> *I will make your horse glitter*
> *A fever of diamonds.*

At times the metaphors are audio-visual:

> *The hooves of your horse,*
> *Four silver sobs.*

---

[1] *Cortijo.* An estate in southern Spain, usually with farmhouse, outhouses and cattle of some kind.

Even when in dramas the horse is used with a symbolic value, the smell of the stable is there. At the beginning of the third act of *The House of Bernarda Alba* there is an abrupt knock that frightens the visiting Prudencia.

BERNARDA ALBA: It's the stallion. He's locked in and is kicking the wall. (*Shouting.*) Shackle him firmly and take him to the courtyard. (*Softly.*) He must be in rut!

PRUDENCIA: Are you going to mate him with the new mares?

BERNARDA ALBA: At dawn.

And on the second kick:

BERNARDA ALBA (*Getting up in a fury*): Must one say everything twice? Let him roll over in the straw. (*Pause and as though talking to labourers.*) Then shut the mares in the stables but set him free, or he will bring down the walls.

That stallion, waiting for the young mares, accentuates or symbolizes the tension of the unmarried daughters of Bernarda waiting for the early arrival of Pepe 'the Roman', but the language is always realistic and direct, the language that the poet heard in his childhood. It is his early contact with the life and work of an Andalusian estate that gives all his work an unmistakable earthy flavour, and endows his daring surrealist imagery with the authenticity of something flowing from nature. If sometimes he invents an expression, automatically it sounds traditional: the reality breathes beneath its transformations.

Over this realistic background one has to project the influence of legends, folk-tales, songs heard in his childhood in which the horse is either the protagonist or an essential element. When in the short poem 'Death of the Petenera' he uses as a refrain the Spanish eight-syllable metre:

> *One hundred mares caracole.*
> *Their riders are dead . . .*

it sounds like a far-off echo of the legends that throughout the fields of Europe carry dead riders away. We find a similar theme in the book *Songs*:

> *Little black horse*
> *Where do you carry your dead rider?*

187

But in this poem the refrain alternates with another one:

> *Little cold horse*
> *What a perfume of knife's flower!*

This particular poem entitled 'Song of the Rider' belongs to the group 'Andalusians', divertissements or variations on Andalusian themes. Here the theme is that of the highwaymen. In five stanzas of three short lines each, separated by the quoted refrains, Lorca uses the essential elements of a crime without any specific reference to the fact he is alluding to: the stabbed highwayman. From the opening:

> *In the black moon*
> *Of the highwaymen*
> *Sing the spurs . . .*

right to:

> *. . . The hard spurs*
> *Of the motionless rider*
> *Who lost the reins.*

(To lose the reins of the horse of life as in 'Facing this body with broken reins' in the *Lament for Ignacio Sánchez Mejías*.)

In the third stanza we encounter one characteristic play of transpositions:

> *In the black moon*
> *Bleeds the side*
> *Of Sierra Morena.*

What was bleeding was, of course, the highwayman's side – his blood 'perfume of knife's flower' – but the poet transfers the blood to the hills of Sierra Morena already coloured by the first lights of dawn. Night is fading quickly:

> *Night spurs*
> *Its black flanks*
> *Piercing them with stars.*

This is not the only instance of Lorca seeing the stars as spurs:

> *Night appears to them*
> *A show window of spurs.*

This he writes in the 'Ballad of the Civil Guard'. The final stanza of the 'Song of the Rider':

> *In the black moon*
> *A shriek and the long*
> *Fire's horn . . .*

refers to the first rays of the rising sun. With great economy Lorca
has extracted the lyrical dramatic essence of an Andalusian cliché.
But the theme is not exhausted. With even greater concentration
and deeper content he uses it again in the second 'Song of the
Rider' beginning 'Cordova./ Far away and alone.' The mare in
this song is black, like the horse in the previous one, and the
horses of the Civil Guard that bring death to the gipsies' town,
like most of the horses in European folk-lore connected with
death, are black. An almost romantic setting – 'From the towers
of Cordova/ Death is gazing at me' – frames the human tragedy of
never arriving: 'Woe! That death waits for me,/ before reaching
Cordova!' Before reaching Cordova, or whatever the ideal destiny
of man may be, Death is waiting in some tower though few see:

> *Let us, then . . . not go . . . or let us wait. Because the alternative is to die
> here and now, and it is much more beautiful to think that tomorrow we shall
> still see the one hundred horns with which the sun raises the clouds*

says the Old Man in *When Five Years Have Passed*.

Not to arrive. In 'Camino', the little poem from the book
Cante Jondo the poet asks:

> *One hundred riders in mourning,*
> *Where will they go*
> *Through the lying sky*
> *Of the orange grove?*
> *Neither Cordova nor Seville*
> *Will they reach.*
> *Neither Granada which sighs*
> *For the sea.*
> *Those dreaming horses*
> *Will take them*
> *To the labryinth of crosses*
> *Where the song trembles.*
> *With seven piercing laments,*
> *Where will they go*
> *The one hundred Andalusian riders*
> *Of the orange grove?*

The themes of never arriving and the mysterious rider of the legends – personifying sometimes death, sometimes the devil – appear in the prose narrative 'Dialogue of the Amargo', the Bitter One. Immediately after the protagonist is left alone on the road, begins a song that sounds like an invocation to death: 'Ay, yayayay. /I asked Death. /Ay yayayay.' And Death disguised as a rider, appears on the road. She speaks to him of her three brothers (as the three card players of *When Five Years Have Passed*). Distracted by the conversation Amargo has lost his way. He begins to give way to the rider's invitation to mount behind her as she cunningly puts to Amargo key questions that lead to 'Once arrived there, then what do you do?' The idea of arriving, or nearly arriving only to meet death, is also the core in the already quoted little song from the *Poem of the Cante Jondo*:

> *I wanted to arrive*
> *Where the good ones had arrived.*
> *And I have arrived, Oh God!*
> *But then,*
> *A candle and a blanket*
> *On the ground.*

In the 'Ballad of the Summoned Man' the author points to a physical and psychic correlation between horse and rider, also with antecedents in folk-lore and literature:

> *The little eyes of my body*
> *And the big ones of my horse*
> *Do not close by night,*
> *Nor do they look to the other side*
> *Where a dream of thirteen boats*
> *Quietly fades away.*

The summoned one rides night and day, wears out his horse's shoes and gipsy smiths replace them in mysterious forges:

> *And over the somnambulistic anvils*
> *The hammers sang*
> *The insomnia of the rider*
> *And the insomnia of his horse.*

The legends of horses announcing the coming of death run throughout the 'Martyrdom of St. Olalla', from a beginning that no doubt would appeal to de Chirico:

> *On the street leaps and runs*
> *A long-tailed horse . . .*

to

> *And while a confused*
> *Passion of manes and swords vibrates . . .*

In the 'Ballad of the Civil Guard' we encounter surrealism and tradition in curious combination. The horse from the legends turns into:

> *A badly wounded horse*
> *Was knocking at every door.*

The Civil Guards charge and he contrasts their horses of fury with the good horses of the old gipsy women:

> *The sabres cut the breeze*
> *Trampled by the hooves.*
> *Through the streets of penumbra*
> *Flee the old gipsy women*
> *With the sleepy horses*
> *And the jars filled with coins.*

Another contributing factor in Lorca's poetic use of the horse-image are the songs he had heard in childhood, especially the cradle songs in which the horse plays an important part. And to illustrate that 'the child's capacity for poetic understanding is far greater than adults like to believe' – he resorts to one of his typical equine images:

> *The child is inside an inaccessible poetic world where neither rhetoric, nor that pander, imagination, nor fantasy can enter: a high plateau with the nervous system exposed, full of acute horror and beauty where the whitest horse, half-nickel, half-smoke, suddenly falls wounded, with a swarm of bees furiously nailed to his eyes.*

But this is already the world of *Poet in New York*, a world of mutations and death, of reality subjected to a process of negative type transformation. There, in order to express the contrast that the poet experienced between his Granada world – old cultural tradition, based on nature – and the triumphant mechanized cold civilization of America, with its back turned to nature, he often projects over the concrete landscape of New York the animals, things and ideas of his childhood, of the Andalusian countryside, of universal nature. The result is the distintegration of forms dear to the poet, none more dramatic than that of the horse.

'1910 (Intermezzo)', the second poem of the book *Poet in New York*, is a flash-back to his childhood in Granada. The poet reviews the things he did not see then and underlines those which attracted his gaze as a child. Amongst the latter, several close-ups and some still-lifes illumined by moonlight: 'The white wall by which little girls urinated,/ the bull's muzzle, the poisonous mushroom . . .', a few pieces of dried lemon next to some bottle and, of course, the vision of the quadruped and the coloured picture of a popular saint.

> *Those eyes of mine in the neck of the mare*
> *In the pierced breast of the sleepy St. Rose . . .*

He recalls his childhood only to contrast it with what he sees and does not see in the great city. Amongst the absences, that of the horse is conspicuous; or rather the awareness of the shape of its disappearance, its void. On the asphalted pavement of Harlem he sees cars crowded with smiling negroes passing quickly under the rain. He will remember them in the 'Ode to the King of Harlem':

> *Its murmur* (that of Harlem) *reaches me . . .*
> *Through grey tears,*
> *Where your cars full of teeth float by,*
> *Through the dead horses and the minute crimes . . .*

The union of those two antithetical worlds, that of nature and that of a modern city living in complete ignorance of nature – wheel of industry versus horse – will only be possible when the dance of death comes:

> *The primitive impulse dances with the mechanical impulse*
> *In their frenzy unaware of the original light.*
> *For if the wheel forgets its formula,*
> *It could sing naked with the herds of horses.*

In the confused labyrinth of the poem 'Nativity by the Hudson', the horses continue to remind him of the real world:

> *The four sailors were struggling with the world,*
> *With the world edges seen by all eyes*
> *With the world that cannot be travelled over without horses.*

And even in his vision of the dead Lorca remembers the animal as a vital form:

> One day
> The horses will live in the taverns . . .

which could well have been a model for Raymond Queneau's *Le Cheval troyen*.

Lorca himself has described the Kafkaesque experience that inspired his poem 'Girl drowned in a well'. In the eye of a horse – a round well – he sees the child:

> Tranquil in my remembrance, star, circle, goal,
> You cry by the shores of a horse's eye.

We have already seen how in New York his obsession with the mutation of forms was intensified, especially with that imposed by death. The first poem in the group 'Introduction to Death' begins with an allusion to his favourite animal:

> What an effort!
> What an effort of the horse to become dog!
>
> . . . .
>
> What an effort of the bee to become horse!
> And the horse,
> What sharp arrow he squeezes from the rose!
> What grey rose rises from his lips!

And in the second part of the second poem 'Void's Nocturnal':

> I.
>
> With the whitest white void of a horse,
> Mane of ashes, pure and folded bull-ring.

Nothing for him conveys more dramatically the impression of the void created by death than this horse's skeleton, once the forms that made him the symbol of energy have gone. White skeleton, calcinated bones, as if abandoned in a desert – here a deserted and folded bull-ring – as if it were the white skeleton of Blake's white horse which so much obsessed Lorca, or the ashen horse's skull which in the already mentioned monochrome by Titian – pursues Cupid round a tree. In that poem the poet sees himself already dead, alone, with no other companion but the white skeleton of the animal. There for a moment his own skeleton fuses with that of the horse and sees his own void in a swift flight 'riding on my life irretrievably anchored'. The brief poem ends with the strange image to which we referred when dealing with the theme of the metamorphosis:

> *There is no new century, nor recent light*
> *Only a blue horse and a dawn.*

The process of disintegration is accentuated. We take part in a nightmarish vision of death over the urban landscape of New York, or of dramatic glimpses – 'The horse had an eye on his neck' – or the conjunction moon-death and horse:

> *Soon it was clear that the moon*
> *Was the skull of a horse . . .*

or

> *At last the moon could roam on the*
> *White curve of the horses.*

That moon-death is the same that in another poem 'burned with its candles the horse's phallus', the same that will wash with water 'the burns of the horses/ and not the living girl silenced by the sand'.

Nothing discloses better the inner anguish experienced in those years by the poet, aggravated by the problems of New York in the years 1929/30 and the fears of a possible new world war, than the distortions that he imposes on his favourite animal. Lorca did not need to wait for the Spanish Civil War before seeing the bull as the symbol of fratricidal struggles, nor for Guernica before using a convulsed horse to portray the horrors of war and of a civilization living with its back to nature.

However, in nearly all his work prior to his year in America the horse is associated with the joy of life, with sexual vigour, and with the natural instincts, tame or otherwise, even if their very strength leads to drama and death. Already in the early poem 'Madrigal' the horse appears as the symbol of virility. After narrating his first amorous experience, the poet rather naively already thinks of himself as an expert:

> *Now grave master*
> *Of the high school of riding*
> *To my love and my dreams*
> *(Little eyeless horses) . . .*

Let us follow the rider and his mount.

The most superficial reader of Lorca will have noticed one of
the many metaphors he uses to describe the sexual act:

> *That night I ran*
> *The best of all roads*
> *Riding a mare of mother of pearl*
> *Without bridle or stirrups.*

He also uses the image of the rider to describe the sexual
problem of 'The Gipsy Nun':

> *Through the nun's eyes*
> *Gallop two horsemen . . .*

Thus at first sight it would seem impertinent to use in connection
with the Archangel Gabriel a symbol with so many sexual connotations, yet this is what he does with total poetic logic. The
ballad 'St. Gabriel' is a tender and graceful lyrical altar-piece of
the Annunciation, a Biblical scene transferred to the contemporary
streets of Seville, just as Crivelli placed his Archangel kneeling in
the streets of Ascona. For Lorca the Archangel's mission to Mary
is fundamentally one of procreation; especially so in the case of a
gipsy virgin. The image of the horse comes to his pen in a precise
play of opposites. The Archangel speaks:

> *Your barren eyes glow*
> *On a landscape of riders . . .*

In the same way he uses the horse-symbol in every manifestation
of the love-theme. The young men of 'Fable and Round Dance
of the Three Friends', were in his hands 'three horses' shadows'.
Whoever may be the person alluded to in the mysterious poem
'Your Childhood in Menton' the allusions are of strength, vitality
and the frenzy of love:

> *There, lion, there heaven's fury,*
> *I will let you graze on my cheeks,*
> *There, blue horse of madness . . .*

And amongst the eulogies bestowed on the love he hides under
'Gacela of the Unexpected Love', our attention is drawn to the
second quatrain:

> *One thousand little Persian horses went to sleep*
> *In the moonlit bull-ring of your forehead,*
> *While I girdled four nights*
> *Your waist, enemy of the snow.*

The Man-rider may mount the horses of the instincts without bridle or stirrup, but the poet is always fully aware of the perils he runs:

> *Oh how the knight cried!*
> *Mounted on an agile*
> *Reinless horse.*
>
> . . . .
>
> *Amongst the saffrons*
> *They found dead*
> *Don Pedro's sombre horse.*

These quotations come from 'Mockery of Don Pedro on Horseback', which in spite of its title so clearly anticipates the world of *When Five Years Have Passed* and of *The Public*. In another ballad – 'The Black Sorrow' – the poet warns Soledad Montoya that:

> *At the end the bolting horse*
> *Finds the sea*
> *And the waves swallow him*

an idea that reappears in the 'Nocturnal Song of the Andalusian Sailors':

> *Oh, lad, my lad,*
> *The waves carry my horse away!*

With this sense of a force that attracts or draws away, we find the horse in the semi-surrealist prose-poem 'Submerged Swimming Girl':

> *One night the devil made my shoes horrible. It was 3 a.m. I had a scalpel across my throat and she had a long silk handkerchief. I am lying. It was a horse's tail. The tail of the invisible horse that was going to drag me. Countess: how right of you to press my hand.*

Almost the same simile is used by Mariana Pineda addressing her servant, in the second act of the historical drama of that name. Pedrosa, the ill-famed *Alcalde del Crimen*,[1] visits her, interrupting the conspirators' meeting:

> *Open, Clavela! I am a woman*
> *Tied to the tail of a horse.*

In surrealist prose-poem or drama, in historical drama, farce or rural tragedy, the horses break in with as much force as in the

---

[1] *Alcalde del Crimen.* Name given to the judges in the old chancelleries of Valladolid and Granada.

196

poems. Very seldom does the horse have a merely realistic value or lose the rich polyvalent quality of Lorca's symbols.

In that same scene, when Mariana Pineda sits at the piano awaiting Pedrosa's entry, the song that comes to her lips is an early 19th-century one which the poet modifies to accentuate the dramatic situation:

> *Oh lads! Oh girls,*
> *Who will buy for me a black thread?*
> *My horse is exhausted*
> *And I am dying of sleep!*
> . . . .
> *Woe! Woe! my little horse*
> *My dapple-faced horse*
>   *Woe!*
> *Woe! Horse, run speedily,*
> *Woe! Horse, for I am dying.*
>   *Woe!*

And in the third act, after the last interview with Pedrosa, Mariana sits exhausted on a bench in her convent-prison and desperately cries for her lover:

> *Pedro, ride on your horse*
> *Or come mounted on the day.*
> *But quick! For already they are coming*
> *To take my life away!*
> *Drive in the hard spurs.*

In the prologue to the *Cachiporra* guignolesque farce there is a popular sally that reflects the association horse-sex:

MOSQUITO: Men and women! Attention. Child, shut that little mouth of yours and you, girl, sit down with one hundred thousand cavalry soldiers.

In *The Prodigious Cobbler's Wife* the references to the horse are at first sight purely realistic, until one realizes that almost all the allusions to the animal come from the Wife's mouth with a precise connotation: they are related in her fantasy world, to the obsessive idea of a young and beautiful woman married to an old man. She wants to incite jealousy in her husband by discussing with him real or imagined suitors from her past:

But the one I fancied above all others was Emiliano . . . who came riding on his

197

black mare, covered with tassels and little mirrors, and with a thin cane in his hand and shining spurs.

When she is alone on the stage she dances with imaginary suitors a little polka or comic rhythmic dance. Then the one she prefers is José María:

You I love, you . . . Oh! Yes . . . tomorrow bring the white mare, it's my favourite.

Something similar happens in the second act when, abandoned by her husband, she is forced to turn his workshop into a little tavern. Alone with a child – her only friend in the village – she gives way to her fantasy. The only difference is that now she idealizes what she no longer has, the absent husband, and the idealization makes him a rider on a vigorous mount:

When I saw him come riding on his white mare . . .

It matters little that the child tries to stop her fleeing from reality: 'You are teasing me. Mr. Cobbler had no mare.' Mare or horse he will have had because it is an essential element in her vision of a virile husband:

He looked at me and I at him. I lay on the grass. I still seem to feel in my face the freshness of the breeze that came through the trees. He stopped his horse and the horse's tail was white and so long that it reached the water of the stream.

And if the old cobbler – disguised as a story-teller with picture-board and pointer – mentions the animal, it will be to illustrate the dangerous suitors his wife once had, in his tale transformed into the cruel wife of a harness-maker:

> *Behold how she is courted*
> *By lads of good appearance*
> *On shining horses*
> *Covered with silky tassels . . .*

or

> *And they caracoled*
> *Their mares over the stones . . .*

And then his own lament:

> *Old but decent husband*
> *Married to a tender lass!*
> *What cunning rider at your door*
> *Steals your love!*

198

Because in that simple world those stealing the honour of saddlers and cobblers will always be young men arriving on their trotting Cordova mares.

Horse, mare, colt and cob. Companions of men, of real males spelling vigour, moral and physical strength. The cobbler's wife knows it well. When alone in her little shop, and surrounded by frustrated admirers she cries out:

Behold, I have my grandfather's blood – God keep him in his glory – he who was a tamer of horses and what can be called a real man.

And later with the whole village about to rise against her, she shows to her disguised husband her untamed courage:

Then, here I am, should they dare to come. And with the calm of one who belongs to a family of good riders who so often crossed the sierra, without women's saddles, bareback!

In spite of all this the horse is kept on a realistic level. What allusions there may be to the virility of its riders are deeply rooted in the popular mind. In the rural dramas the co-existence of two levels is somewhat clearer. In the scene quoted above from *The House of Bernarda Alba* it is obvious that the heat of the stallion symbolizes the desire for a man that consumes the five sisters. It is this symbolic side that needs to be examined in order to establish the relationship between the horses in Lorca's plays or poems and those in his surrealistic dramas, especially in *The Public*. First let us look at *Blood Wedding*.

Leonardo and his horse are so united, so mutually identified that it would be almost impossible to imagine the one without the other; in fact without the horse it would be difficult to visualize the drama:

And when I saw you from afar
I threw sand into my eyes.
But I mounted the horse
And the horse came to your door

says Leonardo to the Bride in the forest scene. A lyrical way of expressing his blind love? Andalusian fatalism when he begins to realize the roots of the drama? That very horse is the one whose harness the Bride changed in order to ride off with him. When in that forest scene the Bride makes a sudden stand against Leonardo he weakens her resistance with three key questions:

'Who was the first to come down the stairs? Who put a new harness on the horse? And what hands fastened my spurs?' Should we take these questions in a literary sense? Do they refer to real actions carried out in the midst of the wedding celebrations when Leonardo was closely watched by his wife, and the Bride by the Bridegroom and all the guests? That may have been the poet's first intention but a careful reading of the play will demonstrate that the author must have been fully conscious of his symbolic use of the horse and of how that plurality of values plays an important part in the structure of his play.

Even before the first entry of Leonardo, his own house appears under the fatalistic sign of a mysterious horse. The scene opens in Leonardo's house. It is morning. The Mother-in-law sings softly to the child in her arms. The Wife knits. The two alternate in singing the lullaby, variation of the famous traditional cradle song:

> To the lullaby, lullaby, lullaby,
> To the lullaby, of that one
> Who took the horse to water
> And left him without drinking.

In his essay on the traditional Spanish lullaby Lorca describes this one as seen from the marvellous, enigmatic world of the child who listens to the song:

> In this lullaby . . . the child plays a lyrical game of pure beauty before he surrenders to sleep. That one and his horse will fade away in a path of dark branches leading to the river, only to start fading anew as the song comes back again and again, always in a silence reborn. The child will never see their faces, but will always imagine in the penumbra the dark suit of that one and the shining rump of his horse.

In order to endow the horse with still more drama Lorca begins by simplifying the components of the song. He suppresses the man thus leaving only the horse and the water, both almost personified, in a strange correlation. Without man it is now the horse by himself who rejects the liquid element:

> Lullaby, child, lullaby
> Of the big horse
> Who did not want water.

The fact that the horse does *not* want to drink gives greater depth to the mystery of the song and at the same time awakens in the attentive reader of Lorca a series of suggestions not difficult to detect. Are not drink and water closely connected with sexual desires? Once again we see Lorca in the centre of a very old cultural tradition. From the mysterious verse in Amos: 'In that day shall the fair virgins and young men faint from thirst,' to the flamenco couplet:

> *I carry you in my heart.*
> *Live at peace, woman,*
> *For even if far away from you*
> *At no other fount will I drink*
> *Though I may be dying of thirst.*

Thirst, fire, drink and water have always been connected with sexual appetites. The old lullaby sets Lorca weaving together all the possible resonances within the apparently natural conjunction of horse and water, animal and element.

The lullaby, which Mother and Mother-in-law turn into an exorcism of the horse who does not want to drink, may have some connection with the marital waters that Leonardo now refuses to drink while in search of other love:

> *His hot lips did not wish to touch*
> *The wet bank*
> *With flies of silver.*
> *To the hard mountains*
> *He only neighed*
> *With the river dead*
> *On his throat*

That ominous horse has:

> *Inside each eye*
> *A silver dagger.*

Just like Leonardo. In the last scene of the first act his wife tells him: 'You have a thorn in each eye', and in the forest scene Leonardo confesses to his bride that:

> *With rusty pins*
> *My blood turns black . . .*

Sheer coincidence, or like the echoes of a musical theme? In any case the horse in the lullaby that both women try to charm away is overlaid by Leonardo's real horse. The lullaby ended, Leonardo enters. After short greetings, the wife asks him whether he did go to the blacksmith's.

LEONARDO: From there I come. Can you believe it? For the past two months I've kept on having him shod and the new shoes always fall off. It seems that he knocks them against the stones.

And when his wife asks him if he was the one whom the women gathering capers saw by the end of the plain:

LEONARDO: No. What should I do in that dry land?

WIFE: That's what I said. But the horse was bursting with sweat.

The sudden entry of the Mother-in-law interrupts the dialogue between Leonardo and his wife:

MOTHER-IN-LAW (*entering*): But who rides a horse like that? There he is in the stable, stretched out, with his eyes starting out of their sockets as if coming from the end of the world.

LEONARDO (*sour*): I.

The Girl, who comes to tell the story of what the Bridegroom's mother is buying as engagement presents breaks for a moment the tension created by the lullaby and accentuated by the arrival of Leonardo. But Leonardo reappears, is violently rude to the Mother-in-law and the young Girl and treats his wife with bitter disdain. His exit coincides with the waking of the child. The tension of the lullaby is redoubled:

MOTHER-IN-LAW: The legs wounded
                The mane frozen
                Within each eye
                A silver dagger.
                They went down to the river.
                The blood ran
                Stronger than water.

Leonardo's wife joins in the song 'turning slowly and as if in a dream':

> *Sleep, my carnation,*
> *The horse is setting to drink . . .*

Instead of 'the horse does not want to drink' in the song and at the beginning of the lullaby.

The Leonardo-horse association persists all through the play.

First scene of Act II: The Servant combs the Bride's hair under the porch of her father's farm, in order to enjoy the cool of dawn. The guests are still far away. Suddenly a loud knock is heard at the door. The Servant opens the heavy gates and is surprised to see Leonardo:

SERVANT: And your wife?

LEONARDO: I came on horseback. They are coming by road.

SERVANT: Did you encounter anybody?

LEONARDO: I overtook them with the horse.

SERVANT: With so much galloping you are going to kill the animal.

LEONARDO: When he dies he'll be dead.

In the violent dialogue that follows between the Bride and Leonardo she says:

A man with his horse knows much and is powerful enough to crush in his hands a girl buried in a desert.

It is not only that characters and spectators noticed the Leonardo-horse relationship, it is that Leonardo himself never imagines himself without his mount. At the end of that scene Leonardo's wife orders her husband to accompany her.

WIFE: But you are not going on horseback. You come with me.

LEONARDO: In the cart?

WIFE: Is there another way?

LEONARDO: I'm not a man to ride in a cart.

For once he gives way but they are the first to return from the wedding. When the Bride's father asks the Servant if he is the first to arrive, she answers:

No. Leonardo and his wife came some time ago. They rode like devils. The wife was scared stiff. They covered the distance as if they had come on horse-back.

The first flash of the storm is seen when Leonardo's Wife asks the newly married couple with some anxiety if they have seen her husband:

But I cannot find him and the horse is not in the stable.

The act ends with a desperate cry from the Bridegroom on

hearing of his wife's elopement with Leonardo, a cry his mother repeats in a frenzy:

Who has a horse, right now? Who has a horse? I will give him everything I have, my eyes, my tongue . . .

which sounds like a rural Spanish echo of Richard III's famous cry in Shakespeare's play.

In Act III the allusions to the animal are loaded with associations. One of the Woodcutters listens attentively. He hears the magic of the night 'but the horse is not heard'. Later, another Woodcutter comments: 'Now he'll be making love to her.' They discuss the possibility of escaping: 'He has a good horse,' says one. For the Bridegroom in pursuit of the fugitives, 'There is only one horse in the whole world and this is it.' The same horse which the Moon, for Death's benefit, will make shine as with 'a fever of diamonds', the same one to which Death, in the disguise of an old beggar-woman, alludes in the plastic nocturne with which she describes the double death:

I saw them; soon they will be here; two torrents
At last still amongst big stones.
Two men under the legs of the horse.
Dead, in the beauty of the night.

Only Death could have separated Leonardo from his mount. Leonardo's wife says it in the closing scene:

He was a handsome horseman,
Now a heap of snow.
He rode through fairs and mountains
And on women's arms.
Now night's moss
Crowns his forehead.

Leonardo, who for his wife became the horse that did not want to drink, was for the Bride a deep river where she could extinguish the fire that consumed her, a crystalline water wherein to quench her thirst. Without shame she confesses it to her Mother-in-law in the last scene:

I was a woman parched, covered with hidden sores. And your son was a little water from whom I expected children, land, health; but the other was like a dark river filled with branches, who brought me the murmur of its reeds and the song between its teeth. And I went with your son who was like a little

child of water, cold; but the other sent hundreds of birds which prevented me
from walking away and laid frost to the wounds of a poor withered woman, a
girl caressed by fire.

The House of Bernarda Alba offers a good example of the double
use of the horse as animal and symbol. Pepe, 'the Roman' who
does not once appear on the stage, is the *lingam* against which the
despotic pride of Bernarda Alba will be shattered. Invisible for
the spectators, but nailed in the eyes of the five unmarried daughters, we will always imagine 'the Roman', too, when not in a
woman's arms, riding over sierras or plains.

'I heard him coughing and I heard his cob's hooves,' says
Amelia a little after the beginning of the second act. And a few
minutes later Martirio affirms that she heard voices in the courtyard much later than the hour Augustias, the fiancé, says 'the
Roman' stopped talking to her through the barred window:

AMELIA: Perhaps it was a young untamed mule.

MARTIRIO (*in a low voice and with double meaning*): That is it. Just that.
A young untamed mule.

Galloping on his cob Pepe 'the Roman' will escape in the small
hours while Adela, thinking him dead, will hang herself from the
window-frame of her room.

All this could be, as Lorca intended, dry realism, and 'the
Roman's' horse, a horse and nothing else. But could the same
thing be said of the stallion whose kicks resound monumentally at
the beginning of the last scene? The horse may be real, but its
reality is loaded with symbolic value. That good breeding horse,
which at dawn will be covering the young mares, is a double of
'the Roman' who, before dawn, will take Adela on a heap of
straw. Once supper is ended Adela and Martirio go out to the
courtyard to find a little fresh air. On returning Adela comments:

The stallion was in the centre of the courtyard, white: double its size, filling
the darkness.

Lastly, when Martirio interrupts the amorous enjoyment of Adela,
the latter describes her newly found strength:

Not you, who are feeble; with only the strength of my little finger I can force a
rearing horse to his knees.

In *Yerma*, as was to be expected, there are no horses, nor could one imagine them in connection with Juan, a shy or sexually timid husband. It may be significant that the first time we hear the animal named it is in a metaphorical sense and from the lips of the old woman, the one Lorca first intended to call 'the Pagan'. In the second scene of Act One Yerma, anxious to find out the reason for her sterility, asks the old woman about it:

OLD WOMAN: I? I know nothing. I lie face upwards and begin to sing. Children come like water. Oh! Who could say that this body of yours is not beautiful? You walk and at the end of the street the horse neighs . . .

The second mention of the animal comes from Yerma when she refers to her restlessness and the palpitation of her breasts:

These two fountains I have of warm milk are in the thickness of my flesh two heart-beats of a horse which set the branch of my anguish a-quiver.

In *Yerma* there is no horse but in compensation there are the corresponding symbols of sexual appetite: thirst and water. In that same scene the old woman comments:

. . . Men must please us, girl. They must undo our tresses and they must give us water from their own mouths. This is the way of the world.

A little later Yerma, alone on the stage, hears the shepherd Victor's voice singing:

Why do you sleep alone, shepherd?

and she varies the song:

And if you hear a woman's voice
It is the broken voice of the water.

But Victor enters and Yerma praises his song:

And what a powerful voice. It seems a flow of water that fills your entire mouth.

Is this not an echo of what, just a moment before, the old woman said to Yerma? In that second act the tension and Yerma's obsession has increased alarmingly. She cries out to her husband that only when she is dead will she accept the idea of not having children. And when Juan asks her what she wants to do, Yerma answers:

I want to drink and there is no glass or water . . .

A moment later María, the good friend, comes to comfort her and Yerma hits back:

When you married women have children you cannot think about those of us without any. There you are all calm, unawares, just as the swimmer in sweet water can have no idea of the meaning of thirst.

In the third act Yerma says to the old woman:

You are old and see everything as in a book already read. I think that I am thirsty and have no liberty . . .

At the beginning of the erotic song-dance performed by the masked Male-Female couple we see once again Lorca playing with the metaphoric meaning of fire and water, as in the ballad of 'Thamar and Amnon' and in many other poems. Finally, when in the last scene the old woman invites Yerma to become her son's mistress, saying he will make her a mother as often as she likes, Yerma retorts fiercely:

OLD WOMAN: When one is thirsty, one is grateful for water.

YERMA: I am like a dried out field capable of holding a thousand oxen pulling their ploughs, and what you offer me is a little glass of water from a well.

Doña Rosita is the real drama of resigned, almost morbid frustration of love, of the acceptance of an endless waiting known to the protagonist herself to be fruitless. Therefore neither horse, nor water, nor thirst could symbolize her desolation. Consequently the only two references to the horse are made in connection with her cousin. When in the first act the aunt blames herself for having allowed the relationship between the two cousins, knowing that sooner or later he would depart for America, she retorts to her nephew:

And you there; the horse and the rifle to hunt the pheasant.

The second mention is in the already quoted scene between the two cousins:

When my horse slowly eats
Stems sprinkled with dew . . .

Quite peculiar is the case of Don Perlimplín, the old impotent man who would like to but cannot behave as husband to the young Belisa whose desires and capabilities are insatiable; over-sexed

Belisa in whom converge thirst and water in a delightful game of dropsical eroticism:

> *Oh! he who looks for me with passion will find me. My thirst cannot be quenched, no more than the thirst of the masks spouting water into the fountains can be quenched . . .*

she says at the beginning of the first scene, while listening to the calls of the five young lovers who will go in and out of her bed on her wedding night and take the place of the happily sleeping husband. In the prologue, before Belisa comes on to the stage, we already hear her singing, inside her house, an erotic dawn-song:

> *Love, oh love.*
> *Between my closed thighs*
> *Swims the sun, like a fish.*
> *Warm water amongst the reeds,*
> *My love.*
> *Cock, the night is going! –*
> *No, do not let it go.*

In the face of Belisa's sexual exuberance what could poor Perlimplín do? 'And if I am honest with you, I feel such a thirst . . .' he confesses to his servant Marcolfa when he sees himself drawn into marriage. But not understanding what is happening to him he adds: 'Why don't you bring me a glass of water?' Marcolfa approaches him and whispers something in his ear. 'Who could believe it?' comments the astonished old man. When he returns from the church, already married, he still does not know what is happening to him:

> *Since you came back from the church my house is full of secret murmurs, and water gets warm in the glasses. Oh! – poor Perlimplín!*

At the end of Act I, Belisa at last subdued by the upheavals of her wedding night, Lorca lets us hear the Perlimplinesque echo to Belisa's dawn song contrasting perfectly character and words:

PERLIMPLIN: Love, oh love!
        I come wounded.
        Wounded by a fleeing love;
        Wounded,
        Dead of love.
        Tell everyone that
        The nightingale did it,

Dagger of four edges
Broken throat and forgetfulness.
Take my hand, love,
For I come badly wounded,
Wounded by fleeing love,
Wounded!
Dead of love.

In the semi-surrealist play *When Five Years Have Passed* fire and water, thirst and horses, cross and intermingle freely. We know that the protagonist of this play is a character difficult to define, but one suspects that there are features of the sexually timid in this young man, possible victim of an onanistic imagination rather than cowardly homosexuality:

I wish to love her just as I wish to be thirsty in front of fountains. I wish . . .

he says in Act I talking to the old man and referring to the Secretary who is in love with him.

What a contrast with his young sweetheart! She is going to elope with the Rugby-player and as she leans her head on his chest she murmurs passionately:

In your chest is a torrent in which I am going to drown . . . Oh! (she kisses him). What white burning coals, what an ivory fire pours from your teeth! My sweetheart's teeth were frozen; he kissed me and his lips were covered with tiny faded leaves.

This is why in the farewell scene she asks the Young Man, her ex-fiancé:

SWEETHEART (*with passion*): And did you carry a horse by his mane and kill three thousand pheasants in one day?

YOUNG MAN: Never.

SWEETHEART: Then, why do you come to fetch me?

And a little later:

SWEETHEART: They are not your arms, they are mine! I am the one who wants to be burnt in another fire!

Lastly, the Mannequin, in the final scene of Act II, draws with precision the character of the protagonist and the roots of the drama by means of the symbols under discussion:

You could have been for me
Colt of feather and foam,
The air broken on your bridle
And the sea tied to your rump.

You could have been a neigh
And you are a sleepy swamp,
With dead leaves and moss
Where this dress will rot.

Before this direct accusation the Mannequin lets escape a significant lament:

Clothes covering the flesh
Will be for the muddy water.
And instead of a warm murmur
The broken torso of rain.

For the two women, the one he thinks he loves, and the one who really loves him, the Young Man is 'sleepy lagoon', 'muddy water', 'broken torso of rain', 'shadow of a river'. This last precise accusation comes from the secretary in the scene preceding the action in the little theatre placed in the centre of the stage: a bad dream within another bad dream. The Young Man tries to entice the Secretary to go with him before nightfall:

> Before the branches moan
> Yellow nightingales.

SECRETARY: Yes; that sun is a bird of prey.
> Better: a falcon of glass.
> No: the sun is a great tree-trunk
> And you the shadow of a river.
> If you embrace me, why, tell me,
> Do not reeds and lilies grow on me
> And your arms not discolour
> The hues of my dress?
> Love! Leave me in the mountain
> Tired of cloud and dew
> To see you huge and sad
> Covering a sleepy sky.

A few minutes later she repeats the accusation in a scene which is an inverted replica of the one between the Bride and the Rugby-player in the second act. In both instances the women lean their heads against the men's chests and hear the beating of their hearts:

SECRETARY: I want to live.

YOUNG MAN: With whom?

SECRETARY: With the shadow of a river. (*In anguish and taking shelter in the Young Man's arms.*) What's that which resounds so far away?

YOUNG MAN: Love,
the blood in my throat.
My love.

Now let us try to clarify to some extent the constant intervention of the horses in *The Public*, not only as symbols, but as characters moving, acting and speaking with the other characters on whatever level the action is taking place.

The play begins with the entry of four horses and a difficult conversation between them and the Director of the Open Air Theatre. After their exit, the drama begins anew with the entry of three men 'dressed in tails and looking exactly alike'. The suspicion that there must be some relation between men and horses is inevitable. Yet there are *four* horses coming to see the Director and only *three* men. May not one of the horses be connected with the Director? If that be so, is it not possible that those four mounts may be, at least in a certain sense, materialization of the four men's instincts taking part in the drama?

The Director not only accepts as normal the appearance of the four animals, but we know that he loves them with a secret impassioned love. On the one hand he expels them, on the other he whispers in an aside: *My little horses*, and, in one of those revealing deletions from the text, *Little horse of my heart*. Shortly after comes a phrase that he repeats in another place: *The bed for sleeping with horses has already been invented.* The four horses know only too well who the Director is, and at all costs want to master him. They begin by begging: *For three hundred pesetas – For two hundred pesetas, for a plate of soup, for a little empty bottle of perfume. For your saliva, for a piece of your fingernail.* But suddenly they change their tune: *For nothing!* and they remind him how, when they were small, they waited for him *in the lavatory . . . behind the doors and then we filled your bed with our tears.* Just as the Director himself hides his 'hare in the briefcase' only to have it reappear later in a more violent way.

But there is something more. One could say that those horses, in the form of a charade, enunciate the core of the drama we are about to see: the power of hidden desires, the normality in abnormal relations, the apparently strange correlations, the intercommunication between different levels and spheres:

THE HORSES (Though the manuscript says *men*, an error that the author forgot to correct): And your shoes were baked with sweat but we learnt to understand that the moon bore the same relation to the apples that rotted on the grass.

Lastly it is worth remembering that the Director's first reaction to the entrance of the horses was one of defence: *My theatre will always be an open air theatre,* that is to say, of apparent realities, in opposition to the theatre *underneath the sand,* a theatre in search of ultimate truths, feelings, instincts that the men and the Director himself will embark upon once they have passed behind the folding screen. If this reading is accepted, it will be only natural that at the end of that first scene, when the real drama is about to start, we hear offstage the horses' triumphal trumpets and that Man 1 should invite them to come and sit on the stage to witness a drama of which they will become part. With the words, *Mercy, mercy,* the horses end the first scene of the play.

In the *cuadro* 'Roman Ruin' the horses are no more than part of the Emperor's retinue. But the two main characters taking part in this scene – the Figure covered with Vine Leaves and the Figure covered with Little Bells – are only two costumes, two doubles engaged in an impossible love-dance. The problem is presented here in the open, within the frame of a historical ruin where Bacchus could have danced with Cyssus and Hadrian have wept for Antinous.

In the *cuadro* that we have provisionally considered to be half of the second act, the horses make a marked intervention and seem at times to contradict our interpretation. More than two thirds of this long *cuadro – Theatre underneath the sand –* takes place in Verona, in Juliet's sepulchre. Once her song is finished we see how Horse 1 enters with a sword in his hand and how he invites Juliet to mount on his rump so that he can show her, in a dark place, the horse's love. Juliet refuses because, among other reasons, she knows that what the horse wants to disclose is just the same as *Men, trees, horses. I know perfectly well all you want to teach me.* This White Horse 1 represents the instincts, or is a double of Man 1, or of the Director (he repeats several sentences of both), just as the other three white horses are related to the other men. The presence of a new horse, this one black, is obviously related to Juliet, not as her double, not even as a representation of her instincts, but as her constant death guardian, as a mysterious angel of death in animal form.

Five people on the stage; five horses. The white ones standing for those still alive, the black one for the dead Juliet. And yet these horses that we believe to be predominantly symbols suddenly reject all idea of the symbolic and demand to be accepted for what they are: *Because we are real horses, cab-horses who have broken down the wooden partitions and the windows of the stable with our pizzles,* says White Horse 1. Reality and dream, representation and symbol are superimposed on one another. A few lines later the horses shout: *We want to resurrect!* And the possibility that they may have been only horses and nothing more, seems to vanish when we hear Horse 1 repeat the very words of Man 1 at the beginning of Act I. *We have inaugurated the real theatre. The theatre underneath the sand.* And even more when Man 1 says to the black horse, referring to the other four white horses:

MAN 1: They must disappear immediately from this place. They are frightened of the public. I know the truth, I know they are not really after Juliet and are hiding a desire which hurts me and which I read in their eyes.

BLACK HORSE: Not one desire; all the desires. Just like you.

MAN 1: I have only one desire.

WHITE HORSE 1: Just like the horses; nobody forgets his mask.

If the horses represent, in part at least, hidden instincts or desires, most psychoanalysts would accept the Lorquian idea that the instincts can also wear a mask. That *cuadro* ends, as we have seen, with the Director escaping with the four white horses. When in *Cuadro V* Student 3 asks about the horses:

STUDENT 1: The horses managed to escape by breaking the ceiling of the stage.

213

STUDENT 4: When I was shut up in the tower I saw them clustered, climbing the hill. They were with the Director of the Theatre.

Flight that brings to mind the final dance of death, as it was later interpreted by Ingmar Bergman in *The Seventh Seal.*

The Public which starts with horses, heralds and shadows of men, ends, partly, on account of the horses. With his Romeo and Juliet the Director wanted to prove that love can be borne with equal intensity on all levels; his failure was due to the revolution that started when the public discovered the real personality of the interpreters. *The masks, the horses, the sea and the army of grass* prevented his success. This is why in the final scene – the Director's dialogue with Death disguised as a Juggler – the main difference in the decoration of the Director's room is a huge horse's head next to the Director's desk. The Juggler, seated on the table, has been tapping the marble head with his fingers, lightly but insistently. Then he whistles gaily while the echo repeats the last words of the Director and of his Servant:

VOICE (*offstage*): Sir!

VOICE (*offstage*): What?

VOICE (*offstage*): The public!

VOICE (*offstage*): Show them in!

What conclusion, if any, can one draw from this confusion? In *The Public* converges all we know of the horse in the work of Lorca. Often he uses it, like all his other symbols, on a series of levels that telescope into each other. The visual fields may change but the figures moving in them may or may not. Symbolic plurality. Those horses are simultaneously the horses of Lorca's childhood, mythological or legendary animals, doubles or portraits of his characters, personifications of the most secret instincts that degrade men, sexual energy, life or death. The poetic imagination receives and transforms a rich pictorial, literary and popular tradition.

The horses that in Lorca's work have a predominantly vital value, end, in *The Public*, by meaning negation and death. This is the usual end of practically all Lorquian symbols related to the theme of love. Take as a further example the transformation that the apple, as symbol of carnal union, undergoes. Lorca naturally associates the fruit with original sin. Defining the soft, dark complexion of a gipsy as 'a nocturnal apple', besides being an exact description of a hue, embodies a temptation to sin. We see it even more clearly in the early poem 'Oriental Song':

> *The apple is the flesh,*
> *Fruit of sin,*
> *A drop of the centuries that retains*
> *Its contact with Satan.*

– or when he says to Estrella, 'the Gipsy':

> *Join your red mouth with mine,*
> . . . .
> *Under the sunny gold of moon*
> *I will bite the apple.*

Or, when referring to Venus, he writes:

> *It shines over its field of pre-kiss as a great apple.*

In his essay on the lullabies he recalls that:

> *In Orense another lullaby is sung by a maid whose breasts, still blind, await the slippery murmur of their cut apple.*

The association apple-carnal union, is also implicit in some of the surrealist prose:

> *An apple will always be a lover, but a lover will never be able to become an apple,*

he writes in 'Lovers Murdered by a Partridge', foreshadowing the plastic symbol that René Magritte used some years later.

In *Poet in New York,* the apple, like all the other Lorquian motif and themes, changes into its opposite:

> *They are the dead, the pheasants and the apples of another hour, which are choking us in our throats.*

He writes in 'Landscape of the Vomiting Multitude' and in 'Dance of Death':

> *The drop of blood was searching for the light of the planet's yoke* referring to the moon *to feign one dead seed of the apple.*

The funeral association – death – seed – apple – will go on taking shape and in 'Landscape of the Urinating Multitude' we read:

> *Landscapes fill with sepulchres producing extremely cold apples.*

Extremely cold apples that only death can produce for her insatiable appetite.

These and other examples from *Poet in New York*, together with what we have already seen in other works, clarify certain passages of *The Public*. The first references to the apple, easier to understand, are in the first *cuadro*. The horses speak to the Director:

> *And your shoes were baked with sweat but we learn to understand that the moon bore the same relation to the apples that rotted on the grass.*

Relation between the moon-woman – or death – and apple-love that is death. We have the next reference to the fruit in 'Roman Ruin':

FIGURE WITH BELLS: If I should turn into an apple.

FIGURE WITH VINE LEAVES: I would turn into a kiss.

The fruit has more connotations in the mouths of those speaking in Juliet's tomb:

WHITE HORSE: By the Dead Sea grow beautiful apples of ash, but the ash is good.

BLACK HORSE: Oh freshness! Oh pulp! Oh dew! I eat ash.

JULIET: No, no, the ash is not good. Who speaks of ash?

WHITE HORSE: I do not speak of ash. I speak of ash which has apple form.

BLACK HORSE: Form, form, blood's longing.

JULIET: Tumult.

BLACK HORSE: Blood's longing and boredom of the wheel.

Double meaning: shores of a sea near to one of the places where the Garden of Eden is supposed to have existed and shores of the sea of death. In both cases there are apples that by giving life become food for Death. Ash is good for the Black Horse (another disguise of Death?) as it was good for the Juggler that the little grains of sand turned, only for a short while, into lively ants. The correlation form-ash is obvious if we refer the reader to what has been said on the section 'form – metamorphosis – void' and if one remembers the ash-whiteness of the apple's flesh. 'Blood's longing and boredom of the wheel' is another form of the motif blood – life – form (longing of blood to live within a form) and to the motif of the wheel of life – or of fortune – crushing everything that is born.

At that very moment the three Horses enter: *Form and ash. Ash and Form*, and Lorca meant White Horse 1 to have added: *Mirror: ZANICE and MAFOR, MAFOR and ZANICE*; (inversion of the Spanish sounds of 'forma' and 'ceniza' as though listening through an acoustic mirror, similar to the horses' inversion at the beginning of the drama in the Director's room.)

Horses and apples: two symbols of energy and life, transformed at the end, as is love itself, into visions or symbols of death. Yet this persistent tendency never touches morbidity or the macabre. From such dangers the poet is saved by the mastery of poetic form and expression and because what moves him at all stages is love. Joy of life is checked by the fragility of every living thing, by his awareness of death's watch from corners and towers.

IV

THEATRE IN THE
WORK OF GARCÍA LORCA

More about Cultural Tradition

Few statements by Lorca have been more misleading than the answer to the question put by the poet Gerardo Diego to his friends and colleagues taking part in his now famous *Anthology of Contemporary Spanish Poetry* (1915–1930): 'Neither you nor I nor any other poet know what Poetry is.' To this, one has to add Lorca's natural anti-pedantism, willingness to learn from child, concierge or professor and his subtle Andalusian irony: 'Jesus, how much you know!' I often heard him say when somebody tried to make a show of his reading. All contributed, no doubt, to the legend of Lorca 'poet by the grace of God', because 'it had to be', with little or no personal effort, little cultural background and scanty reading.

'None amongst his contemporaries has read fewer books,' states J. F. Montesinos. Angel del Río, who quotes that sentence in his book,[1] softens it a little when he adds 'though to a lesser degree than his contemporaries, he was a fully conscious and studious artist'. But a few pages later: 'there is not a single clear idea in his (Lorca's) poetry,' and to sum up he writes what is meant to be a panegyric of the poet: 'Lorca is a further proof of what we might call Spanish radical anti-intellectualism. Only one world was for him completely alien: the world of abstract ideas.'

Those who wrote these and similar statements were intimate friends of the poet, unconditional admirers of the man and of the

[1] Angel del Río: *Federico García Lorca* (1899–1936), Hispanic Institute in the United States, New York, 1941, p. 54.

artist, university teachers, critics and scholars of great reputation. Whether Lorca really read more or less than other poets of his period is not possible or useful to ascertain. What is puzzling about that early unanimity of judgment is that it precisely contradicts the fact that all Lorca's work radiates traditional and learned culture (acknowledged, curiously enough, by all those who spoke of his limited reading) with an intensity and variety rarely equalled by any of his contemporaries. When a properly annotated edition of his work is published it will be seen how from his first book down to the pages written a few days before his death, there is a remarkable list of cultural echoes and allusions. They range from the 12th-century 'Cantar de Mío Cid' right up to Lorca's contemporaries Ramón Pérez de Ayala and Ramón Gómez de la Serna; from the Bible and old Greek tragedies to Pirandello and O'Casey; from folk songs and dances to a fine appreciation of classical or modern music, from folk art to painting by Vermeer or Picasso. Our purpose is not to study influences – pitfall of the erudite – but to delineate how Lorca carries on, recreates or transforms a great cultural tradition not only Spanish but universal.

Perhaps those early assessments of his work were due to the fact that the cultural content seems to flow without conscious effort. Only in his first youthful book may it be possible to detect the juvenile desire to 'show off' knowledge. In the prose piece 'Canephorous of Nightmare' he describes a prostitute as 'Goya's dream or St. John's vision. Beloved by Valdés Leal, or Martyrdom of Jan Weenix'. But as soon as the poet masters his form erudite facts are treated with irony. Thus a village foot-path becomes 'Flammarion of footsteps' and the donkeys 'Buddhas of the Fauna'. In another prose piece he describes one of Granada's gardens: 'The gardens of the Martyrs were full of cocks. It was Breughel's earthly paradise . . .' Erudite allusions always come to his pen as easily as words learned in childhood. Even in his paper on Góngora's poetry, so loaded with cultural allusions, the standpoint taken and the use made of the material at his disposal are radically different from those customary in a professor or critic. 'For a metaphor to be fully alive,' writes Lorca, 'two conditions are essential: form and field of action.' He illustrates what he means:

Even the most evanescent English poets, like Keats, need to design and limit their metaphors or dreams, and Keats is 'safe' from the dangerous world of poetic vision thanks to his admirable plasticity. Afterwards he could say with calm: 'Only Poetry can tell its dreams.'

In Buenos Aires, during the performance of his adaptation of Lope de Vega's comedy *La Dama Boba* he was warned that at the end of the evening he would be asked to speak from the stage. He quickly drafted a few lines on a piece of paper:

Lope de Vega, 'monster of nature' and father of the theatre . . . He attains a Shakespearean landscape in his tragedy 'The Gentleman of Olmedo' and opens the door of his 'Dama Boba' to the air of mirrors and yellow violins which Molière breathes or into the air full of pepper where Goldoni's jingling bells are heard.

In *When Five Years Have Passed* the Harlequin alludes to one of the many legends attributed to Virgil's magic power:

The poet Virgil made a gold fly and all the flies that were poisoning the air of Naples died. There inside, in the circus, there is enough soft gold to make a statue of the same size . . . as you.

And in *Poet in New York* Lorca alludes to an anecdote in the life of St. Ignatius of Loyola:

> *Saint Ignatius of Loyola*
> *Assassinated a little rabbit*
> *And still his lips moan*
> *From the church towers.*

Examples such as these, elaborations or allusions to cultural themes like those we have in *The Public*, are abundant throughout the poet's work.

No less clear and persistent is the preoccupation with the ethical and aesthetic ideas that should rule literary creation, at least his own. We find it not only in letters to his friends, in press interviews, after-dinner speeches and in lectures, but also in his own creative work. That such evident phenomena have until very recently passed unnoticed[1] can only be explained by that early image of the spontaneous poet, nature's prodigy, a vehicle, almost unconscious, of telluric forces. Let us first limit ourselves to delineating Lorca's attitude towards the theatre in general and to *The Public* in particular.

---

[1] See Marie Lafranque's *Les idées esthétiques de Federico García Lorca.* Centre de recherches hispaniques, Paris, 1967.

Passion for the Theatre

— *What was your favourite game as a child?*
— *The game of all children who are on the way to becoming fools, poets: making little theatres . . .*

This answer to the question put to him in an interview with his fellow-writer Giménez Caballero confirms the testimony of those who knew him as an infant and took part in his games or partook as actors or spectators in the home performances he improvised and directed as a child. These performances culminated in the 'Festivity for Children' on the Eve of Epiphany 1923, to which we have already referred.

'To say mass, to make altars . . .' The rich Catholic rite and the popular songs of Andalusia were the first things to awaken his sensibility. 'When Federiquito could not yet talk, and he began to talk very late' – his mother told me one day – 'he got terribly excited when he saw the processions pass by . . .' The enthusiasm for popular religious spectacles never abandoned him. It was well known to all those friends who accompanied him to some religious festival or to the Easter processions. Even as late as 1936, speaking from the Madrid broadcasting station, he evoked Holy Week in the Granada of his childhood:

> *Then all the city was like a slow merry-go-round, going in and out of the churches, dazzlingly beautiful; a fantasy twin to Death's grottoes or theatrical apotheosis.*

On a more conventional occasion, from the stage of the principal theatre of Buenos Aires he spoke of theatre as of something intimately consubstantial with man. To illustrate his thesis he resorted to a religious example:

> *. . . theatre is an art, a great art, born with man, who carries it high in his soul. When he wants to express the deepest recesses of his history and of his own being he expresses it by representation, by repeating words, gestures and movements. The Holy Office of Mass is still the most perfect theatrical performance that can be seen.*

From what is known of his infancy and childhood, one feels that for the child-poet – to a great extent for the man too – reality lay in the processions, the mass, the little theatres; the rest would become more real as it approached theatrical reality.

With language borrowed from the little popular theatres, he opens the first book of his adolescence: 'The curtain rises', a sentence that he repeats at the end of the short paragraph with which he begins *Impressions and Landscapes*. Here as elsewhere in his work, we find a vision of reality referring to the stage:

> *The tragedy, the reality, is what speaks to the people's heart.*
> *Over the broken arches . . . fallen capitals . . . the decorative vision of a magnificent ruin . . . the stage is sunk, the legend is over.*
> *. . . and all with that admirable rhythm, with solemn theatricality preserving the huge strength of the ancient liturgy.*

Theatre and life; imagination and reality: not opposing or different worlds but two forms of reality equally true. Over this idiosyncrasy, which evolves without ever quite disappearing, he will later project his vital and artistic experience and his studies of theatrical art both from books and from the actual stage.

Various writings bear witness, also, to constant and reasoned meditation on these problems. They are far from being notes for a new art of writing comedies, not even notes for one or several volumes on theatrical art in the manner of Brecht. Yet what stands out from the totality of these Lorquian texts are some general but clear and precise ideas of what is or should be the theatre of today, of its educative function, both social and artistic. The rigour of such ideas is increased by the fact that the artist was not writing under any political label or with the intent of aligning himself with any literature of 'commitment'.

> *Otherwise, the beliefs, the aesthetic schools, do not worry me. I have not the slightest intention of pretending to be old or modern, I am only me, myself, quite naturally. I know perfectly well how the semi-intellectual drama is written but that has no importance. In our time the poet must open his veins for the benefit of others.*

Lorca approaches the theatre through a need to communicate. In that same interview given to a Madrid newspaper he added:

> *I have thrown myself into the theatre because it allows us more direct contact with the masses.*

And in another interview:

I have embraced the theatre because I feel the need of expression in a dramatic form.

And in a dialogue with the greatest Spanish cartoonist of the time, Bagaría, published in *El Sol*, the well-known Madrid liberal paper of the day, Lorca declared a few days before the beginning of the Spanish Civil War:

At this dramatic moment of the world, the artist must cry or laugh with his people . . . I have a true longing to communicate with others. This is why I knocked at the doors of the theatre . . .

He confesses a passion for the theatre because the stage is a unique medium of expression and, for glory or shame, a school for the masses:

I do not speak tonight as author or poet . . . but as a fiercely passionate lover of a drama of social action . . . A sensitive drama well orientated in all its branches, from tragedy to musical comedy, can in a few years change the sensibility of the people; and a corrupt drama, where cloven hooves have taken the place of wings, can corrupt and stultify a whole nation.

He explains with great clarity the didactic function of the theatre since urgency to communicate has a didactic as well as artistic value, assuming it is possible to separate the two.

Thus a little further:

The theatre is a school of tears and laughter and a free tribunal where men could show us the old or mistaken morality and explain with living examples eternal norms of man's heart and feelings.

In order to prevent any confusion between the role of the theatre and that of an academic chair, public tribunal or pulpit, he emphasizes another essential requisite of the free theatre that completes the two-way flow.

. . . The theatre that does not reflect the heart-beat of society or of history and the real colour of its landscape and of its spirit . . . has no right to call itself theatre.

The last three quotations come from a talk delivered in the Madrid National Theatre early on the morning of 2nd February, 1935. The occasion deserves mention. The actors of Madrid had asked the famous actress Margarita Xirgu to give a special performance of *Yerma*. But in order that all actors might be present such a performance had to start early in the morning, when all the other theatres of the capital were closed. This spontaneous homage seemingly without precedent in Spain, was proof of a contagious interest in a play thought to bring new life to the stage. After the performance in a theatre full to overflowing with 'the great theatrical family' – authors, actors, critics, stage hands – Lorca outlined a few principles which to many seemed new or daring though they belong to all times.

A year earlier, at the Teatro de la Comedia of Buenos Aires, in a performance in honour of Lola Membrives, interpreter there of several plays written by Lorca or arranged by him, the author had already put forward similar arguments.

I do not wish to speak today as a poet . . . but as an impassioned lover of the theatre, as a firm believer in its unchangeable efficacy and its future glory.

It was on that occasion that he outlined the causes which, according to him, were hampering the normal development of the whole Spanish-speaking theatre:

When they talk to me about the decadence of the theatre I think of the young dramatic authors who, because of the present organisation, leave the world of their dreams and do something else, tired of fighting; when they talk to me about the decadence of the stage I think of the millions of men who in fields and in the poor quarters of towns wait to see with their own eyes, fresh with astonishment, that idyll with nightingale, 'Romeo and Juliet'; Falstaff's belly full of wine or the lament of our Segismundo,[1] struggling face to face with Heaven. I do not believe in the decadence of the theatre, just as I do not believe in the decadence of painting or music.

He sees two main reasons for the present state of affairs that reacted upon each other. On the one hand there was the financial side of the theatre. Lorca does not forget that for the time being the theatre was a business which, in order to survive, needed money. But this was only half the truth.

The other half is purification, beauty, care, sacrifice for a superior aim of emotion and culture.

He does not refer, of course, to the artistic or experimental theatre. These types of theatre always lose money and as a result should be supported by the State, the municipalities or by some

[1] Prince Segismundo is the protagonist in *Life's a Dream*, the famous play by Calderón de la Barca.

individual patron. Lorca was referring exclusively to the box-office theatre:

> *One must demand from it a minimum degree of honesty and must continually remind it of its artistic function, of its educational role.*

The other cause, closely linked to the financial one, is what he terms the 'crisis of authority':

> *There is neither authority nor spirit of sacrifice to impose* ... (the necessary innovations) *on a public that must be tamed by nobility, contradicted, and at times attacked.*

And this brings us to one of Lorca's main ideas on the subject.

Author and Public

The constituent elements of the theatre are the author, the actors who represent what the author has written and the public who listen and judge the performance. The public: an amorphous mass, made up of all those who have paid to witness the spectacle, a mass that may be cultured or vulgar, receptive or violent, childish or authoritative. Lorca believes that through fear of that mass, authors often impose upon themselves a kind of auto-censorship and in tacit conspiracy with actors and management devote themselves to the low office of giving pleasure by invoking the easy, cheap, or vulgar themes they think the masses will like. For Lorca this is one of the worst forms of prostitution:

> *Theatre must impose itself on the public and not the public on the theatre. The public can be taught* ...

And in support of his statement he quotes the examples of Debussy and Ravel in music, and of Wedekind and Pirandello in the theatre, all of them bitterly attacked at first by a public which a few years later regarded them as idols. This is why Lorca lays no blame on the public.

> *The public is not to blame; the public can be attracted, deceived, educated and given not cat instead of hare but gold instead of hare. Yet nobody should lose sight of the fact that the theatre is superior to the public and not inferior, as happens with lamentable frequency.*

And a little later:

> *The common man attends with emotion spectacles that he considers superior to him, where he can learn, where he finds authority.*

The poet spoke backed by the successes of his own plays and of the classic plays he himself had directed. Besides, he had already witnessed the reaction of the popular masses, of illiterate peasants, on his tours through Spain with the university theatre 'La Barraca'.

> *The public in little villages always show a respect, a curiosity and a desire to understand not always matched by spectators in big cities.*

This facet of the poet, unpretentious but sure of himself, courageous without being boastful, speaking to the general public or to 'the great theatrical family' does not fit the image of 'a big child', 'without a clear idea in his head', that his first biographers and critics have left us.

Of course these words were pronounced from the position of strength won with the success of *Blood Wedding* and *Yerma* and with his tours to Argentina and throughout Spain. But let us remember that those ideas and attitudes were already clearly manifested in the young author and in his early works.

For his debut as playwright in the Madrid of 1920, he wrote an introduction to his *Malefice of the Butterfly*, a naive play from a technical point of view, but daring in ideas and approach. It would be impossible in that prologue to detect the slightest intention to flatter his audience. What we do find is the enunciation of typically Lorquian ideas which could only irritate the normal theatre-goers of those days: fusion of love and death, equality of everything and everybody in nature. In all this, and in sentences such as: 'Tell man to be humble. What reason do you have to despise the minute in nature?' there was, still in minor key, a courageous didactic intention.

It can also be detected in his guignolesque farce, though here, of course, on a humorous note; Mosquito speaks:

> *We, I and my company, come from the theatre of the bourgeoisie; from the theatre of counts and marquises, a gold and crystal theatre where men go to sleep and ladies . . . sleep too.*

Or at the end of the *Don Cristóbal* puppet play, when the

Director appears on the stage with his puppets still in his hands, and addresses the audience:

Among the staring mules' eyes, which are as hard as blows from a fist, among the tender wet sheaves, we hear bursting with gaiety and delightful innocence curses and expressions that we do not tolerate in the city atmosphere, heavy with alcohol and gambling. These strong words become naive and fresh in the mouths of these puppets who mime the charm of this very old rural farce.

We find a clearer exposition of the attitude we are discussing in the prologue to *The Prodigious Cobbler's Wife*, read by Lorca himself at its first performance, Christmas Eve, 1930:

The Author:
Esteemed public . . . (pause). No; esteemed public, no; only public. Not because the author does not consider the public worthy of esteem. Just the opposite. But because behind that word lurks something like a delicate tremor of fear, a sort of plea to the audience to be generous with the work of the actors and the artistry of the invention. The poet does not ask for benevolence, only attention, since he has long since jumped the thorny barrier of fear that authors have for audiences. Due to this absurd fear, and due to the fact that too often the theatre is nothing more than a business, poetry has withdrawn from the stage in search of other media where people are not frightened of seeing, for example, how a tree turns into a smoke ball, or how three fishes, by the grace of a hand and a word, turned into three million fishes to calm the hunger of a multitude . . .

and when the Cobbler's wife, still half-puppet, half-woman, comes on to the stage which depicts a gay Andalusian morning:

Each day dawns over cities, just like this one, and the public forgets its half-world of dreams to enter the market place as you enter your house, the stage, prodigious little cobbler's wife.

On the one side author and actors; on the other the public: a separation, a barrier which the poet seeks to eliminate by establishing a direct contact not with the masks and dresses sitting in the stalls or boxes but with the public hidden behind the disguises. The poet then addresses the other half.

'The public forgets its half-world of dreams': another example of how the author always remains linked to a very old cultural tradition. Lorca did not have to read Freud or Jung to be aware that dreaming and waking, sun and shadow, night and day are two halves of a whole. Neither did he discover it perhaps – to quote some of the authors I know he was reading at that time – in Plato or Plotinus, nor in Shakespeare nor in the 'evanescent' English poets of the 19th century, not even in Cervantes or Calderón, in Bécquer or Rosalía de Castro – evanescent Spanish poets – not even in Antonio Machado, author of the lines 'the only valuable gift of memory /is that of remembering dreams', that Lorca often used to quote. Perhaps he only learned it by 'remembering' the dreams of his childhood, always alive in Lorca the man.

Reality and Dream

The Prodigious Cobbler's Wife is the first Lorquian attempt to bring to the stage the world of dreams. It is the author himself who from the stage warns the public that what they are going to see is the representation of a dream, a collective dream. In the guise of a gay farce the intention seems relatively straightforward. Some years later, in an interview with a Buenos Aires journalist, Lorca said of this play that it was:

a simple classic-type farce which portrays a woman's mind, the mind common to all women, and where there is a simultaneous and delicate attempt to present a fable of the human soul.

Not so simple, therefore. The wife in the play was conceived and realized as a type and as an archetype; in the words of the author himself a 'primary creature', 'a myth of our pure unsatisfied illusion'.

Yet in the farce the barrier between stage and public persists. *The Public* is an experiment aiming to turn the audience itself into theme and protagonist without allowing it to cease being the spectator. The procedure used has nothing to do with the technique of the 'living theatre'. It is not a question of 'forcing' the public to take part in 'improvised' interventions but of bringing on to the stage 'dreams' and such intimate secrets of man that the audience will intervene in protest at seeing itself the spectator of its own shame. The true *public* is not the men, the horses, or the other characters appearing on the stage, but the real public that every night fills the theatre. In an interview he gave to *La Nación* in Buenos Aires, on the night of his arrival in the Argentinian capital,

Lorca alluded to *The Public* when listing his unpublished works. After saying that nobody would dare to produce the play, he explained:

> *It is the mirror of the public. That is to say, it parades on the stage the real drama which each spectator may have at the back of his mind while looking absentmindedly at the performance, often without paying the slightest attention to what is going on. And since usually the personal drama within each one of us is very poignant and generally nothing to be proud of . . . the spectators will immediately rise in fury from their seats and prevent the performance from continuing. Yes. My play is not to be performed but, as I have already said, it is 'A poem to be booed'.*

And this is what happens in the play. We saw in *Cuadro* V how the Judge demanded the repetition of the performance before the assassination of the man who plays Romeo and of the 15-year-old boy playing Juliet. Through the Students, we learn that the public during the first performance discovered the identity of the impassioned lovers and how this set off the revolution which at that very moment reaches the cathedral. The act missing from the manuscript was, I think, the one containing the revolution. The Spanish writer José Luis Cano, who also heard Lorca reading the play, remembers:

> *There was a clash between a character hidden in one of the galleries and the actors on the stage at whom the disguised actor was firing a revolver while, in an atmosphere of revolution, aeroplane-engines could be heard as though they were flying over the roof of the theatre.*[1]

Not a mere theatrical trick, but a desire to emphasize that *The Public* was in the gallery and stalls. Lorca offers that public the chance of joining the actors and voicing their protest. Although the intention is quite different this is a theatrical resource which can be compared in this context with the technique used by clowns and harlequins when they intermingle with the public at the circus. But it has an even closer connection with the very personal use Lorca has made of the well-known formula of the theatre within the theatre as an auxiliary dramatic agent of the central plot. This formula offers obvious possibilities in a play whose central theme is precisely the public and the performance of characters on and off the stage. It would perhaps be opportune to look a little more closely at this Lorquian technique.

[1] José Luis Cano in *Gaceta del Fondo de Cultura*. México, August 1961.

Theatre within the Theatre

In the dramatic work of Lorca, and in many of his poems too, we find several examples of superimposition of levels, themes and actions. At times there is a mere leap out of time and action, such as the brief monologue of 'The Hour' in the puppet play *Los Titeres de Cachiporra*; at times, as in *Mariana Pineda*, one has the impression that an approaching 'camera' animates a romantic print:

> *Prologue. Curtain representing the vanished Arab arch in the Cucharas and perspective of Bibarrambla square, in Granada, framed in yellow like an old print illumined in blue, green, yellow, rose and light blue over a background of black walls. One of the houses to be painted with marine scenes and garlands of fruit. Moonlight. Behind the curtain young girls singing to the accompaniment of popular music the traditional ballad that begins:*
> Oh, what a sad day in Granada . . .

Within the play itself the ballad of the Duke of Lucena, recited in the second act in three voices by the nurse Clavela and Mariana's two children, is a parenthesis, a variation on a folk theme which accentuates the tension of the drama, in the same way as the lullaby sung by the Grandmother and Mother in *Blood Wedding*. Yet the best examples of the theatre within the theatre are to be found in *The Prodigious Cobbler's Wife* – a farce, in *The Love of Don Perlimplín and Belisa in his Garden*, a tragic farce, in *When Five Years Have Passed* and in *The Public* – both 'surrealist' dramas.

In *The Prodigious Cobbler's Wife* the author himself comes on stage to introduce his characters as if they were puppets in a play soon to acquire real life. 'Let's start!' – he orders the protagonist – 'You come in from the street.' In the second act, the *romance de ciego* – recited by the disguised Cobbler with pictureboard and pointer in his former workshop, now the little tavern – is a short play, a distorted farce within the main one.

In *Don Perlimplín* the invention is more original. The play within the play is performed by the protagonist himself. Don Perlimplín 'plays' the role of the mysterious handsome young man in a scarlet cloak passionately in love with his wife and with whom she, without ever having seen him, falls madly in love. Once Perlimplín is sure of her passion he rushes out of the house to kill the young man by stabbing himself to death. Thus Don Per-limplín introduces into what was a gay, piquant farce, his own dramatic 'representation', and by his self-sacrifice turns into drama something that was until then a very gay farce, half-Italianate, half-Cervantesque.

In *When Five Years Have Passed* the different levels on which the play moves, together with its atemporal character, allow a series of simultaneous actions, independent in appearance. In Act I we have the dialogue between the Dead Cat and the Dead Boy, super-imposed on the discussion that the storm has interrupted between the Young Man, his friends and the mysterious old Man:

> (*Another clap of thunder is heard. The light fades and a stormy blue luminosity invades the stage. The three characters hide behind a black folding screen with embroidered stars.*
> *Through the left door comes the Dead Child with the Dead Cat . . .*)

In the second act the dialogue btween the Young Man and the Mannequin supplies another dream parenthesis in the only act that is realistic. The third act is full of isolated units, actually small sketches within the main plot.

> ('*Cuadro I*'. *Forest. Big tree trunks. In the centre a theatre surrounded by baroque curtains.*)

Throughout this *Cuadro* the Harlequin behaves as a real producer. At the beginning the Fool and the Girl play a sort of *paso*,[1] subtly connected to the main plot but truly an independent performance, a transformation of a children's song and game:

GIRL: Who says it,
      Who will say it?
      My lover awaits me
      Far down in the sea.

HARLEQUIN (*humorously*): Lie!
GIRL: True
      I lost my desire,
      I lost my thimble,
      And by the big trees
      I found them again.

---

[1] *Paso.* Name given by the sixteenth-century playwright Lope de Rueda to short sketches interspersed in his comedies. These superb farces with only two or three stock characters and a simple plot told in quick, racy dialogue are the origin of the best Spanish popular drama.

HARLEQUIN (*with irony*): A big long rope,
      Long to descend.
GIRL: Sharks and fishes
      And coral trees.

So independent is this whole scene that at one moment the Fool shouts: 'Now to the performance!' A few minutes later comes the dialogue between the Secretary and the Mask (the Concierge, mother of the Dead Child), both 'performing' their respective dreams or transformations of reality. Finally, when the young man appears in search of the Secretary, there begins a strange dialogue that gradually changes in tone as the Secretary climbs the short stairs leading to the little stage, in the centre of the main one:

The curtain rises and we are in the library of Act I, though much reduced in size and lighter in colour . . .

The Young Man also climbs the stairs and we witness a performance which is in reality an inverted re-enactment, with some changes and variations, of the first scene of the play.

Yet it is in *The Public* that the best examples of the use of the old theatrical device are to be found. Even in the first act, when the Director and two of the Men pass behind the folding screen we already find ourselves on quite a different level. More than representation one could speak of 'de-representation', of veracity versus theatrical fiction. The *cuadro* 'Roman Ruin' is a performance witnessed from 'outside', from the Director's room, at least by two of the characters whose corresponding doubles wear vine leaves or little bells.

As the background wall opens, half way through the un-numbered *cuadro*, we face Juliet's sepulchre in Verona. A scene within a scene. Somnambulist repetition, somnambulist gallery of mirrors, through which actors filter and are transformed as they pass from one to the other. Finally we see how in *Cuadro* V Lorca employs three simultaneous actions, though two of them – the one round the perpendicular bed and the one taking place inside the theatre in the background – are one and the same: a representation and its fable. The theatre at the back of the stage and in front are one and the same. Between, the fable: the Red Nude with a crown of blue thorns dying on the bed-cross; notable example of how technique is never in Lorca mere imitation or simple device. In his hands the theatre within the theatre has a precise function similar to the superimposition of levels we find in many of his poems.

In *The Public* converge, accentuated, all Lorca's main ideas on the theatre. In it didacticism has a special quality. If the author highlights vices and human failures it is not to bring man to shame or repentance, but to awaken understanding and sympathy towards man's nature and utter loneliness. No fear of the audience deters him from that task. Often the lesson is given through one of those characters – double of doubles – who at times speaks with the poet's own voice. The students discuss the causes of the revolution:

STUDENT 4: People forget the dresses during the performance and the revolution started when they found the true Juliet gagged under the chairs and covered with cotton wool to prevent her from shouting.

STUDENT 1: This is everybody's great mistake and this is why the theatre is dying: the public should not penetrate the silks and cardboards the poet builds in his bedroom.

And a few minutes later, after the deaths inside the theatre and in the perpendicular bed, the students speak again.

STUDENT 4: The behaviour of the public has been intolerable.

STUDENT 1: Detestable. A spectator must never form part of the drama. When people go to the aquarium they do not murder the sea-serpents or the water-rats or the leprous fish but gaze through the glass and learn.

In his often-quoted talk about theatre, Lorca, who had refused to accept the homage offered him to mark the success of his tragedy *Yerma*, said:

> As for poets and playwrights, instead of homage I would organise attacks or challenges in which we will be told courageously and in anger: 'Bet you have not the courage to do this.' 'Bet you are not capable of expressing the anguish of the sea in one character.' 'Bet you dare not relate the despair of the soldiers, enemies of war.'

In *The Public* Lorca had the courage to handle themes never expressed on the stage before, to explore motivations as yet unformulated, to experiment with techniques, daring even today. However all this is of relative import. The real value of this still unpublished play lies in the fact that its study discloses a new and unexpected dimension in the poet, confirmed by the rest of his work when read in the new light of this difficult text.

The Public also gives us the key to what may be the main reason for Lorca's uncanny success: underneath this and other 'surrealist' texts, as well as underneath the brilliance of image and metaphor, the gaiety of his farces, the so-called 'popular' elements in the *Gipsy Ballads* and some of his dramas, flows an old cultural tradition which the poet at times transforms, at times recreates or enriches, projecting it with confidence towards the future.

> *I know truth is not in the hands of him who says, 'Today, today, today', eating his bread by the fire, but in the hands of him who looks serenely towards the distant first light of dawn in the fields.*
> *I know that he who says, 'Now, now, now' with his eyes fixed on the little red throat of the box-office is wrong, but right is he who says, 'Tomorrow, tomorrow, tomorrow' and feels the imminence of new life soaring above the whole world.*

LORCA'S MAIN WORKS

The dates listed refer to first publication of books and to first performance of plays. The actual writing often belongs to a much earlier date than that of publication, or, in the case of plays, of their first performance.

Prose

Impressions and Landscapes (*Impresiones y paisajes*) Granada, 1918

Poems

Book of Poems (*Libro de poemas*) 1921
Songs (*Canciones*) Málaga, 1927
Gipsy Ballads (*Romancero gitano*) 1928
Poem of the 'Cante Jondo' (*Poema del Cante Jondo*) 1931
Ode to Walt Whitman (*Oda a Walt Whitman*) México, 1933
Lament for Ignacio Sánchez Mejías (*Llanto por Ignacio Sánchez Mejías*) 1935
Poet in New York (*Poeta en Nueva York*) (Written in 1929–30) México, 1940
Diván del Tamarit (Only a small group of its *Gacelas* and *Casidas* has been published posthumously)

Plays

The Malefice of the Butterfly (*El maleficio de la mariposa*) (An insect play) 1920
Mariana Pineda (Historical drama) 1927
Retablillo de Don Cristóbal (A puppet play) 1935
Los títeres de cachiporra (A guignolesque farce) 1937
The Prodigious Cobbler's Wife (*La zapatera prodigiosa*) (A poetic farce) 1930

The Love of Don Perlimplín and Belisa in his Garden (*Amor de Don Perlimplín con Belisa en su jardín*) (Erotic tragi-farce) 1933

The Public (*El público*) Still unpublished. Written in 1930

When Five Years Have Passed (*Así que pasen cinco años*) (Performed posthumously. Written in 1931)

Blood Wedding (*Bodas de sangre*) (A rural tragedy) 1933

Yerma (A rural tragedy) 1934

The House of Bernarda Alba (*La casa de Bernarda Alba*) (A rural tragedy. Finished in 1936. Published posthumously)

Doña Rosita the Spinster or the Language of Flowers (*Doña Rosita la soltera o el lenguage de las flores*) 1935

Unless otherwise indicated all the works listed above were published in Madrid. Other works by Lorca mentioned in this book are to be found in *Obras Completas*. (Aguilar, Madrid; Losada, Buenos Aires.)

WORKS BY LORCA
MENTIONED IN THE BOOK

Books

Ballads (see *Gipsy Ballads*)
Book of Poems 108, 127, 128, 155, 164, 168
First Songs 85
Gipsy Ballads 12, 30, 85, 94, 118, 130, 133, 135, 156, 161, 234
Impressions and Landscapes 86, 108, 114, 128, 144, 163, 222
Poem of the Cante Jondo 85, 156, 166, 189, 190
Poet in New York 30, 69, 73, 86, 91n., 93, 94, 97, 98, 103, 108, 109, 127,
    130, 153, 156, 158, 166, 167, 168, 169, 173, 176, 177, 182, 183, 191,
    192, 215, 216, 220
Songs 68, 85, 117, 130, 131, 145, 153, 155, 157, 166, 187

Plays

Blood Wedding 15, 23n., 28, 59, 69, 95, 112, 119, 120, 125, 126, 127, 138,
    156, 166, 199–205, 226, 230
Doña Rosita the Spinster or the Language of Flowers 12, 59, 101, 113, 115,
    116, 118, 121–124, 127, 151, 207
Los Títeres de Cachiporra 77, 141, 197, 230
Mariana Pineda 67, 95, 112, 181, 196–197, 230
The House of Bernarda Alba 59, 103, 112, 118, 119, 127, 167, 187, 199, 205
The Love of Don Perlimplín and Belisa in his Garden 59, 124, 125–126, 127,
    141, 207–209, 230
The Malefice of the Butterfly 77, 108, 144, 152, 164, 176, 226
The Prodigious Cobbler's Wife 59, 124, 126, 141, 197, 227, 228, 230
The Public 17, 19–103, 111, 112, 135, 142, 147, 148, 150, 151, 153, 159,
    168, 173, 174, 177, 196, 199, 211–217, 220, 228, 229, 230, 232, 233,
    234
Retablillo de Don Cristóbal 141, 181, 226
When Five Years Have Passed 43, 59, 63, 66, 67, 70, 73, 76, 86, 94, 95, 96–
    103, 113, 125, 126, 127, 135, 141, 147, 148, 151, 156, 173, 174, 189,
    190, 196, 209–211, 220, 230, 231
Yerma 28, 59, 101, 113, 118–120, 139, 140, 166, 205, 206, 223, 226, 233

Adam 68, 147, 168
Albaicín 93
Andalusians 188
Another Convent 115
Antoñito el Camborio 111, 134, 135
At Last the Moon could Come to a Halt 168
August Noon 128
Autumn Rhythm 109

Baeza 93
Ballad of the Black Sorrow 118, 196
Ballad of the Little Square 87, 153
Ballad of the Spanish Civil Guard 135, 188, 191
Ballad of the Summoned Man 94, 190
Ballad of the Unfaithful Wife, (See Unfaithful Wife)
Beehive 79
Beheading of the Baptist 96, 162
Betrothal 146, 147
Birth of Christ 162, 167
Brawl 90

Cain and Abel 16n.
Camino 189
Canephorous of Nightmare 219
Cante Jondo, (Paper on) 109
La Cartuja 114
Casida of the Bunch of Flowers 158
Casida of the Dark Doves 158
Casida of the Impossible Hand 153, 184
Casida of the Recumbent Woman 151, 152
Casidas 30, 93, 103, 127, 130, 151, 153, 156
Christs 162, 175
City without Sleep 173
Cock, The 94
Crucifixion 162, 168

Dance of Death 215
Dead with Love 94
Death of the Petenera 187
Destruction of Sodom, The 15, 16
Dialogue of the Amargo 190
Diván del Tamarit 30, 151

Don Pedro on Horseback, (See Mockery of)
Double Poem of Edem's Lake 110, 155

Elegy 116, 117
Elegy to Doña Juana, the Mad 116
Encounters of an Adventurous Snail 164
Eros with Walking Stick 131, 158

Fable and Round Dance of the Three Friends 91n., 111, 151, 195
Fresdelval 93
Fright in the Dining-Room 131

Gacelas 30, 93, 103, 127, 130, 151, 153
Gacela of the Dark Death 95, 174
Gacela of the Dead Child 95
Gacela of the Desperate Love 151
Gacela of the Market at Dawn 151, 158
Gacela of the Flight 160
Gacela of the Terrible Presence 151
Gacela of the Unexpected Love 151, 195
Gipsy Nun, The 115, 117, 195
Girl Drowned in a Well 193

The Hen, (A tale for dotty children) 97
Herbalists 95, 100
Holy Week in Granada 115
Hunter 155, 166

Interior, (Eros with Walking Stick) 131
Interlude 97
1910, (Intermezzo) 192
Introduction to Death 89, 90, 174, 193
Invocation to the Laurel 85

Jewish Cemetery 173

Lament for Ignacio Sánchez Mejías 88, 95, 149, 156, 169–172, 183, 188
Landscape of the Urinating Multitude 98, 173, 215
Landscape of the Vomiting Multitude 215
Little Infinite Poem 79
Living Sky 69
Love 158
Lovers Murdered by a Partridge 215

Madrigal de Verano 194
Manantial 85
Market at Dawn 151
Martyrdom of St. Olalla, The 63, 68, 94, 133, 190
Massacre of the Innocents, The 96, 162
Mockery of Don Pedro on Horseback 94, 135, 196
Moon and Panorama of the Insects 91n., 162, 176
Morning 163
Most Holy Virgin Speaks, The 177

Nativity by the Hudson 162, 167, 192
Nocturnal of the Void 92
Nocturnal Song of the Andalusian Sailors 142, 196
Norm and Paradise of the Negroes 88
Norms 143, 144

Ode to the Blessed Sacrament 162, 163, 177
Ode to the King of Harlem 69, 98, 192
Ode to Salvador Dalí 87, 163
Ode from the Tower of the Chrysler Building 177
Ode to Walt Whitman 59, 60, 111, 142, 147, 149, 150, 169
Office and Accusation 98
Omega 95
Oriental Song 215

Poem of the Cante Jondo 85, 156
Poetic Image, The Don Luis de Góngora in 72, 82
Prologue 165

Return from a Walk 87, 91n., 97
Ribereñas 145
Rose's Prayer, The 174
Ruin 95, 173
Ruins 93

Sad Ballad 147
St. Gabriel 111, 134, 135, 195
St. Lucy and St. Lazarus 162
St. Miguel's Ballad 132
Samson and Delilah 23, 24
San Pedro de Cardeña 68, 115
Scene 146
St. Olalla, (See Martyrdom of)

Sol y Sombra 78
Somnambulistic Ballad 118
Son Negro 158
Song to Honey 128
Song of the Little Pansy 145
Song of the Rider 188, 189
Song to the Moon 165
Songs for Children 158
Sonnets of Dark Love 128, 136, 151
Station Gardens 86
Submerged Church 173
Submerged Swimming Girl 196
Summer Madrigal 111, 129, 136
Sun and Shadow 78n.

Thamar and Amnon 137, 138, 207
Theory and Divertissement of the Duende 87, 159–161, 175, 181
They cut Three Trees 69, 166
Trasmundo 146, 166
Two Waltzes 158

Unfaithful Wife, The 111, 129, 132, 136
Unmarried Woman at Mass, The 117

Void's Nocturnal 193

Your Childhood in Menton 88, 92, 111, 137, 151, 195

INDEX

Abu Nuas, 80
Albéniz, Isaac 172
Alberti, Rafael 73
'Albertine' 111
Aleixandre, Vicente 73
Alfredo (Martínez Nadal) 12
Alice in wonderland (Lewis Carroll)
40
Amic de les Arts, L' 74
Amos, Book of 201
Amour, la poésie, L' (P. Eluard) 73
Angelico, Fra 134
Anthology of Contemporary
Spanish Poetry 218
Antinous 61, 212
Aragon, Louis 71, 73
Auclair, Marcelle 10n., 78n., 84,
84n.
Azorín, José Martínez Ruiz 100

Bacchus 82, 84, 85, 212
Bagaría 223
Barcelona, Atheneum of 109
Barraca, La (University Theatre)
181, 226
Beckett, Samuel 27
Bécquer, Gustavo Adolfo 228
Bellini, Giovanni 136
Berceo, Gonzalo de 177
Bergman, Ingmar 214
'Birth of Venus' (Botticelli) 144
Blake, William 90, 172, 193
Bonnard, Pierre 131

Bonnes, Les (Genet) 37
Book of the Dead 160
*Book of the Thousand and One Nights,
The* (tran. Richard F. Burton)
80, 80n.
Bosch, Hieronymus 31, 71, 75,
172
Botticelli, Sandro 31, 134, 136,
144, 167
Brecht, Bertold 222
Brenan, Gerald 172n.
Breton, André 71, 72, 73
Brueghel, Pieter, The Elder 71,
219
Buñuel, Luis 71, 73, 74, 146
Burton, Richard F. 80n.

Calderón de la Barca 224n., 228
Calvo Sotelo, José 12, 12n.
Campbell, Roy 117
Cano, José Luis 10n., 229, 229n.
Cante Jondo 109, 175
Čapek, Karel 77
Castillejo, Jacinta 10
Castillo, Lieutenant 12n.
Castro, Rosalía de 228
Cernuda, Luis 182n., 185
Cervantes, Miguel de 119, 124,
125, 126, 140, 172, 228
Cézanne, Paul 128
Chaises, Les (Ionesco) 41
Chekhov, Anton Pavlovich 119,
124

Cheval Troyen Le (Raymond Queneau) 193
Chien Andalou, Le (LuisBuñuel) 71
Chirico, Giorgio de 185, 190
Cid, Mío 115
Cirlot, J. E. 38
'Clarín' (Leopoldo Alas) 119
Cocteau, Jean 29
Cocu Magnifique, Le (F. K. Crommelynck) 125
Commedia dell' Arte 125, 141
Compte-Rendu de la Commission imperiale Archéologique pour l Année 1862, 80
Cosi e se vi para (L. Pirandello) 123
Coventry Cathedral 162
Crivelli, Carlo 195
Crosland, Margaret 10
Crucifixion (Filippo Lippi) 136
Cuatro Vientos, Los 19, 21
Cyrano de Bergerac (Edmond Rostand) 125
Cyssus 82, 212
Czerny, Charles 122

Dali, Salvador 65, 71, 73, 74, 74n., 87, 107, 163
Dama Boba, La (Lope de Vega) 220
Dance of Death 127, 159
Darío, Rubén 45n.
Debussy, Claude 225
Dethorey, Ernesto 17
Dictionary of Symbols (Cirlot) 38
Diego, Gerardo 72, 218
Dominga de los negritos 45n.
Domínguez, Oscar 65
Dream of the Skulls, The (Quevedo) 159
Duarte of Portugal, Don 181n.
Duende 87, 112

Eluard, Paul 73

Empedocles, 107
En España con Federico García Lorca (Carlos Morla Lynch) 12n.
Enfances et Mort de García Lorca (Marcelle Auclair) 10n., 84n.
Ernst, Max 71
Espadas como Labios (Vicente Aleixandre) 73

Falla, Manuel de 162, 180
Falstaff 224
Faust (Goethe) 170n.
Faustus (Dr.) 169, 169n.
Federico, Don (Lorca's father) 13
Ferrant, Angel 77
Fiscowich, Alfonso 13, 17
Franco, Generalísimo 9
Fränger, Wilhelm 81
Frazer, Sir James G. 69
Freud, Sigmund 227

Gaceta del Fondo de Cultura (Cano) 229n.
Galatians, Epistle to the 114
Galdós (See Pérez Galdós)
Garcilaso (de la Vega) 87
Garden of Earthly Delights, The (H. Bosch) 31, 81
Gash, Sebastián 71, 72, 176
Genesis, 15
Genet, Jean 27, 37
Gentleman of Olmedo, The (Lope de Vega) 220
George, Stefan 7
Gibson, Ian 10n.
Gide, André 163
Gili, J. L. 114n.
Gimenéz Caballero 221
Ginido 84
Ginsberg, Alan 51
Giotto (di Bondone) 15

Giraudoux, Jean 174
Gnido 84
Goethe, Johann Wolfgang von 170n.
Gogh, Vincent Van 155
Golden Bough, The (Frazer) 69
Gómez de la Serna, Ramón 74, 172, 173, 219
Góngora y Argote, Luis de 74n., 82, 83, 84, 96, 136, 219
Goya (Francisco de) 75, 90, 172, 219
Granada (Fray Luis of) 107
Grande Gaieté, La (Aragon) 73
Guillén, Jorge 75, 110, 158, 185
Guisando (Bulls of) 169

Hackforth-Jones, Campbell 7
Hadrian 61, 212
Hesiod 83, 86
Homage to Lautréamont (Man Ray) 71

Ibáñez, Paco 74n.
Ibsen, Henrik 119
Idées esthétiques de F. García Lorca, Les (Marie Laffranque) 220n.
Intermezzo (Jean Giraudoux) 174
Ionesco 27, 41
Isabelita (Isabel García Lorca) 13
Isaiah 172

Jealous Estremaduran, The (Cervantes) 125, 126
Jeremiah 172
Jeremiah (The Book of the Prophet) 160
Jimena (Wife of El Cid) 115
Job (Book of) 171n.
Joyce, James 163
Juan I 114
Jung, Carl Gustav 119, 227

Kafka, Franz 96, 100, 172
Keaton, Buster 96
Keats, John 219

Lady of the Hare, The (John Layard) 80
Laffranque, Marie 220n.
Lautréamont (Comte de) 172
Lawrence, D. H. 185
Layard, John 80, 81
Life's a Dream (Calderón de la Barca) 224n.
Lippi, Filippo 134, 136
Lola (Nadal), Doña 12, 17
Lolita (Martínez Nadal) 13
Lot 15, 16
Loti, Pierre 136

Machado, Antonio 100, 108, 228
Maeterlinck, Maurice 102
Magnus, 17
Magritte, René 71, 215
Manrique, Gómez 167
Manrique, Jorge 170
Marienbad, Last Year at 51
Marini, Marino 185
Marx Brothers 49
Maurois, André 185
Membrives, Lola 224
Metamorphoses (Ovid) 86
Midsummer Night's Dream, A (William Shakespeare) 31, 53, 77, 78
Millennium of Hieronymus Bosch, The (W. Fränger) 81
Mío Cid, Cantar de 219
Miró, Joan 65, 73
Molière, Jean-Baptiste 220
Molinari, Ricardo E. 7
Montesinos, J. F. 218
Morla, Lynch, Carlos 12, 12n., 19, 20, 175
Morla (Bebé) 12n.

245

Muir, Edwin 185

Nabokov, Vladimir 136
Nación, La (Buenos Aires newspaper) 228
National Gallery, London 167
National Gallery, Washington 70
Nativity (Botticelli) 167
Neruda, Pablo 73, 109
'New Yorker' 49
Nielsen, Jacob 17
Nightingale and the Rose, The (Oscar Wilde) 149
'Niña de los Peines' 87
Noailles, Comtesse de 185

O'Casey 219
Oedipus (Sophocles) 78
One Hundred Years of Solitude (Márquez) 174
Orlando 85
Orphée (Cocteau) 29
Othello (Shakespeare) 78
Ovid 86

Paco (Francisco García Lorca) 13
Patinir, Joachim de 172
Pérez de Ayala, Ramón 219
Pérez Galdós, Benito 119
Philip, The Fair 164
Picasso, Pablo 23, 185, 219
Pietá (Giovanni Bellini) 136
Pirandello, Luigi 27, 100, 123, 135, 219, 225
Plato 228
Plotinus 228
Poussin, Nicholas 128
Primo de Rivera (General) 12n., 181
Proust, Marcel 185

Queneau, Raymond 193
Quevedo, Francisco de 75, 136, 159, 170, 172
Quintero brothers, 121
Quixote, Don 76, 115

Raine, Kathleen 10, 78n., 174n.
Raphael, Raffaello Santi 171
Ravel, Maurice 225
Ray, Man 71
Residencia (de Estudiantes) 73, 109, 181
Revolver à cheveux blancs Le (Andre Breton) 73
Ribera, José 153
Richard the Third 204
Río, Angel del 169, 218, 218n.
Romeo and Juliet (Shakespeare) 30, 33, 50, 63, 77, 78, 224
Rueda, Lope de 231n.

St. Ignatius of Loyola 220
St. John the Baptist 167
St. John of the Cross 143, 172
St. John the Divine 172, 219
St. Manuel the Good (Unamuno) 164
St. Paul 114
St. Teresa 160, 175
Salinas, Pedro 84
Samuel (Book II) 138
Schneider, Marius 38
Selene 80
Seventh Seal, The (Bergman) 214
Shakespeare, William 30, 31, 50, 62, 76, 77, 78, 87, 119, 204, 228
Silos, Monastery of 115
Simmias 160
Six Characters in Search of an Author (Pirandello) 29
Sobre Pos Ángeles (Rafael Alberti) 73
Socrates 160
Sol El (newspaper) 13, 223
Solitudes of Don Luis de Góngora,

246

The (A text with translation by E. M. Wilson) 82n.
Solomon (King) 136
Spanish Civil War 9, 11, 12n., 20, 90, 179, 194, 223
Spender, Stephen 114n.
Spring (Botticelli) 31
Stravinsky, Igor 180
Los Sueños (Quevedo) 75
'Los sueños de la razón producen monstruos' (Goya) 75
Synge, John M. 185

Thamar and Amnon (Tirso de Molina) 15, 138
Theogony (Hesiod) 83, 86
Tirso de Molina 15, 119, 138
Titian (Tiziano Vecellio) 70, 193

Unamuno, Miguel de 99, 135, 160, 164
Unión, La (Hotel in Havana) 21, 22

Valdés Leal 219
Valdivieso, Joseph 159, 182
Valle-Inclán, Ramón del 172, 173
Vega (Lope de) 119, 181, 220
Vermeer, Jan 107, 219
Virgil 220
Víznar (Valley of) 9, 90

Waiting for Godot 24
Walt Disney 40
Wedekind, Franz 225
Weenix, Jan 219
Whitman, Walt 149, 150
Wilde, Oscar 149
Williams, Tennessee 27
Wilson, Edward Meryon 82n.

Xirgu, Margarita 12, 157, 223

Yeats, W. B. 174n.

Zalamea, Jorge 158, 169n.
Zend-Avesta 185